ASP 2.0
Programmer's Reference

Alex Fedorov
Brian Francis
Daniel Maharry
David Sussman
Chris Ullman

Wrox Press Ltd. ®

ASP Programmer's Reference

wrox

PROGRAMMER TO PROGRAMMER™

Published by Wrox Press Ltd, 30 Lincoln Road, Olton, Birmingham, B27 6PA
Printed in USA
ISBN 1-861002-4-59

Trademark Acknowledgements

Credits

Authors
Alex Fedorov
Brian Francis
Daniel Maharry
David Sussman
Chris Ullman

Additional Material
Chris Blexrud
Matt Brown
Richard Harrison
Juan T Llibre

Development Editor
Anthea Elston

Editors
Joanna Mason
Ian Nutt

Technical Reviewers
Chris Blexrud
Philip Carmichael
Brian Francis
Richard Harrison
Juan T Llibre
David Sussman

Cover
Andrew Guillaume
Image by Rita Ruban

Design/Layout
Noel Donnelly

Index
Julian Skinner

About the Authors

Alex Fedorov

Alex Fedorov works as an executive editor for "Computer Press" magazine – a monthly software and hardware magazine, published in Moscow, Russia. During his work in magazines Alex has authored more than 150 articles on various programming topics, including Delphi programming, Internet programming, COM/OLE and other technologies. Alex was one of the co-authors of Professional ASP 2.0, and has written several other books, published in Russian.

Brian Francis

Brian Francis is the Technical Evangelist for NCR's Retail Self Service Solutions. From his office in Duluth, Georgia, Brian is responsible for enlightening NCR and their customers in the technologies and tools used for Self Service Applications. Brian also uses the tools that he evangelizes in developing solutions for NCR's customers.

He has worked extensively with Wrox Press as a technical reviewer and has also co-authored on a number of projects including Professional IE4 Programming, Professional ASP and Professional ASP 2.0. He is also one of the five strong author team behind the best-selling Beginning Active Server Pages 2.0. His latest works include the ASP Programmers Reference, a forthcoming IE5 book, and a series of articles for ASP Today. *I wish all the love and happiness in the world to my wife Kristi, for her love and support, and for being my best friend in the whole world. I Love You!*

Daniel Maharry

Daniel Maharry currently lives in Birmingham with two of his co-workers at Wrox Press. If you can't find him online, you're likely to find him either in the cinema or somewhere near loud music, if he's not making any himself. Daniel would like to thank his family, friends and all those at Wrox for being there. Currently his favourite website is http://www.linux.org.

David Sussman

David is a developer, trainer and author, living in a quiet country village in Oxfordshire. He was one of the authors of Professional ASP 2.0, and co-author of the bestselling Professional MTS/MSMQ and, most recently, ADO 2.0 Programer's Reference. He is currently working on an Access 2000 VBA Tutorial book.

Chris Ullman

Chris Ullman is a computer science graduate who has not let this handicap prevent him becoming a programmer fluent in Visual Basic, Java, SQL, DHTML and ASP. When not cutting up pictures by old masters to re-assemble them as dynamic jigsaws on his preferred browser, he's either found down at his local soccer ground urging on his favorite team, Birmingham City, or at home trying to prevent his two young cats from tearing up the house, or each other.

Table of Contents

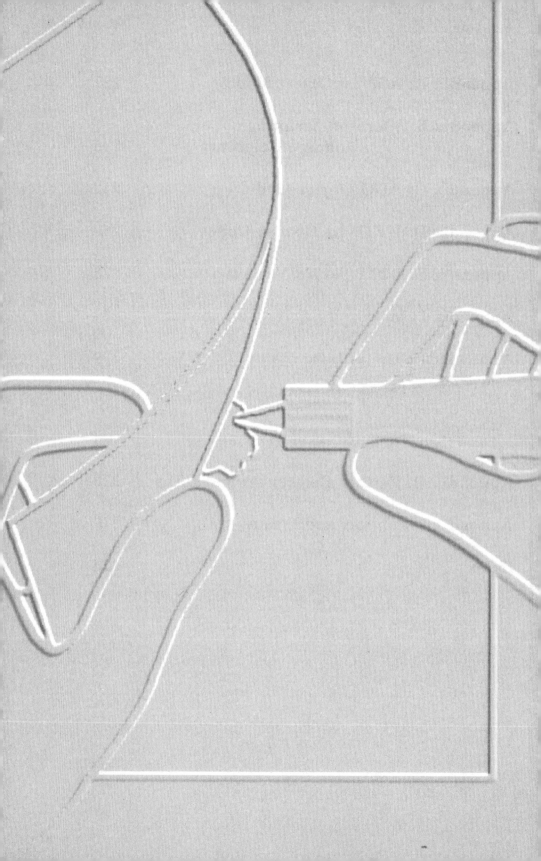

Introduction

This book provides a desktop reference to version 2.0 of Microsoft's *Active Server Pages* technology. It's a guide to the ASP object model (with which we communicate with the client browser), and the scripting objects (with which we communicate with the server-side file system). We'll cover all the properties, methods, collections and events that provide us with this accessible server-side scripting functionality through these objects.

We'll also look at how we can extend ASP, via technologies like ADO, CDO, ADSI and ASP components. The result, we hope, is a book that provides a quick (yet concise) dictionary of ASP, with relevant and useful tips and tricks.

A Potted History of ASP

Around the turn of 1996, Microsoft identified the need for a server-side scripting framework that would work with and complement the client-side script languages of the time – JavaScript, JScript and VBScript. They figured that such a technology would offer webmasters the ability to create web pages dynamically, and would also provide more people with the incentive to select Microsoft's Internet Information Server (IIS) as their web server of choice.

Project 'Denali' (as it was known before release) was officially announced to the world in July 1996. Active Server Pages (as it was rechristened) was released to beta in November 1996, and released to the public on December 12, 1996, bundled with version 3.0 of IIS. While it was certainly not perfect, it was enough to whet the appetite – and consequently version 2.0 was received with open arms when it was released with IIS 4.0 in the Windows NT4 Option Pack in December 1997. Because of ASP 2.0's extensibility, and its integration of 'regular' programming concepts (persistent storage, application state, modularity via components, client-server interaction) into web applications, it remains the most popular set of server-side extensions for the PC web server market.

Looking to the future, ASP 3.0 is nearly ready to ship as part of IIS 5.0 in Windows 2000; with this new version comes the promise of a faster, more scalable, more robust environment in which to set our web applications.

Interestingly, Microsoft now markets ASP as a 'glue' technology. We can query, update or build a database that contains our data; we can access and use the business logic for our data in custom-built components; then we can create an interactive and customizable front-end presentation. And we can do all this using ASP. Visual Basic was at this stage a couple of years ago and is now one of Redmond's major products. It would seem safe to say that ASP is here to stay.

What Is This Book About?

This book is about ASP – its current state and its future. We cover all of the ASP vocabulary, and (where applicable) how individual commands work and how they affect the system – both server and client. We describe the syntax of the associated scripting objects, that are available to ASP users as part of the VBScript engine.

We cover the basic ASP components that are installed with IIS and PWS – what each component is designed to do, and the syntax and calls that invoke them. We also point you in the direction of third party ASP components, and step through the basics of creating your own components.

Continuing the theme of extending ASP pages through other technologies, we'll look at five sets of APIs – namely ADO, RDS, CDO, ADSI and XML. Between them, these APIs allow the ASP programmer to write any type information into his pages, regardless of the format in which it's stored. We'll take a very brief look at what each one does, and we'll demonstrate its capability through code samples that perform some of the basic functions. For good measure we've included some useful resources for each of these topics, so that you can delve further into them.

Finally, we'll look forward to the next incarnation of ASP and its associated scripting languages; Chapter 10 talks about the added functionality that we'll gain with the advent of Windows 2000 and IIS version 5.0.

We've endeavored to present a 'pure' ASP reference, before covering other aspects of ASP development. Extensions to ASP (things like ADO) are covered in the latter part of the book, but with an ASP flavor. As a result, the example code in the book is short but precise – we try to give you a flavor for how these techniques are used, rather than demonstrating how to build complete applications. Finally, we have provided a cornucopia of further resources – and there's certainly plenty out there.

Who This Book Is For?

This book *isn't* designed to be a novice's guide to ASP. However, if you're familiar with client-side scripting languages, this book should provide you with enough to get you up to speed with ASP. If you're an established ASP programmer, it's a handy and straightforward reference guide – and a viable alternative to a 1000-page book if you need to carry it around in your satchel. Finally, if you're a budding ASP programmer and you want to learn more about the capabilities of ASP and its extensions, then this book should give you plenty of ideas.

What This Book Contains

The structure of the book is as follows:

❑ Chapter 1 is an introduction to ASP. We'll cover its presence on the Internet, good coding practice and an overview of the ASP object model.

❑ Chapters 2 and 3 look at the `Response` and `Request` objects, and how they allow interaction between the browser and server.

❑ Chapter 4 covers the `Application` and `Session` objects, and how they give a web application some form of 'memory'.

❑ Chapter 5 discusses the `Server` object, and how it gives the developer another level of control over the virtual aspects of the server.

❑ Chapter 6 moves on to the Scripting objects and how they allow a developer control over the physical aspects of the server.

❑ In Chapter 7, we look at ASP components: what they are, how to use them and the functionality they can add to your applications.

❑ Chapters 8 and 9 venture into the supporting technologies and what they do.

❑ Chapter 10 looks at ASP 3.0: what's new and what's improved.

❑ There's also a comprehensive collection of appendices, designed to support you as you dip into the book and as you work on your applications.

The object reference chapters (Chapers 2-6) all follow a similar structure. In order, we identify the collections, properties, methods and events that make up the object's interface. For each of these, we'll give an outline description and syntax, and we'll provide example code some specific points of note. We hope that the uniformity of these chapters will make it easier to find what you are looking for.

Finally, you need to bear in mind that practically every piece of ASP code you write will have bugs, and that it's quite normal to spend a fair amount of your time debugging the aforementioned code. Therefore, Chapter 1 also explains how to set up a basic script debugger, and outlines some good coding practices that should ease the debugging process, if not totally eradicate the more obvious bugs.

What Do I Need to Use this Book?

The first thing you need is a text editor of some description (to write your code). The other thing you need is a functioning web server that supports ASP. At time of writing, this means one of the following: Microsoft's Internet Information Server; or Microsoft's Personal Web Server; or a PC or Solaris version of the Apache web server (with Chili!ASP installed). If you're wondering where to get hold of these, you'll find the answer in Chapter 1.

What Language Should I Use?

ASP itself is not a language – rather, it's a framework that can be manipulated with the use of any scripting language. Chapter 1 discusses the basic differences in ASP syntax with respect to Javascript, JScript and VBScript, but the rest of the book utilizes VBScript in its code, since this is the default language of ASP.

At some point, it may occur to you that it is easier to code certain aspects of your application in different languages. While using multiple languages within a single *application* is certainly not an issue, may we suggest that juggling two or more languages within a single *page* is not a good idea.

Samples and Updates

We provide the source code for the samples you'll see in this book on our web site; and if you don't fancy installing them on your own server, you can also run most of them directly from our site. To access the main samples menu page for this book, you have two choices. You can navigate to `http://www.wrox.com`, follow the **Source Code** link and select **ASP Programmer's Reference**, or you can navigate directly to `http://webdev.wrox.co.uk/books/2459/`. This second option also contains a range of other resources and reference material that you might find useful – articles, links to useful websites, and information on other books that demonstrate how to apply ASP in different settings.

If you plan to run the samples yourself, download the `.zip` file and extract all the `.asp` files to a virtual directory set up on your web server. (The code in Chapter 7 will require the presence of the relevant ASP components, and the code for Chapters 8 and 9 requires the relevant technology to be installed – we'll explain where to get these resources in the chapters themselves.) The base for the code in Chapter 10 is beta 2 of Windows 2000 and IIS5.0 – but you'll be able to follow the examples without too much trouble, even without this setup.

Conventions

There are conventions you should be aware of. The first concerns the notation that we use to illustrate the syntax of ASP. We will use square brackets [ ] around an item to indicate that its presence is optional.

Second, we have used a number of different styles of text and layout in the book to help differentiate between the different kinds of information. Here are examples of the styles we use and an explanation of what they mean:

Advice, hints and background information comes in this type of font.

Important pieces of information come in boxes like this.

Bullets appear indented, with each new bullet marked as follows:

- **Important Words** are in a bold type font
- Words that appear on the screen, in menus like the File or Window, are in a similar font to that which you see on screen
- Keys that you press on the keyboard, like *Ctrl* and *Enter*, are in italics

Code has several fonts. If it's a word that we're talking about in the text – for example, when discussing the **For...Next** loop – it's in a bold font. If it's a block of code that you can type in as a program and run, then it's also in a gray box:

```
Response.Write("Hello World")
```

Sometimes you'll see code in a mixture of styles, like this:

```
<%
   Dim strLastName
   strLastName = Request.Form("LastName")
   Response.Write("Your surname is " & strLastName)
%>
```

The code with a white background is code we've already looked at and that we don't wish to examine further.

Tell Us What You Think

We've worked hard on this book to make it useful. We've tried to understand what you're willing to exchange hard-earned money for, and we've tried to make the book live up to your expectations.

Please let us know what you think about this book. Tell us what we did wrong, and what we did right. We take your feedback seriously – if you don't believe us, then send us a note. We'll answer, and we'll take on board whatever you say for future editions. The easiest way is to use email:

```
feedback@wrox.com
```

You can also find more details about Wrox Press on our web site. There, you'll find the code from our latest books, sneak previews of forthcoming titles, and information about the authors and editors.

Customer Support

If you find a mistake, please have a look at the errata page for this book on our web site first. Appendix I gives more details of how to submit an errata, if you are unsure. You'll find the errata page on our main web site, at

```
http://www.wrox.com
```

If you can't find an answer there, tell us about the problem and we'll do everything we can to answer promptly!

Just send us an email to support@wrox.com or check out the advice on our website:

```
http://www.wrox.com/contacts.asp
```

What Is ASP?

It wouldn't be any use to you if we just wrote down what's in ASP. We could just sell you a cheat sheet. Syntax is nothing if you don't know what surrounds that code, how the code fits into the environment it's built for and how to fix the code when it's broken. So in this chapter, before we hit the specifics, we'll cover the generalities, namely:

❏   What ASP is and where to get it
❏   What you'll find in an Active Server Page
❏   An overview of the ASP object model
❏   Scripting objects and components
❏   How ASP works
❏   What languages we can use to write an Active Server Page
❏   Good ASP coding techniques
❏   Where else to look for help with your ASP

Let's start with one of the key questions...

What is ASP?

In the dim and distant past, web developers wishing to create more than just static displays of information turned to CGI (Common Gateway Interface) and Perl to introduce some sort of interaction to their pages. While this approach worked (and indeed, many sites still use it today), CGI was not by any means fast and the quest for an alternative means to create a page dynamically continued. ISAPI came and went – primarily because it required more knowledge to create a dynamic filter than web programmers were prepared to learn. Finally came web scripting languages and with them Microsoft's Active Server Pages: a server-side scripting technology for building web pages that are both dynamic and interactive.

An Active Server Page itself is simply a text file script with the extension .asp containing HTML, client- and server-side script. The implementation behind the ASP page was created by Microsoft and intended as an open technology server-side framework, giving web developers the freedom to develop dynamic web sites using information accessed from the many COM-compliant data sources available to them.

The syntax and grammar of ASP is easy to comprehend, and yet powerful enough to:

- ❑ support some interaction between page user and server
- ❑ allow web page access to databases and directory services
- ❑ incorporate and make use of high-powered COM components

It's also server-based, and therefore browser-independent, leaving you only the problems of which cross-browser client-side script and stylesheet you want to use.

Writing ASP pages is straightforward:

- ❑ **The static content of the page is created using HTML and text.** We can also use standard HTML forms to question the client and, using ASP, create a page that incorporates their answers into the text. This is the simplest form of client-server interactivity using ASP.
- ❑ **We make calls to one or several of the ASP intrinsic objects to create the dynamic element of the page.** ASP provides a set of intrinsic objects – Response, Request, Application, Server and Session – that allow us to access information about the request being made of the server, as well as the response that the server will send.
- ❑ **We also have access to the functionality of our standard scripting languages** (VBScript, JScript and JavaScript) and the scripting objects they expose.
- ❑ Finally, **we can incorporate any standard COM object** (or active server component, as we call them) **into a page.** There are many third-party companies who specialize in writing such components and if you do use them, then you have the added guarantee that they've been stress-tested and fully debugged. On the other hand, if you need your component to do something unique, COM components are easy to develop in any established language. Visual Studio would be a good investment at this point.

So now that we know what ASP is, where can I get an ASP scripting engine from?

Where Can I Get ASP?

ASP is a web enhancement tool that was developed and distributed by Microsoft. As such, the ASP scripting host (which translates ASP into HTML) is distributed within Microsoft's web-specific products – its web servers, Internet Information Server (IIS) and Personal Web Server (PWS) and its HTML editors (FrontPage 9x and Visual Interdev, though not Notepad ;-). In the spirit of the open standard that ASP wants to be, the scripting host has also been taken by third parties and rewritten for use with other, non-Microsoft web servers – more on that later.

To date, there have been two versions of ASP for development use. The first, ASP 1.0, appeared in 1996 with Windows NT4 Service Pack 3 as part of IIS 3.0. ASP 2.0 reared its head about nine months later, much improving on its previous incarnation – it is this version which is available for installation with a web server/html editor from quite a few sources. The latest version, ASP 3.0, is due to ship some time in the first half of 1999 with IIS 5.0 (as part of Windows 2000. Since ASP 3.0 is currently not widely available (and is still in beta), we'll concentrate on ASP 2.0 in this book, which you can install from the following sources.

Windows NT 4.0 Option Pack

Contrary to its rather specific name, the **Windows NT 4.0 Option Pack** comes in two different flavors (the choice depends on which operating system you are using). If your system set-up is based upon Windows 95 or Windows NT 4 Workstation, then ASP will be installed with Personal Web Server. If you use Windows NT 4 Server, then ASP is installed with Internet Information Server.

The Option Pack is available from several different sources:

❑   MSDN subscribers will find it on Disk 2 of the BackOffice Test Platform or Disk 13 of the Development Platform.

❑   Other users can download it from the Microsoft home site at `http://www.microsoft.com/windows/downloads/contents/Update s/NT40ptPk/default.asp`. The total pack is 27Mb, so be prepared for a long wait – and no, there isn't an option to download just IIS and ASP.

Windows 98 Install Disk

The Windows 98 Install Disk includes a version of Personal Web Server and ASP as an extra to the operating system itself. Simply run `setup.exe` from the `add-ons/pws` directory of the disk and all will be well.

Visual Studio 6

Personal Web Server and IIS, and therefore ASP, are included with this product.

Installation and Setup under Windows NT 4.0

Windows NT4.0 can be a tricky beast to set up, and getting the latest version of ASP running with the latest hotfixes for security holes and other bugs can be a matter of trial and error unless you know the right order in which to install your software. For an NT 4.0 web server running ASP, it would be preferable to get a copy of the NT 4.0 Option Pack and then install in this order:

❑   Windows NT 4.0 Server/Workstation
❑   NT 4.0 Service Pack 3
❑   Internet Explorer 4.01 (or later)
❑   NT 4.0 Option Pack (or other source of ASP)
❑   NT 4.0 Service Pack 4

Service Pack 3 is required to install the Option Pack, but in its turn the Option Pack contains older files than SP4 which contains the latest hotfixes (upto November 1998 anyway). Check out the Microsoft security or downloads sites for the fixes after SP4 (see Appendix H for URLs).

Setting up ASP under IIS

If you've installed Internet Information Server, there's a couple of other things you need to do in order to make sure ASP is running and will run in your test code. Checking that ASP has been installed properly is simplicity itself. IIS documentation comes installed as a set of .asp files – you can test your ASP installation simply by choosing to run those help files from the Start menu (at Programs | NT 4.0 Option Pack | Product Documentation). If the help files display correctly, then ASP is running. If they don't, then it isn't.

The other quick check to make is to ensure that the virtual root for your web site is set up to run .asp files. In the MMC, expand the IIS folder and select either a web site or a virtual directory beneath it. Bring up the Properties dialog for that virtual directory by right-clicking on it and selecting Properties from the menu that appears. Select the Documents tab, add Default.asp to the default documents listbox and promote it above Default.htm using the arrows on the right-hand side.

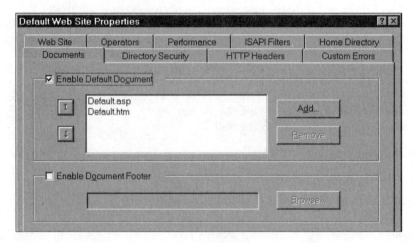

Finally, click on the Home Directory tab (this will be the Virtual Directory tab if you are setting the properties of a virtual directory instead of a web site). Under the Permissions heading at the bottom of the dialog, make sure the Script radio button is checked – this ensures the ASP scripting host will parse the page when it is requested by a client.

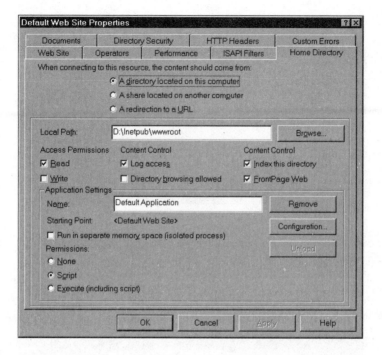

*This applies to IIS4.0 only. In IIS3.0 the **Script** button doesn't exist, so you have to select the **Execute** button. It was only when IIS3.0 was being used in production setups, that anyone noticed that selecting **Execute** allows any executable file to be run in that directory – which imposed a security threat on the website . Thus, in IIS4.0 the **Script** button appears in the **Permissions** dialog to allow only the 'secure' execution of scripts in the relevant directory.*

Setting Up ASP Under PWS

Personal Web Server is really just a scaled down version of Internet Information Server and to ensure that ASP is running correctly and is available for your site, the checks are the same. The PWS documentation can be run from the Start menu under Programs | Personal Web Server | Product Documentation to confirm that ASP is running, and once you have created a virtual directory for your web site, the default document dialog can be found in the Advanced Options window of PWS.

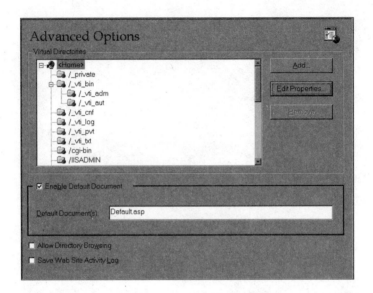

Meanwhile, the Scripts permission button can be found by selecting Edit Properties. Again, make sure that Scripts is checked along with Read.

ASP is not just for IIS

The core of ASP is the ASP Scripting Host, which you can find in `asp.dll` – without it, we would have no working `.asp` files. However, although the vast majority of ASP developers are currently using either Personal Web Server or Internet Information Server to base their pages on, these web servers are no longer the only products that contain a productive ASP engine for us to work with.

The really attractive part of having open standards – even wannabe ones like ASP – for the Internet is that once a standard has been released, it can be implemented by anyone. Soon after Microsoft's release of ASP 1.0, a company called Chili!Soft began to develop a fully-functional parser for other web servers besides IIS and PWS.

On the Windows NT platform, Netscape's Enterprise and Fasttrack servers are now ASP-enabled thanks to their product **Chili!ASP,** as are Lotus' Domino and Go Webservers. A version for NT Apache is currently in beta. Chili!ASP also offers ASP and ADO to Netscape servers on the Sun Solaris platform and has plans in the works for more non-PC-based servers too. It will be interesting to see how Chili!soft react to the release of ASP 3.0. The question of whether or not they'll upgrade their current products is pressing, but whatever the answer there, ASP is no longer just for IIS.

The ASP Object Model

We mentioned earlier, that "we make calls to one or several of the ASP intrinsic objects to create the dynamic element of an active server page". These objects are immediately accessible to the ASP developer and neatly cover all the key aspects of creating dynamic and interactive pages. Together, the five intrinsics and their parent object form the hierarchy that is the ASP Object Model, which looks something like this:

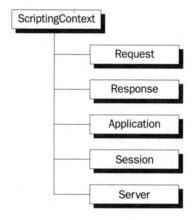

Each of the objects has a set of collections, methods, properties and events which provide them with all their functionality. The following chapters will take you through the calls and syntax of the five objects, but for now we'll have a brief look at how the objects divide up their work.

The Scripting Context Object

It's a bit of a cheat to include the scripting context object at the root of the ASP object model. Even though this is its rightful place, you'll never have to reference it directly because it simply represents the scope under which any scripting in ASP runs. Whenever a block of ASP code is run, ScriptingContext is created automatically, making the ASP intrinsics available to the scripting host along with the scripting objects. Similarly, when the scripting host finishes parsing an ASP page, it destroys the instance of ScriptingContext automatically.

In Visual Basic you can create an instance of the ScriptingContext object to get access to the ASP object model – this is what Visual Basic's new WebClass feature does.

The Conversation Objects - Request and Response

One of the main reasons that first scripting languages and then ASP were developed was that by themselves, HTML pages did not 'respond' to the client. They were static. The advent of scripting languages brought us the ability to determine what was going on within a page and react to that but these 'interactions' were limited to a developer second-guessing a user's actions and pre-programming a reaction. Only with ASP did the technology come into being that allowed a client's action (his *response*) to be 'seen' *by the server* and dealt with *by the server*. For an ASP developer, a website 'listens' to the client browser with the Request object and then answers using the Response object.

The Objects of State - Application and Session

As time has gone by, we have seen the transformation of static web content into fully competent web-based applications. We can now check our bank account, buy a computer, or hire a llama over the web – and most of the web applications (or *weblications*, if you prefer hideous contractions) online today are written and developed just as they would be if they were to be packaged in a box. ASP pages provide the user interface while COM components encapsulate the necessary business logic and let us access databases where our business information is stored. The only difference between developing applications for commercial distribution and web applications is the question of state.

The protocol over which web applications are run – HTTP – is stateless. It cannot remember from one page request to the next who you are, what you are doing or even what page you last looked at. Nor can it retain, for example, what items you're currently buying from amazon.com or CDNow. This is where the Application and Session objects come in, providing the virtual memory for a web application to run correctly and retain state.

The Server Object

Finally, we have the Server object, the least populated but arguably most useful object of them all. This contains four miscellaneous methods that the server performs, the most utilized of which is CreateObject – which allows us to create an instance of an ASP component.

The Scripting Objects

The third ingredient(s) in our ASP recipe are the Scripting Objects, which are available to us through the VBScript scripting engine – the FileSystemObject object, the TextStream object and the Dictionary object.

The FileSystemObject object allows us to code a page that accesses the file system of the web server itself. If we use the FileSystemObject object correctly we could create a website with the same functionality as Windows Explorer if we so wished. The key to this ability is the hierarchy of collections and objects of which it is the root:

FileSystemObject Object

```
                    ┌─────────────────────┐
        ┌───────────│  Drives Collection  │
        │           └─────────────────────┘
        │                   ┌─────────────────────┐
        │           ┌───────│     Drive Object    │
        │           │       └─────────────────────┘
        │           │
        │           ┌─────────────────────┐
        ├───────────│  Folders Collection │
        │           └─────────────────────┘
        │                   ┌─────────────────────┐
        │           ┌───────│    Folder Object    │
        │           │       └─────────────────────┘
        │           │
        │           ┌─────────────────────┐
        └───────────│   Files Collection  │
                    └─────────────────────┘
                            ┌─────────────────────┐
                    ┌───────│     File Object     │
                            └─────────────────────┘
```

FSO hierarchy diagram

A `Textstream` object is created by a call to one of `FileSystemObject` methods, `OpenTextFile` or `CreateTextFile`, or to a `File` object's `OpenAsTextStream` method. Once created, it gives you read/write access to the contents of the text file specified in the method. Of course, this will only work if the file actually contains valid ASCII characters. Naturally, `.txt` files work with `TextStream`, and so will `.htm` or `.asp` files, which are displayed as source code. You might also wish to inspect `.log` files with this object as well. But don't expect decent results using `TextStream` to inspect a `.dll` or a `.bin` file.

The last of the three scripting objects, the `Dictionary` object, acts as aneasily accessible store for name/value (or key/item as they are properly known) pairs, generated by the application during a session. `Dictionary` objects usually last for the duration of the page but can be stored in a `Session` object for use in a more 'mobile' role.

We'll look at the Scripting objects again in Chapter 6.

Using ASP Components

The final piece to the core-ASP puzzle is the use of ASP Components in a web application to encapsulate some or all of the key actions and rules that the application runs under. Heavily-hit sites become much more efficient when some or all of their functionality is coded within components, with ASP used as the adhesive to synchronize the program flow and integrate the components' functionality together.

The phrase *ASP Components* is a bit of a misnomer, because they're actually COM objects – written not in ASP but in C++, Visual Basic or Java. They are standalone `.dll` or `.exe` files that have entries in the Windows registry and make available extra properties and methods to the developer using them. At a low level, practically everything in the Windows world is based on COM (Microsoft's Component Object Model architecture) – even ASP. The intrinsics are also COM objects, stored in `asp.dll`, and can be used by any programmer who knows the correct way to reference them.

The key to ASP components is that the functionality within them has been pre-compiled and will run faster than if the code was parsed by the ASP Scripting Host. The performance gain is quite noticeable and, of course, they can be reused on many different sites as well.

There are four broad 'categories' of ASP component, as follows:

- **Presentation Components**. The one aspect of an application seen from the moment it starts is its user interface. Presentation components take the trouble out of the graphic side of web application creation and allow a developer to code the invisible back-end part of his site.

- **Business Components**. Developers building applications for the web may use ASP components to encapsulate their business logic rather than put it in an ASP page with the presentation code or in with the data server. The advantage to this approach is that if business logic needs to be updated, you only need to alter it within the component – you can leave both the data access and presentation code alone. A good example here is a component that encapsulates standard rules to validate credit card information for an e-commerce site.

- **Data Components**. Rather than use a great deal of code in a page querying (for example) an SQL database, a developer may choose to use a component to perform the queries and just call the component from the code. Alternatively, he could use a data component to access information from another non-database type of system.

- **Utility Components**. There are plenty of ASP components that perform some function that does not fall neatly into any of the three tiers of the classic application development model. We refer to these as utility components. For example, consider a component that allows us to upload files from one location to another over HTTP. It might even let us store these files within a database for good measure.

ASP components are fairly easy to come by. Some are automatically installed along with PWS and IIS, others are available from the IIS Resource Kit, and many more are available for download free of charge from the web. There is a thriving market in reliable third-party components too – however, these ones cost – or you can of course write your own. We'll look further at ASP components in Chapter 7.

How Does ASP Work?

How does an `.asp` file, full of calls to the ASP intrinsic objects and other components, get translated into an HTML page that a standard browser can view (and execute)? In fact, the process is reasonably simple:

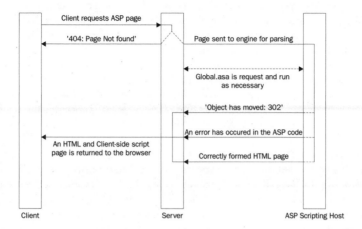

The client requests an ASP page by sending an HTTP Get or Post Request to the server. All things being equal, one of two things will happen here. If the server cannot find the file then it responds with the familiar **HTTP 404 Not Found** message. If the file is found, it will be recognized as an Active Server Page because of its .asp extension and sent to the ASP Scripting engine to be parsed. (All things *not* being equal, then something untoward – like a Server Error – may occur.)

The Scripting Host, located in asp.dll, can now do two things. If this is the first ASP page to be sent to this client from the server, this means a new session, and possibly a new application too, has begun and it will check global.asa for anything to do before it gets to the requested page. Once that has been done, or if this is not the first ASP page the client has requested, the host then executes all the server-side scripting code in the page as delimited by either <% ... %> or <SCRIPT RUNAT=SERVER> ... </SCRIPT> tags. Once this has been done, the engine passes back one of three things: an error page, an object moved status code, or an HTML page.

If either an error page or a correctly-formed HTML page is passed back, it is then displayed. If the ASP page contained a call to Response.Redirect, the server will pass back to the client the HTTP code 302 telling it that the page requested has moved temporarily. Note that if response buffering had previously been set to true, it will seem to the client that the server automatically transferred him to the new location of the page. If response buffering is set to false, which is the current ASP default, they will see an error page telling them the page they wanted has moved temporarily.

ASP Applications

Before we go any further, it would be a good idea to tie a few loose ends together and explain a few of the concepts that we've encountered in a little more detail, starting with exactly what a web application is. As we mentioned earlier, more sites are being developed for the web that mimic the functionality of an application you would go and buy from a shop.

A **web application** is really no more than a collection of ASP pages and server components, and a website can contain several. The distinction between them is made by the definition of the application's starting-point or root directory within the site. All the content within this directory and the physical directory structure underneath it is considered to be part of the application until another application root directory is found (although ideally one application shouldn't exist below another – we'll come to this in a moment). Thus the *scope* of an application is defined by the directories under the root not belonging to another application. The scope itself specifies the reach of changes to application state or to server-related attributes.

Each application has its own set of variables and attributes that define its current state, and these are maintained throughout the lifetime of the application from the moment it is first run until the end of the last session is closed. As we pointed out earlier, the problem with web-based applications is that the under-lying protocol of the web, HTTP, has less memory than a goldfish and retains no information from one client request to the next. ASP gets around this by using the `Application` and `Session` objects to store information for the duration of the application, and for the duration of a user's session, respectively. Both application and session states are initialized and destroyed by code contained in the `global.asa` file. `Global.asa` can be found in the root directory of any web application. Code in `global.asa` is triggered off at the initialization and termination of the application, and also at the beginning and end of each user session, governing the lifecycle of the state variables. `Global.asa` might also contain some 'global code' for use throughout the application.

An application's `global.asa` file is valid throughout the scope of that application, i.e. the application root directory and its physical subdirectories. If at all possible, you should avoid creating another application below an existing application, because this new application's root directory will be a subdirectory of the existing application. If both application root directories contain `global.asa` files, it's possible that they will conflict, with the wrong `global.asa` being executed. The safest option is to preserve a separate directory structure for each application.

Which Language for ASP?

Now that we've seen what goes into an ASP page, and how ASP pages are interpreted by the ASP Script Host, it's time to consider some practicalities. First up, what language do we create our ASP pages with?

Aside from the rule that it must be a scripting language, the ASP scripting host is language-independent. So if you're already familiar with, say, Python, Rexx or PerlScript, you could very well use them. For the purposes of this book however, we'll restrict our attention to the two scripting languages most associated with ASP – JScript and VBScript.

From an ASP point of view, both languages support the `object.method` syntax and the naming convention for procedures fired by an event. The main difference is how we access the various collections attached to, for example, the `Response` object.

Iterating through Collections

You may recall from earlier that the `Dictionary` scripting object is simply a collection of miscellaneous key/value pairs that you may want to make use of within a page (or possibly during an entire session). Like the `Dictionary`, the *collections* associated with the intrinsic objects also hold a number of key/value pairs but in these cases, those pairs are created in association with something specific. For example, the `Response.ClientCertificate` collection automatically contains information about the certificate a client has that allows access to your site.

As we do for the `Dictionary`, to retrieve the value of a specific key we need to know its name:

```
strValue = objDictionary.Item("KeyName")
```

This syntax works in both languages and we'll see plenty of examples of this later in the book.

Sometimes, though, we will also need to extract the contents of the entire collection – for example, to iterate through all the values stored in it. The approach here depends on our choice of scripting language, as we'll see next.

In VBScript

Iterating through a collection in VBScript is made very easy thanks to the `For Each ... Next` construct. Consider the following code fragment that displays each key in the `Response.Form` collection together with the stored within it.

```
For Each Item In Response.Form
    strKeyName = Item
    strValue = Response.Form(Item)
    Response.Write strKeyName & "  " & strValue & "<BR>"
Next
```

For every key/value pair in the collection, we store the name of the key in `strKeyName` and its value in `strValue` and then display them to the screen using `Response.Write`, separating the two with a couple of spaces for clarity's sake.

In JScript

In JScript (Microsoft's implementation of the ECMAScript scripting language standard), the `For Each ... Next` construct does not exist. Instead we make use of a special JScript object whose sole reason for being is to provide access to collections - the `Enumerator` object.

First we create an Enumerator for the collection that we want to access:

```
new Enumerator(collection)
```

Now we have access to its methods, `moveFirst` and `moveNext` and its properties `AtEnd` and `Item`. A fragment that performs the same task as the one we saw in VBScript would look like this:

```
FormItems = new Enumerator(Response.Form)
while (!FormItems.atEnd())
{
  i = FormItems.item();
  strKeyName = i
  strValue = Response.Form(i)
  Response.Write (strKeyName + "  " + strValue + "<BR>");
  FormItems.moveNext();
}
```

Once we've created an Enumerator that will run through the `Response.Form` collection, we use a `while` loop instead of the `for each ... next` loop to get each item, checking each time that we haven't reached the end of the collection. If not, then we `MoveNext` to retrieve the next key/value pair. The rest of the code within the loop is basically the same with only a few syntactical differences.

Which Language is Best?

Which language should you choose? Really, it's up to you. The language you choose should be one that you are comfortable with and that offers you the most functionality with respect to your project. The releases of VBScript and JScript version 5 are just around the corner and both offer some new features (like error-catching and support for regular expressions) that you should take into consideration. There's no reason why you can't use more than one language on the same page – however, for the sake of readability and maintenance it's not recommended.

Most of the code samples in this book are written in VBScript, because it's currently the preset default language for writing ASP pages.

Writing Good ASP

Knowing the vocabulary, grammar and syntax of a language does not mean you are automatically a best-selling novelist. You may make mistakes, use inelegant and inefficient code, not consider scalability issues and not document your code well enough for it to be maintained by others, to name but a few things. We don't pretend to be any better at it either (Response.Wirte? Doh!) but we have spotted a few things that do make for a good page. Most of these you should do already, but a little memory-jogging never hurts.

Give Your Site A Structure

People are getting employed these days as 'information architects' to come into to an organization and devise a data infrastructure that allows information in different geographical locations, different devices and different formats to be integrated into one easily accessible whole. The adoption of an intranet (or extranet) is often at the forefront of their ideas and it's then up to developers to implement their grand scheme.

Usually, when a website is begun, little consideration is given to problems that will be faced when they become medium or large sized. Developers who begin their construction with a well-organized and easily navigable directory structure are already one step ahead of those whose random page locations are hard to discern and impossible to scale with under the strain of a great deal of information. Even if you don't anticipate your site containing a great deal of content (things change!), you will still benefit from this approach.

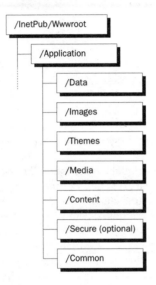

You may want to consider this example structure as a place to start.

Here, the root of the application hangs off the InetPub/Wwwroot directory and contains just a couple of files; probably global.asa and the default home page for the application. Underneath this root are a number of directories that contain the contents of the site according to what type of content a file contains.

- ❑ /Common will contain server-side include files that can help to make site development and maintenance less of a chore. More on these in a minute.
- ❑ /Content will contain all the .htm and .asp files that this site can display. Thus scripting permission will be enabled for this directory and disabled for all others.
- ❑ /Data will contain all the rich data sources that ASP makes use of. For example, this directory might hold a couple of .mdb Access databases.
- ❑ /Images will contain all the graphics files used in the site.
- ❑ /Media will hold all the video and sound files
- ❑ /Secure will hold the subset of the site that is to be sent to a client using the secure HTTPS protocol, for example the section of an e-commerce site that asks for credit-card details.
- ❑ /Themes holds the template graphic files that give the site a regular look and feel.

It is a simple matter to create a strong directory structure like this for your application, which you can then only benefit from as your site content grows larger.

At The Top Of The Page

The first lines of your ASP page (as opposed to `global.asa`) are very important – they can define the basic handling instructions for the rest of your page. Consider this segment of code:

```
<% @Language = "VBScript" %>
<%
    Option Explicit
    Response.Buffer  = true
    Response.Expires = -1000
%>
```

The first line – `<% @Language = "VBScript" %>` – declares the default language in which the server-side script on the page is to be written. Even if you are using VBScript (which is the default anyway), it is good programming practice to use this line.

Following on (not unlike the English national cricket team), the use of `Option Explicit` in your pages will save you a great deal of time when debugging your pages. How? The VBScript scripting engine allows you to use variables without first declaring them. This is great until you misspell one of your variables – VBScript simply treats it as a new variable and carries on as if there's nothing wrong. For example, suppose you declare `NoOfHorses` as a variable and use it throughout your page; then when you try to display the final tally of our four-legged friends, you accidentally mistype `Response.Write(NoOfForses)`. This will echo '0' to the screen because the engine thinks you've specified a new variable, `NoOfForses`.

The `Option Explicit` command gives us control over this – by writing `Option Explicit` at the top of your page, you force the parser to throw an error if it comes across an undeclared variable in the ASP code.

By setting `Response.Buffer = true`, we tell the server not to send a page and its contents down to the client until it has finished processing all the server-side script on the page. The server then has only to send one set of HTTP headers down to the client along with the requested page instead of perhaps two or three, making the communication between client and server more efficient.

Buffering is also useful in debugging, allowing you to hold back content from your test client until you `Flush` it at a point you think a bug might have occurred. With ASP 2.0, the default for response buffering is off (`false`) although in the next release of ASP, the default will be on (`true`). There's more about buffering in Chapters 3 and 10.

Finally, if you know that your page will change at regular intervals, don't forget to expire your page accordingly. When your ASP is 'translated' into a static page and stored in the client's cache, it is given an expiry date after which the client requests an up-to-date page from the server. On the other hand, if your pages *don't* change often then it's not worth setting a short expiry period – the shorter the expiry period, the more work your server will have to do to redeliver requested pages.

You can force a client's request to call a fresh version of your page (i.e. from your server, not from the client's cache) by making the page expire the instant it is received by the client. To do this, declare `Response.Expires=-1441`. Why -1441? This declares that the page expired twenty-four hours and one minute ago, *with respect to the internal clock on the server and not the client.* Why doesn't `Response.Expires=0` work? Well, it *might* work – but (for example) if the server delivers a page to a client 5.00pm, then the page will expire at 5.00pm on the client; if the client's internal clock is running behind the server's internal clock, then you won't get immediate expiry. By setting the expiry period to at least 24 hours will almost certainly ensure the client expires the page instantly.

In General

Within the `<BODY>  </BODY>` of the page, there are a few more tips and tricks to be aware of.

Use Include Files

By including frequently-used pieces of code within server-side include files, your pages become easier to read and easier to create. Instead of 10 or 15 lines of code that, for example, setup your HTML meta tags, you would instead write the simple line:

```
#include virtual="/Common/metatags.inc"
```

This gets those tags from the file `metatags.inc`. In the above statement, this is assumed to be found in the `Common` subdirectory of the website's root folder. We can also specify its location in a physical directory on the server's hard drive with the line:

```
#include file="d:\wwwroot\includes\metatags.inc"
```

Consistent use of one of these lines throughout your site would also mean that you can update the tags for all those pages simply by updating the include file. Thus, the use of server-side include files makes it easier to handle and maintain code, and also brings the web developer closer to the programming ideal of modular code and reusable code components.

Note that it's a bit safer to use the `.asp` extension for include files. With this, you do not have to worry about turning off Script permissions for the directory that holds them, as you should do if you use the `.inc` extension shown above. On the other hand, using `.inc` does distinguish include files from ASP pages.

Remove Comments From Live Pages

Comments in your code seriously reduce the ability of the ASP parser to zip through pages and serve them up to the client. Make sure to keep copies of your work that are well commented so you can maintain and improve them, but when you are ready to release your work to a live production server, remove all the comments from your site.

Minimize Context Switching

There is a time cost involved in the switch between parsing server-side scripting code and looking through HTML and client-side script for the next <% .. %> block. Consider this code:

```
<% Response.Write ("Hello Mum") %>
<% Response.Write ("<BR>") %>
<% Response.Write ("I'm fine thanks") %>
```

The code above will incur six time penalties when being parsed. Now consider this:

```
<%
  Response.Write ("Hello Mum")
  Response.Write ("<BR>")
  Response.Write ("I'm fine thanks")
%>
```

This incurs only two time penalties, because we've used fewer ASP <% .. %> blocks.

Don't Rely On Cookies

Cookies are undoubtedly very useful. They allow us to query the client machine for a user identity with which we can personalize our ASP pages. However, there remains a myth that cookies are inherently unsafe – consequently, some users may prohibit a server from placing cookies on their machine. Alternatively, the cookie may have been deleted from the client machine or have been tampered with, rendering it invalid. If your site does use cookies for some purpose, try to minimize what you put in them. For example, a user's complete identity could be stored in a database on the server, while the cookie at the user's end would solely contain a unique key in that database which references the correct ID.

Performance Testing

Your task is not done, even when you've finished writing your pages. It is the developer's responsibility to make sure that his code is as robust, reliable, tight and efficient as he can make it.

Try and Break Your Own Code

The people who have created a site are generally the most likely to know where the possible problems and weaknesses are. They should see if they can break the site and cause it to produce unaccounted-for results, errors and other faults. Web sites should not be exempt from alpha testing – they're still just code.

Load Testing

These days, several utilities, like InetMonitor 3.0 (available from http://www.microsoft.com/msdownload/#itool), are available which can stress test your site and the server that hosts it. They do this by simulating very large numbers of clients trying to access the site at the same time and present very detailed results about the degradation of performance as more clients are introduced. Those of you creating a commercial site should give serious thought to acquiring a copy of such load testing software and using it before you put the site live.

Summary

In this chapter, we tried to cover the massive topic of ASP in as concise a form as possible. You should now have some idea of what ASP is, how it works, how you might use it and how you might want to code with it. The rest of the book should now serve as a reference as you put your plan of ASP development into action.

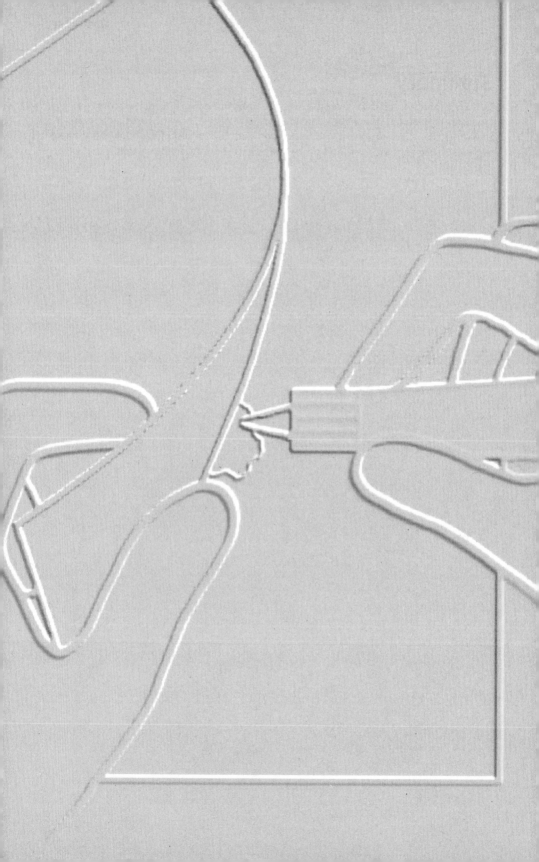

2

The Request Object

In Chapter 1, we saw that ASP provides us with a number of built-in (intrinsic) objects. As ASP developers, these objects help us with much of the grunt work needed to deal with HTTP requests and responses, and with generating web content dynamically. In the early days of the Internet, many such tasks required a lot of code – now, with ASP, we can perform the same tasks through a single method call on one of these objects.

In this chapter we shall focus on one of these ASP intrinsic objects – the Request object. As we go down that road, we'll also consider:

❑   The HTTP protocol
❑   What a client certificate is
❑   A brief overview of cookies
❑   HTML forms, and the difference between the POST and GET methods
❑   What a query string is, and how to use them
❑   Server variables and their uses

Before we discuss the various collections, properties and the methods of the Request object, we'll give a quick overview of how a client and a server communicate using requests and responses.

The HTTP Protocol

The Internet is based upon a set of transport protocols and networking protocols, which are collectively known as **TCP/IP**. Above TCP/IP sits an application-layer protocol called **HTTP** – the **HyperText Transfer Protocol**. The HTTP protocol specification includes definitions for the following:

❑   **The HTTP Request:** this is the format of any message that is sent from the client to the server (e.g. from the browser to the web server). This message includes the URL of the required web resource and information about the client hardware platform. In some cases it also contains information about the user.

❑ **The HTTP Response:** this is the format of any message that is sent from the server to the client. This message includes the web content that has been requested.

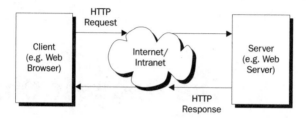

ASP and HTTP

So how do we get at the information passed in the HTTP Request and Response messages? ASP provides us with a quick and simple way of getting at the information programmatically:

❑ We use the ASP Request object to extract the information stored in the HTTP Request message. The Request object is the subject of this chapter.

❑ We use the Response object to handle the information returned in the HTTP Response message. The Response object is the subject of Chapter 3.

Because we can use the Request and Response objects, we'll never need to write any message-parsing code to extract information from the HTTP Request and Response messages. In fact, we don't even need to *know* the exact format of the HTTP Request and Response.

To track communications between the browser and the server, ASP must capture and store the information from the HTTP Requests that the client makes as he references ASP pages. To do this, a host of information (the details of the browser, the URL, and a whole bunch of other stuff) is placed in a Request object. Having collected this information, our scripts can then use the Request object's methods and properties to access the information and thus determine what action to take, and what kind of information to return.

The Request Object

Let's start with a clear definition. The Request **object** enables our web application to access the information contained in an HTTP Request. The information wrapped up in the HTTP Request message is then received and handled by the web server. If the requested web resource in an ASP page, the ASP Scripting Host analyses the HTTP Request message and places information into specially designed data containers, called **collections**.

In a collection, each piece of information is stored as a name/value pair. Put simply, a collection is like a two-column array. The first column is a list of names; the second column contains the values associated to those names. What's special about a collection is that each name is unique within that collection – thus, we can access a value by referring to its name. Collections are good for storing properties and attributes of objects.

> *The name/value pair is a also known as a key/item pair, as these pairs can be stored in the* Dictionary *object with the names (or keys) in one array and the values (or items) in another. We discuss the* Dictionary *object in greater detail in Chapter 6.*

The Request object contains five collections, which store the information retrieved from the HTTP request message. Here's the full interface that the Request object makes available to us:

REQUEST	
Collections	
ClientCertificate	QueryString
Cookies	ServerVariables
Form	
Properties	
TotalBytes	
Methods	
BinaryRead	
Events	

The Requests object's five collections present us with an organized storage system for the information retrieved from the HTTP Request message. When a client sends an HTTP Request, he provides four basic sources of information that the web server may want to access via the Request object:

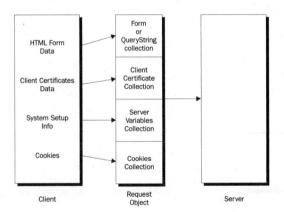

We'll have a closer look at these collections now, and then we'll tackle the TotalBytes property and the BinaryRead method.

The Request Object Collections

In this section we'll look at the five collections of the Request object. We'll explain what each collection represents, and we'll also give syntax and examples.

Client Certificates

When the client makes contact with a web server over a secured channel, either end can gain high levels of assurance over the identity of the other by inspecting their **digital certificate**. A digital certificate contains a number of items of information about an individual or an organization and this is generated by a trusted third party called a **Certificate Authority** (CA). The CA is responsible for checking the credentials of the certificate owner.

> *A secured channel is a communications protocol that provides strong levels of security by providing encryption, message tampering detection and end-point authentication. The common secured channel protocol used by web servers and web browsers is the **Secure Sockets Layer (SSL)** – this is a variation of the HTTP protocol used when a web application required high levels of security.*
>
> *An SSL connection is instantiated by the client specifying a URL with an* https:// *protocol prefix. In fact, HTTPS is simply SSL underlying HTTP. This protocol defines how servers request certifications and browsers send the appropriate certification fields.*

The format of a digital certificate is defined by the X.509 specification. You can find this at http://www.ietf.cnri.reston.va.us/html.charters/pkix-charter.html, and there's an explanation of X.509 at http://poetry-server.cc.columbia.edu/acis/rad/columbiaca/more-info-cert.html. Secured channels and digital certificates rely on complex cryptographic algorithms that are far beyond the scope of this book. All an ASP developer needs to know is that a client-side digital certificate contains various items of information about the certificate holder, such as the holder's key, name and address, the length of time the certificate is valid for.

The ClientCertificate Collection

The ClientCertificate collection is used to access the information located in a client-side digital certificate. These certificates are optional and the contents are only available to ASP when a client and server have established a secured channel and the web server has been configured to insist that clients make their digital certificates available when establishing the connection.

The ClientCertificate collection holds these items of data which are retrieved from the **certification fields** of the client request. The ClientCertificate collection will be empty if the protocol is HTTP, or if the protocol is HTTPS but the server does not require the client to send the client-side digital certificate details (this is an administration configuration option in IIS).

The ClientCertificate collection is read-only. In order to access the elements of the ClientCertificate collection, use the following syntax:

```
[varRetValue = ]Request.ClientCertificate(key[subField])
```

Name	Type	Description
key	String	A field from the digital certificate
subField	String (optional)	Can be used to extract individual items in place of the whole Subject or Issuer keys

The key parameter can take any of the following values:

Key	Type of associated Value	Description of Name/Value Pair
Certificate	String	Contains the certificate contents in its entirety, in ASN.1 format. (ASN.1 is Abstract Syntax Notation One – a notation for describing abstract types and values – see http://auchentoshan.cs.ucl.ac.uk:8877/htm/pkcs/layman.htm)
Flags	Variant	Contains either the value 1 (indicates that a client certificate is present) or 2 (indicates that the issuer of the certificate was unknown). The constants ceCertPresent and ceUnrecognizedIssuer are commonly used to represent these integer values – they are defined in the server-side include file cervbs.inc
Issuer	String	Contains information about the trusted third party that issued the certificate. Consists of a number of separate items called subfields, which (as we shall see shortly) can be extracted individually
SerialNumber	String	Contains a unique serial number for the certificate that is allocated by the trusted third party that issued the certificate. It is formatted as an ASCII representation of its hexadecimal value separated by hyphens (-)
Subject	String	Contains information about the owner of the certificate. Like Issuer, this contains a number of separate items that can be extracted individually.
ValidFrom	Date	Specifies when the certificate becomes valid
ValidUntil	Date	Specifies when the certificate expires

The `subField` parameter is used together with the `Subject` or `Issuer` keys to extract the following individual items, in place of the whole field:

Name	Description
C	The name of the **country** of origin
O	The name of the company or **organization**
OU	The name of the **organization unit**
CN	The **common name** of the user. Used only with the **Subject** key
L	The **locality**
S	The **state** or province
T	The **title** of the person or organization
GN	The **given name** of the person
I	The set of **initials**

The `subField` parameter, when used, is appended as a suffix to the `key` parameter. For example, to retrieve the name of the organization from the `Subject` field, you use `SubjectO`.

Some client certificates contain extra `subField` values (other than those listed above). All of the available values can be identified by their **ASN.1 identifier** – a list of numbers separated by a period (e.g. `2.64.328.01`).

For example, here's how you might retrieve all keys in the `ClientCertificate` collection in VBScript:

```
<%
  For Each Item in Request.ClientCertificate
    Response.Write(Item & " = " & Request.ClientCertificate(Item) & "<BR>")
  Next
%>
```

To check whether the client certificate is presented, you can use the following code:

```
<%
  If Len(Request.ClientCertificate("Subject")) = 0
    Response.Write("Error - There is no client certificate available.")
  End if
%>
```

> You should check that the certificate is available *before* accessing the certificate's fields.

To retrieve the value of any field of the certificate, you simply use its full name. We can use the following to write the value of the `ValidUntil` field to the browser:

```
<%
   Response.Write(Request.ClientCertificate("ValidUntil"))
%>
```

To check the value of the `Flags` key, you should make sure that these two constants `ceCertPresent` and `ceUnrecognizedIssuer` are defined:

```
<!--#include file="cervbs.inc"-->
```

Now, we can find out whether the issuer of the certificate is known:

```
<%
   If Request.ClientCertificate("Flags") AND ceUnrecognizedIssuer Then
      ' The issuer of the certificate is unknown
   End If
%>
```

As we already mentioned, to get the values of the `subField` parameter, we should add it as a suffix to the `key` parameter:

```
<%
   strCommonName = Request.ClientCertificate("SubjectCN")
   strOrg = Request.ClientCertificate("SubjectO")
   Response.Write("Hello " & strCommonName & "! Still working for " _
                       & strOrg & " ?")
%>
```

Reading From A Cookie

The cookies mechanism was first introduced by Netscape in their Netscape 2.0 browser. It allows the web server to store a small packet of information – a cookie – in a file on the client for later access and use. A cookie may contain information that was sent from the client to the server, or information that was created by the server without client intervention. For example, a cookie may contain a `CustomerID` number that's generated by the server and used exclusively by the server for admin purposes.

The cookie is written to the client by including the cookie name and its value (and, optionally, a domain/path name and expiry date) within an HTTP response. With ASP, this is done using the `Response` object –we'll look at this in the next chapter.

When the server wants to access the information contained within a cookie, it does so through the `Request.Cookies` collection, which we'll look at now.

The Cookies Collection

Any HTTP request for a URL will append all cookies that are associated with the requested domain/path name; a cookie will also be appended if the URL is for a file beneath the cookie's path name. By using the `Request` object's `Cookies` collection, we can detect the presence of a particular cookie and determine its value.

The syntax for using the `Cookies` collection is:

```
[varCookieValue = ]Request.Cookies("cookie")[("key")]
```

Name	Type	Description
cookie	String	The name of the cookie to be retrieved
key	String (optional)	Used to retrieve individual items from a cookie that contains multiple values

> Cookies with multiple values are stored as key/item pairs, as in the
> `Dictionary` object. We'll discuss this in Chapter 6.

Each cookie has a single attribute, called `HasKeys`. This is read-only and specifies whether the cookie contains multiple values (the different values are distinguished by the use of keys). Also, the `Request.Cookies` collection itself has a single attribute, called `Count` – this counts the number of cookies that the user currently has stored:

```
[boolHasKeys = ]Request.Cookies("cookie").HasKeys
[intCookieCount = ]Request.Cookies.Count
```

Iterating through the `Cookies` collection is easy. The following fragment uses `Response.Write` to write the cookie name and value (`Item` and `Request.Cookies(Item)`, respectively) to the browser:

```
<%
  For Each Item in Request.Cookies
    Response.Write("Cookie: " & Item & _ " = " & _
                                   Request.Cookies(Item) & "<BR>")
  Next
%>
```

We can check the value of the `HasKeys` attribute in order to get the subkeys from the cookie:

```
<%
  For Each Item in Request.Cookies
    If Request.Cookies(Item).HasKeys Then
      For Each ItemKey in Request.Cookies(Item)
        Response.Write("SubItem " & Item & "." & ItemKey & _
                        " = " & Request.Cookies(Item)(ItemKey)) & "<BR>"
      Next ItemKey
    Else
      Response.Write("Item " & Item & " = " & Request.Cookies(Item) & "<BR>")
    End If
  Next
%>
```

Here again, we've used the `Response` object simply to display our cookie values on the screen.

Because cookies are stored on the client, they can tell us about what the client user did when he last visited our site. On the next visit, we can read this information from the cookie and use it to determine the course of action. This example reacts according to the number of previous visits the user has made:

```
<%
  If Request.Cookies("User1") ="" Then
    Response.Write "Hello doubty newcomer!"
    Response.Cookies("User1") = 1
    Response.Cookies("User1").Expires = DateAdd("m", 3, Now)
  ElseIf Request.Cookies("User1") <= 3 Then
    Response.Write "Welcome back!"
    Response.Cookies("User1") = Request.Cookies("User1") + 1
  Else
    Response.Write "How goes it, old timer?"
  End If%>
```

This rather simplistic script (whose purpose could be achieved in other ways, admittedly) counts the number of times a user has visited a site. It checks to see if the there is a cookie called User stored in the Cookies collection. If not, then it displays the first message and then sets the value of the cookie. Then when the user returns to our site, he gets the second message, and if he comes back four times then he gets a different message again.

Cookies are often used together with Session and Application objects (discussed in Chapter 4), which retain information between different web pages. You could use this code to determine the number of first-time visitors currently visiting a page (this assumes the global variable Application("NoOfUsers") had been previously defined in global.asa):

```
<%
  If Request.Cookies("User1") ="" Then
    Application("NoOfUsers") = Application("NoOfUsers")+ 1
    Response.Cookies("User1") = "Old"
    Response.Cookies("User1") = DateAdd("m", 3, Now)
  End If
%>
```

This code checks to see whether the user has visited the site before; if not, it adds one to an Application variable storing the number of users, and changes their cookie. Of course, you'll also need to write a method that decrements the Application variable every time a user leaves the page.

If your web application is prone to attracting many users, then Session variables can eat up your server resources. One solution is to use cookies instead of Session variables because they distribute the cost of memory among the clients.

In addition to the properties described, a cookie can have attributes that describe its lifetime and availability. We'll leave this discussion to the Response object, where we can actually set these values using script, rather than just being able to read them.

Reading From an HTML Form

From the client's point of view, the most frequently used of these sources is the standard **HTML form** – we've all encountered them at some time. Each element of a form is named, and the name is paired with the data given in that form element. Then the name/value pairs are sent back to the server, in the form of a string, which can then be accessed either by the `Form` collection or by the `QueryString` collection.

Submitting a form in HTML is easy: the client simply enters the information into text boxes or select boxes and clicks on the SUBMIT button. When the HTML Form is SUBMITted, the web browser initiates an HTTP Request for the URL specified in the form's ACTION attribute (specified in the <FORM> tag – see the examples below).

The browser also notes the METHOD attribute of the <FORM> tag, which specifies how the elements in the form are to be packaged within the HTTP Request message. The METHOD attribute will determine how the form's values are sent. Also, if the page specified in the form's ACTION attribute is an .asp page, the form's METHOD attribute determines the appropriate `Request` object collection to be populated with the HTML form data. The METHOD attribute takes one of the following values:

METHOD attribute	How are form elements sent?	Request collection used to read data
POST	Inside HTTP Request body (the free format area of the HTTP Request)	Form
GET	Tagged onto the end of the URL	QueryString

The GET method is the older method, and has a drawback that there is a limit on how long the submission can be. Let's look at a couple of examples. First, here's an HTML <FORM> tag for a form that is sent to the server using the POST method:

```
<FORM NAME="BirthdayCard" ACTION="InMailbox.asp" METHOD="POST">
```

Here, the name/value pairs are sent in the body of the HTTP Request that requests `InMailbox.asp`. The HTML form information is then accessible via the `Request` object's `Form` collection.

Now here's a <FORM> tag for a form sent to the server using the GET method:

```
<FORM NAME="CureAmnesia" ACTION="memory.asp" METHOD="GET">
```

Here, the URL (specified by the ACTION attribute) is suffixed with a question mark delimiter, followed by the name/value pairs from the HTML form:

```
http://testserver.com/memory.asp?FirstName=Abraham&LastName=Lincoln
```

This section of the URL that follows the ? is called the **query string**. The HTML form information (in this case, the values FirstName and LastName) are then accessible in the Request object's QueryString collection.

Should I Use POST or GET?

So which method should you use – POST or GET? In older browsers there is a 255-character limit on the length of a URL – so this imposes a limit on the amount of information you can send with a GET. Also, sending a Form using GET means that the form data shows up as part of the URL – exposing it to users' eyes. (The URL would show up in log files, as well, so you're showing this information quite freely.) Further, every HTTP request drags along the referral URL (i.e. where the client came from). This poses a potential security risk if you have information contained in the URL and then have a link to another site – that other site sees the referral URL and the form information. Given these criteria, you're probably better off using POST whenever possible – as it's more secure.

So we've looked at how an HTML form is created, and the information sent in the HTTP Request. Now let's look at the Request.Form and Request.QueryString collections, which make this information accessible to our ASP scripts.

The Form Collection

The Form collection allows our ASP script logic to retrieve the values of any HTML form elements posted with the HTTP request (when the METHOD type specified in the <FORM> tag is POST). The syntax is:

```
[varValue = ]Request.Form(element)[(index)]
[varValue = ]Request.Form(num)
```

Name	Type	Description
element	String	A string enclosed in quotes, specifying the name of the form element
index	Integer (optional)	Enables access to multiple values – can take any value in the range 1 to Request.Form(element).Count
num	Integer	Enables access to the num-th element of the form

There's also an attribute, `Count`:

[*varEltsCount* =]Request.Form[(*element*)].Count

This returns an integer. If you include the optional *element* parameter then this returns the number of values associated with *element*. Otherwise, it returns the number of form elements on the page that have been submitted (even if empty).

Working with Simple Forms

Let's handle the data that's sent through form using the POST method. Here is the HTML code that makes a form:

```
<FORM NAME="SimpleForm" ACTION="DealWithForm.asp" METHOD="POST">
Type your name here: <INPUT TYPE="TEXT" NAME="USERNAME"> <BR>
Type your phone number here: <INPUT TYPE="TEXT" NAME="PHONENO"> <P>
<INPUT TYPE=RESET   VALUE="Clear">
<INPUT TYPE=SUBMIT VALUE="Submit">
</FORM>
```

As you can see, we have two input lines implemented with `<INPUT>` HTML elements of the type "TEXT", and two buttons with default actions – RESET and SUBMIT. In this form., we use the POST method to send data from the client browser to an ASP application; so the data is placed in the `Request` object's `Form` collection.

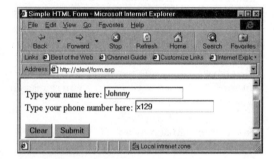

Now it's up to the ASP script logic to process the data sent from the client. Because we've used the POST method on the client side, we extract the data from the `Form` collection. As with other collections, we can simply use an iterator (as discussed in Chapter 1), as shown in the example below:

```
<%
  For Each Item in Request.Form
    Response.Write("For element '" & Item &_
            "' you've entered the value '" & Request.Form(Item) &_
            "'<BR>")
  Next
%>
```

The generated HTML will produce the following output for our simple form:

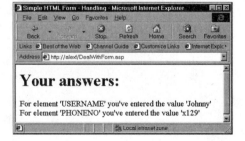

As you can see, we can determine the name of each element (which was set using the NAME attribute of the appropriate HTML tag), and the value of that element.

It's easy to dump the entire contents of the form onto the browser display; but we can also access the values of individual elements. Assuming we know the names of the elements in the form, we can simply use these names to access their values:

```
Response.Write("Hello, <i>" & Request.Form("USERNAME") & "</i>!<BR>")
```

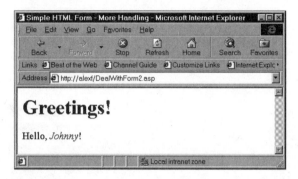

Dealing with Multi-Selection Controls

There are some controls that allow users to choose more than one value from a list of options. We can see this in action by looking at the <SELECT> control. Consider the following example:

```
<FORM NAME="MultiChoice" ACTION="DealWithForm3.asp" METHOD="POST">
  <H2>Which continents have you visited? </H2><BR>
  <INPUT NAME="Cnent" TYPE=CHECKBOX VALUE="Africa"> Africa <BR>
  <INPUT NAME="Cnent" TYPE=CHECKBOX VALUE="North America"> North America <BR>
  <INPUT NAME="Cnent" TYPE=CHECKBOX VALUE="South America"> South America <BR>
  <INPUT NAME="Cnent" TYPE=CHECKBOX VALUE="Antarctica"> Antarctica <BR>
  <INPUT NAME="Cnent" TYPE=CHECKBOX VALUE="The Arctic"> The Arctic <BR>
  <INPUT NAME="Cnent" TYPE=CHECKBOX VALUE="Asia"> Asia <BR>
  <INPUT NAME="Cnent" TYPE=CHECKBOX VALUE="Australasia"> Australasia <BR>
  <INPUT NAME="Cnent" TYPE=CHECKBOX VALUE="Europe"> Europe  <P>
  <INPUT TYPE=RESET  VALUE="Clear">
  <INPUT TYPE=SUBMIT VALUE="Submit">
</FORM>
```

The user is permitted to choose any number of options in the list. When the form is submitted, we can use the `Request.Form` collection's `Count` property to determine the number of selected element items:

```
<%
    If Request.Form("Cnent").Count<=1 Then
        Response.Write("Not too well-traveled, huh?")
    Else
        Response.Write("You've really been to all these places?" & "<BR>")
        For i = 1 To Request.Form("Cnent").Count
            Response.Write (Request.Form("Cnent")(i) & "<BR>")
        Next
        Response.Write("<BR>" & "Impressive...")
    End If
%>
```

As we've mentioned already, the `Form` collection holds data sent through the `POST` method. Now let's look at the `QueryString` collection – that allows us to retrieve data sent with the `GET` method, or `HREF` method of the Anchor `<A>` tag.

The QueryString Collection

The QueryString collection allows our ASP script logic to retrieve the values of query strings – the parameters tagged onto the end of a requested URL:

```
http://www.wrox.com/Store/Support.asp?Code=2459
http://www.sportsite.com/news.asp?sport=football&team=seagulls
```

The syntax for the QueryString collection is:

[*varValue* =]Request.QueryString(*variable*)[(*index*)]

Name	Type	Description
variable	String	A string enclosed in quotes, specifying the name of the variable in the HTTP query string to be retrieved
index	Integer (optional)	Enables access to multiple values contained in the variable. Can take any value in the range 1 to Request.QueryString(variable).

There's also an attribute, Count:

[*varEltsCount* =]Request.QueryString[(*variable*)].Count

This returns an integer. If you include the optional *variable* parameter then this returns the number of values associated with *variable*. Otherwise, it returns the number of name/value pairs that have been submitted in the query string (even if empty).

> Note that the QueryString collection is a parsed version of the QUERY_STRING variable ,which is found in the ServerVariables collection – we'll come to that later in the chapter.

As we've seen, we can generate a query string using an HTML form, by setting the METHOD attribute of the FORM tag to GET:

```
<FORM NAME="MainStories" ACTION="news.asp" METHOD="GET">
```

We can also generate a query string explicitly by using the HTML anchor tag:

```
<A HREF= "news.asp?sport=football">Football - Latest</A>
```

Of course, the user can generate a query string manually by adding it to the URL that they type into the address box of the web browser.

QueryString and Anchor Tags

Let's look at a simple example which demonstrates how to pass a query string using an anchor tag, and how to retrieve the values of specific names sent. The following code will generate a query string when the user answers the question:

```
<H2>Question 2 </H2><BR>
What is the capital city of Sweden? <BR>
<A HREF="q2answer.asp?answer=Reykavik&rw=wrong">Reykavik</A><BR>
<A HREF="q2answer.asp?answer=Stockholm&rw=right">Stockholm</A><BR>
<A HREF="q2answer.asp?answer=Oslo&rw=wrong">Oslo</A><BR>
<A HREF="q2answer.asp?answer=Copenhagen&rw=wrong">Copenhagen</A><BR>
```

Of course, the user could cheat by looking at the source code! In this case, we'll depend on the user's integrity – but it's worth noting again that the information sent in the query string isn't secure.

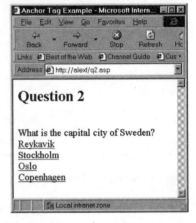

When the user clicks on a link, the `<A>` tag sends a query string that consists of the two variables — `answer` and `rw`. The ASP code that handles the query string looks like this:

```
<%
  Response.Write("Your answer was " & _
                 Request.QueryString("answer") & "...<BR>")
  If Request.QueryString("rw")="right" Then
    Response.Write("That's the correct answer!")
  Else
    Response.Write("No, that's the wrong answer.")
  End If
%>
```

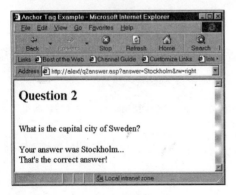

Note that we can see the query string's data in the address box – which affirms again that this isn't a secure way to send information.

Unparsed Query Strings

If you want to use the unparsed version of the query string, simply refer to the `QueryString` collection without specifying a value for the index:

```
dim strUnparsedQS
strUnparsedQS = Request.QueryString
```

This will place the string `answer=Stockholm&rw=right` into the variable `strUnparsedQS`.

Multiple Values

If a parameter can hold multiple values, we use the `Count` property to count the number of values. Let's briefly return to our "How many continents..." example (from earlier in this chapter). This time, we'll pass the information using the `GET` method:

```
<FORM NAME="MultiChoiceQS" ACTION="DealWithQS.asp" METHOD="GET">
  <H2>Which continents have you visited? </H2><BR>
  <INPUT NAME="Cnent" TYPE=CHECKBOX VALUE="Africa"> Africa <BR>
'...snip...
  <INPUT NAME="Cnent" TYPE=CHECKBOX VALUE="Europe"> Europe  <P>
  <INPUT TYPE=RESET  VALUE="Clear">
  <INPUT TYPE=SUBMIT VALUE="Submit">
</FORM>
```

The only change we've made is to the first line — the values for the `ACTION` and `METHOD` attributes of the `<FORM>` tag. To the user, the resulting form looks much the same as before. When the form is submitted, the information is sent to `DealWithQS.asp` in the URL:

```
http://alexf/DealWithQS.asp?Cnent=North+America&Cnent=Asia
```

The code that we use to handle this info is similar to what we've seen before:

```
<%
  If Request.QueryString("Cnent").Count<=1 Then
     Response.Write("Not too well-traveled, huh?")
  Else
     Response.Write("You've really been to all these places?" &
"<BR>")
     For i = 1 To Request.QueryString("Cnent").Count
       Response.Write (Request.QueryString("Cnent")(i) & "<BR>")
     Next
     Response.Write("<BR>" & "Impressive...")
  End If
%>
```

The last collection the `Request` object has is the `ServerVariables` collection. This collection holds the values of some server variables which are commonly termed environment variables.

Using The Server Variables

When an ASP application is executed, there's a plethora of information that is passed across. It's not just info about the application, but also things like who ran the application, where the application is located, the server name, what port the request was sent to – in fact, the whole environment in which the application was executed. These important bits of information are all stored in individual variables known as **environment variables**. This list of variables is predefined by the server.

The ServerVariables Collection

The ServerVariables collection makes it possible to retrieve the values of these variables. The syntax is:

[*varValue* =]Request.ServerVariables(*EnvVarName*)

Name	Type	Description
EnvVarName	String	A string enclosed in quotes, specifying the name of the server environment variable to be retrieved.

You can find the list of all 43 variables in Appendix E of this book, along with a short description of each.

The ServerVariables collection contains a lot of information. In fact, much of the information that we've seen in other collections of the Request object originates here, in the ServerVariables collection.

Any HTTP header that is sent by a client browser is available in this collection. HTTP headers are used to exchange information between the client and the server, such as the identity of the client, type of client, type of connection, and so on. The standard HTTP headers are automatically defined as members of the ServerVariables collection. For example, we can determine how the form data was sent to the server by checking the REQUEST_METHOD member of the ServerVariables collection:

```
dim strSendMeth
strSendMeth = Request.ServerVariables("REQUEST_METHOD")
```

This will set the value of the strSendMeth variable to either GET or POST, depending on how the data was sent from the client browser.

There are many ways that the ServerVariables collection can be used; we'll look at two examples here.

Using the HTTP_USER_AGENT Header

The `ServerVariables` collection's HTTP_USER_AGENT member allows us to check the type of the client browser – and hence to perform appropriate actions based on this information. For example, various versions and platforms use plain HTML, HTML plus JavaScript, browser-independent Dynamic HTML, Microsoft- or Netscape-specific Dynamic HTML, and so on. We could have a set of pages that all deliver the same content, but are fine-tuned to do so in a platform-specific way. By establishing the type and version of the user agent (i.e. the web browser), we can redirect the user to the page that is designed to work for that particular web browser.

We can easily capture the value of the HTTP_USER_AGENT member of the `ServerVariables` collection:

```
dim strUserAgent
strUserAgent = Request.ServerVariables("HTTP_USER_AGENT")
```

For example, if the user is running Microsoft Internet Explorer 4.01 under Windows 98, this code places the following string into `strUserAgent`:

```
Mozilla/4.0 (compatible; MSIE 4.01; Windows 98)
```

We can parse the string contained in the HTTP_USER_AGENT member, using built-in functions of either VBScript or JavaScript. For example, the following code sample uses the `inStr()` VBScript function to search for the substring "4.", and acts according to whether or not the search is successful:

```
<%
  strUserAgent = Request.ServerVariables("HTTP_USER_AGENT")
  If inStr(strUserAgent, "MSIE 4.01") >= 0 Then
    ' User is using Microsoft's IE 4.01 web browser
    ' Act accordingly...
  Else
    ' Use inStr() again to establish browser type...
  End If
%>
```

Here, we could redirect the client to another page, displaying appropriate messages, or whatever. We can also determine the client's platform type (Windows, Macintosh or OS/2), and so on.

> The list of possible values for HTTP_USER_AGENT is contained in the file `browscap.ini`. Check the URL in Appendix H for updates.

It's also possible to get all the information about the client browser by using the **Browser Capabilities** component. We'll discuss that in Chapter 7.

Using the *HTTP_ACCEPT_LANGUAGE* Header

The `ServerVariables` collection's `HTTP_ACCEPT_LANGUAGE` member allows us to determine which human language is supported by the client's browser and software. For example, if the client supports the Russian language (which can be set via appropriate settings in the browser), the `HTTP_ACCEPT_LANGUAGE` member will return the string `ru`. We can use this information to redirect users to localized pages and sites that contain local information. See Appendix G for the list of possible values for `HTTP_ACCEPT_LANGUAGE`.

Using the *AUTH_TYPE* Header

If you're using a CDO or an ADSI site (see Chapter 9) then, ideally, it should be contained in its own virtual directory with IIS Anonymous Access turned off – this forces users to log on. However, if Anonymous Access is switched on, we can write a line to query `AUTH_TYPE` from the `Request.ServerVariables` collection for `_BasicNTLM` – either Basic or Challenge/Response authentication – and force a log on box to appear if necessary.

Using Custom Headers

Sometimes, clients can send extended headers other than the 43 that are specified in Appendix E. To retrieve the value of such a header, we should prefix the header name with `HTTP_` in the call to `Request.ServerVariables`. For example, suppose the client sends the `ExtraInfo` header. We can retrieve this by using the following code:

```
dim strExtraInfo
strExtraInfo = Request.ServerVariables("HTTP_ExtraInfo")
```

Getting all HTTP Server Variables

The following ASP script can be used to retrieve the values of all HTTP server variables:

```
<% @language = JavaScript %>
<HTML>
<HEAD><TITLE>HTTP Server Variables</TITLE>
</HEAD>
<BODY>
  <P ALIGN=CENTER><FONT SIZE=5><B>HTTP Server Variables</B></FONT></P>
  <TABLE BORDER>
  <TR><TH>Variable</TH><TH>Value</TH></TR>
  <%
    // create new Enumerator object
    http = new Enumerator(Request.ServerVariables)
  %>
  <%
    // iterate through collection
    while (!http.atEnd(http))
    {
      // get one item
      i = http.item();
      // show it and it's value
      Response.Write('<TR><TD>' + i + '</TD><TD>' +
                      Request.ServerVariables(i) +
```

```
'</TD></TR>')
    // get next item
    http.moveNext()
    }
%>
</TABLE>
</BODY>
</HTML>
```

Here's what you should see when running this script on your server:

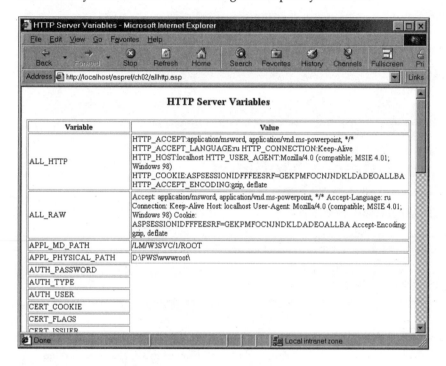

Referring to Collections

It's possible to access the Request object's variables directly by calling Request(variable) (i.e. without specifying the collection name). In this case, the web server searches the collections in the following order: QueryString, Form, Cookies, ClientCertificate, ServerVariables. If you try to reference a variable which shares its name with another variable in a different collection, the web server resolves the ambiguity by consulting the collections in the order above, and returning the first match.

Generally, it's good programming practice to specify the name of the variable's collection. In particular, it's a good idea to specify the collection name when referring to members of the ServerVariables collection – for example, you should write Request.ServerVariables("AUTH_USER") instead of Request("AUTH_USER").

Request Object Properties

The TotalBytes Property

The Request object has only one property – TotalBytes – which specifies the number of bytes that the client is sending in the body of the HTTP request. TotalBytes is a read-only property.

[*varTotalBytes* =]Request.TotalBytes

Here's an example of the TotalBytes property in action:

```
<%
   dim varBinRead
   dim varByteCount
   varByteCount = Request.TotalBytes               ' get the size of request
   varBinRead   = Request.BinaryRead(varByteCount) ' get raw data
   Response.Write(CStr(varByteCount) & " byte(s) received from client."
%>
```

Request Object Methods

The BinaryRead Method

The Request object also has a single method – BinaryRead – which is used to retrieve data sent to the server as part of the POST request.

[*varBinRead* =]Request.BinaryRead(*varCount*)

Name	Type	Description
varCount	Variant	Specifies the number of bytes to be read from the client when execution of this method is invoked. When the BinaryRead method is complete, then intCount returns the number of bytes actually read from the client. This will usually be less than or equal to the value returned by Request.TotalBytes.

The BinaryRead method returns a safe array of bytes (a safe array is an array that specifies the number of dimensions and the bounds of its dimensions). The BinaryRead method gives access to unparsed data sent to the server by a form. In order to read the whole block of data that has been sent, we need to get the total number of bytes. We can do this using the TotalBytes property, as demonstrated in the code sample above.

Typically, scripting languages are only equipped to deal with variants and safe arrays of variants – therefore, you might find that you don't have much use for this method. Its real use is in uploading files – for more information, see the excellent article at http://www.15seconds.com/Issue/981121.htm.

Summary

This chapter has focused on the Request object – its collections, properties and methods. We saw that the Request object has five collections (all read-only), which hold different kinds of information that the client sends to the server in the HTTP Request:

❑ The ClientCertificate collection holds client certificate values
❑ The Cookies collection holds the values of cookies that live on the client machine
❑ The Form collection holds the values of any of HTML <FORM> elements sent by the browser
❑ The QueryString collection holds any variables sent in the HTTP query string (i.e. apended to the URL by a form or ASP request)
❑ The ServerVariables collection holds values of the HTTP headers and environment variables

We talked about retrieving information sent to the server through a client request, how to access data sent through forms with POST and GET methods, how to accept cookies, how to check for client certificate and we've seen examples using colletions in conjunction with both VBScript and JavaScript.

In the next chapter we will take a look at the Response object – the counterpart of the Request object – which plays its own crucial part in the client–server conversation.

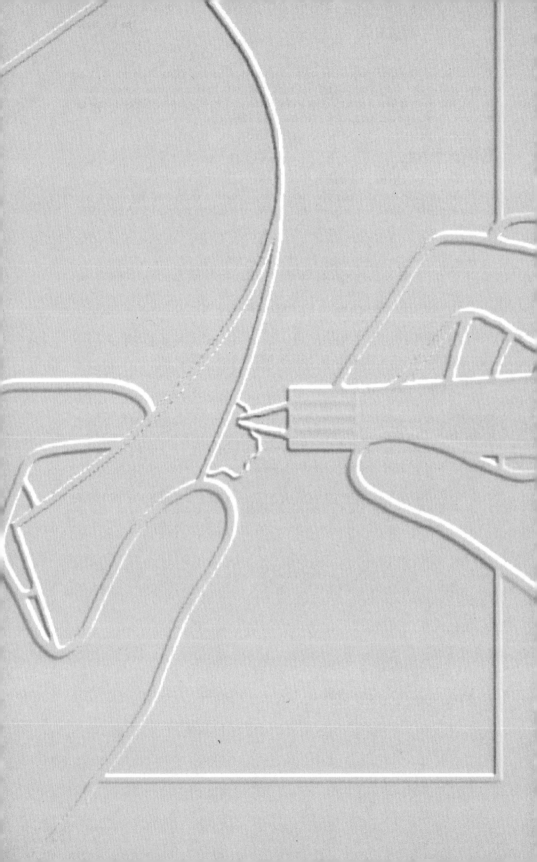

3

The Response Object

In Chapter 2, we saw how our ASP script logic can use the `Request` object to access the information sent by the client in an HTTP request. In this chapter, we'll focus on its partner, the `Response` object, which we use to control the contents of the HTTP Response that our ASP script returns to the client.

With the assistance of the `Response` object, we can enable our ASP script logic to:

❑   Insert information into the HTTP Response body (often, this is information that contributes directly to an HTML web page – but it could also be some other type of web content, such as XML or binary data files)

❑   Send cookies to the browser

❑   Redirect the browser to another URL

❑   Control the buffering of the generated web content and then flush the buffers at strategic points in the script logic

❑   Check the status of the client connection

❑   Write to the web server's log file

The interface of the `Response` object consists of one collection, eight properties and nine methods:

RESPONSE	
Collections	
Cookies	
Properties	
Buffer	Expires
CacheControl	ExpiresAbsolute
CharSet	IsClientConnected
ContentType	Status
Methods	
AddHeader	Flush
AppendToLog	PICS
BinaryWrite	Redirect
Clear	Write
End	
Events	

Response Object Collections

The Response object has just a single collection –the Cookies collection.

The Cookies Collection

In Chapter 2 we discussed the purpose of cookies and how the Request.Cookies collection is used to retrieve the values of cookies stored at the client. The Response object *also* provides a Cookies collection, that is used to *set* the values of cookies. When the client receives the HTTP response, the machine builds and stores cookies according to the values contained in the Response.Cookies collection. If the client has existing cookies with the same names as those in the Response.Cookies collection, the client uses these new values to overwrite the old ones.

Here's the syntax for setting cookie values via the Response object's Cookies collection:

```
Response.Cookies("cookie")[("key")] = value
```

Name	Type	Description
cookie	String	String delimited by double-quotes, specifying the name of the cookie to be set
key	String (optional)	String delimited by double-quotes. If key is specified then cookie will contain a Dictionary object (Chapter 6), which allows the cookies to take multiple values. Then, the key subscript allows an individual item in the cookie to be identified

The following code writes values to two cookies (called FirstName and LastName) that are to be stored in a client's cookie set (if these cookies already exist on the client, then this code writes new values to the cookies):

```
<% Response.Buffer = true %>
    ' ... other HTML / Script ...
<%
  Response.Cookies("FirstName") = "Alex"
  Response.Cookies("LastName")  = "Fedorov"
%>
```

When the Response object makes modifications to a cookie, this causes HTTP headers to be sent to the client. Therefore, these modifications must be made *before* any text or HTML is written to the client. It is for this reason that we use the Response.Buffer = true statement *before* setting the cookie's values. We'll look at the Buffer property later in this chapter.

As the syntax above suggests, there are two forms of cookie. A **simple cookie**, as in the example above, is like a name/value pair: we associate the name of the cookie with its value and we set these as shown in the example. A **dictionary cookie** is a single cookie that can hold several values. In this case, the cookie takes the form of a `Dictionary` object (see Chapter 6) – the `Dictionary` object contains key/item pairs, in which each item is a cookie value. The following example sets a dictionary cookie called `Name`, which contains two keys (`Given` and `Family`):

```
<%
   Response.Cookies("Name")("Given") = "Chris"
   Response.Cookies("Name")("Family" ) = "Ullman"
%>
```

It's up to the `Request` object's code to check whether it's dealing with a simple cookie or a dictionary cookie. For this task, the `Request` object's `Cookies` collection provides the `HasKeys` property, which we discussed in Chapter 2.

Response.Cookies Collection's Attributes

The `Cookies` collection itself has five properties, relating to the lifetime and availability of individual cookies. The syntax for these properties is:

```
Response.Cookies("cookie").property = propValue
```

Here, `property` specifies one of the five properties:

Property	Meaning
Domain	Indicates whether the cookie is only returned to the pages within the domain from which it was created. The default value is the current domain of the page – you should change this if you want to specify the scope of the cookie "visibility". Write-only
Expires	Sets the expiration date of the cookie. If the Expires attribute is not set to a time beyond the current time, the cookie will expire when the browser is closed. Write-only
HasKeys	Specifies whether the cookie is a Dictionary object. Read-only
Path	If specified, the cookie is *only* sent in response to requests for pages within this path. The default value is the root directory of the current ASP application. Write-only
Secure	Specifies whether the cookie is 'secure'. The 'secure' cookie is sent only if the HTTPS protocol (HTTP over Secure Socket Layer, SSL) is being used. 'Insecure' cookies can be sent via either the HTTP or HTTPS protocols. In both cases, the cookie itself is stored as is: i.e. there is no encryption provided. Write-only

The Expires Property

The `Expires` attribute allows us to extend the life of the cookie past the moment when user closes the browser (and thus ends his current session). This is particularly useful if we think that we might want to go back to the cookie at some later date, to read its contents or add more info. The expiry date is set in the following format:

```
Wkdy, DD-Mon-YY hh:mm:ss
```

Here, `Wkdy` is the day of the week (Mon, Tues, etc.); `Mon` is a three-letter abbreviation representing the month; and `DD`, `YY`, `hh`, `mm` and `ss` are integer values representing other aspects of the date and time. Here's how to set the expiry date of a cookie called `CurrentYear`:

```
<%
  Response.Cookies("CurrentYear") = "Nineteen-Ninety-Eight"
  Response.Cookies("CurrentYear").Expires = #January 01, 1999#
%>
```

The # symbol is used to indicate that the `Expires` property is being set a value of the date/time data type. Another way to set the `Expires` property is to use the VBScript `Date` function:

```
<%
  Response.Cookies("USUKExchange") = "1.66"
  Response.Cookies("USUKExchange").Expires = Date + 30
%>
```

This would set the expiration date to 30 days on from the present date. In this example, the ever-changing exchange rate might demand that we set the cookie to expire after a shorter period – say, one hour:

```
Response.Cookies("USUKExchange").Expires = Date + 1/24
```

To ensure that a cookie expires (and hence is deleted) at the end of the current session, simply set its `Expires` property to some date in the past. For example:

```
' This will delete a cookie
Response.Cookies("MyCookie").Expires = Date - 1000
```

We could subtract 1 from the date, but there's no harm in subtracting a larger number, just to make sure.

> Be sure not to confuse the `Response.Cookies("cookie").Expires` property with the `Response.Expires` property – their effects are different. We'll look at `Response.Expires` later in this chapter.

Cookie Security

The `Domain`, `Path` and `Secure` attributes are used to prevent other web sites from accessing the information that we put into cookies – the browser decides whether to send cookies to the server after checking the values of the `Domain` and `Path` attributes.

Setting the value of `Domain` to `/webdev.wrox.co.uk/` ensures that only ASP pages existing on that particular machine can receive the cookie from the browser. The default value for the `Domain` attribute is the domain in which the page is running. We can be more specific, for example, by setting the `Path` attribute to `/Books/2459`. This will ensure that cookies will be only returned to the ASP pages that are running within this path.

The `Secure` attribute is a Boolean value whose value is `true` if the cookie is only be transmitted to be to the server over a SSL connection (the `https://` protocol), and `false` otherwise.

Here's how we might set these properties:

```
<%
  Response.Cookies("MyCookie") = "MyCookie"
  Response.Cookies("MyCookie").Expires = #January 01, 1999#
  Response.Cookies("MyCookie").Domain  = "/webdev.wrox.co.uk/"
  Response.Cookies("MyCookie").Path    = "/Books/2459"
  Response.Cookies("MyCookie").Secure  = true
%>
```

There are limits to the number and size of cookies that the client browser is prepared to accept and store: it's usually 300 cookies in total, with at most 20 cookies per server (or domain) and at most 4 kbytes per cookie. These figures are based on a W3C specification for browser design. There's more information at `http://home.netscape.com/newsref/std/cookie_spec.html`.

Accessing Cookies on the Client Side

While this book is about ASP (server-side scripting), it is worth mentioning how to access cookies through client-side code.

Cookies are available to the client-side JavaScript or VBScript as the property of the `Document` object. Here's some code to illustrate this:

```
<HTML>
<HEAD><TITLE>Cookies</TITLE>
  <SCRIPT LANGUAGE="JavaScript">
    function doCookie()
    {
      var strName = "Name=";
      if (document.cookie.indexOf(strName) != -1)
      {
        intStart = document.cookie.indexOf(strName);
        intEnd   = document.cookie.length;
        intLen   = intStart + strName.length;
        strValue = document.cookie.substring(intLen, intEnd);
        alert("Welcome, " + unescape(strValue));
      }
      else
      {
        name = prompt("Enter your name please...", "...in this box");
        document.cookie = strName + escape(name) + ";";
        document.location.reload();
      }
    }
  </SCRIPT>
</HEAD>
<BODY onLoad=doCookie()>
</BODY>
</HTML>
```

This HTML page tries to find the cookie called Name. If the cookie is found, it produces the greeting such as **Welcome, Jack** – the name of the user is taken from the cookie. If the cookie is not found, user receives a prompt to supply his name – this information is then stored in the cookie.

Handling cookies on the client side requires a lot of code – particularly if you're trying to set a cookie. Bill Dortch has implemented a set of cookie functions that can be found at http://www.hidaho.com/cookies/cookie.txt. You can also find a discussion about using cookies in Wrox's *Professional IE4 Programming* (see Appendix H).

> *If your browser doesn't support cookies, or refuses to accept them, you might like to look at a filter supplied by Microsoft, called Cookie Munger. This filter detects any browsers that can't (or won't) use cookies. It checks for a cookie called* ASPSESSIONID *(this is a cookie that ASP sends with each request). If* ASPSESSIONID *is not found, then it rewrites the HTTP header, 'munges' any URLs embedded in the page and appends them to the HTTP header. You can find more information about Cookie Munger (and download it) from* http://backoffice.microsoft.com/downtrial/moreinfo/i issamples/CkyMunge.asp.

Response Object Properties

Let's look at the properties available for the Response object.

The Buffer Property

The ASP Scripting Host's task is to process an .asp file's HTML statements and script logic and dynamically generate the HTML page to send to the browser. Before it can do this, an empty HTML output stream is created. The HTML output stream is essentially a receptacle or **buffer** where the web server can create the HTML pages dynamically. In order, each line of HTML is added to the end of the buffer; and if the ASP script logic generates HTML statements, they too are appended to the end of the buffer. When the page is sent to the browser, the HTML headers are written first – followed by the contents of the page, in the HTML output stream.

If the output is buffered, as described above, the buffered page output is not sent to the client until *all* of the ASP scripts have been processed, or the Flush method or the End method is called. If the output is not buffered, the server sends output to the client as it is processed.

Thus, we can use buffering to control when we send output to the browser. The output stream is stored (or **buffered**) until we want to release it to the browser. By default, buffering is switched off; but we can turn it on by setting the Buffer property to true. The syntax for this property is as follows:

```
Response.Buffer = flag
```

where flag is either true (output is buffered) or false (output is not buffered). The default value for Response.Buffer is false. You can expect future versions of IIS to have these defaults reversed.

The call to the Response.Buffer should be the first line of your .asp file (apart from any <%@...%> directive – see the example below).

By setting the Buffer property to true, we have access to the Clear, Flush and End methods (discussed later in this chapter). If you try to use these methods without first setting the Buffer property to true, you'll cause a run-time error.

We can use buffering to output large reports step by step, to avoid error messages, and in other situations where control of the HTML output is needed. Here is an example in which we use the Buffer property to trap errors:

```
<%@ Language = "VBScript" %>
<% Response.Buffer = True %>
'   . . .
<%
   If Err Then            ' If an error occurred
      Response.Clear      ' Clear the current buffered output
                          ' (including the error message itself)
      Response.Write ("There has been an error : please try again")
                          ' Show error message
      Response.End        ' Stop processing the page and send it to the client
'   . . .
   End If
%>
```

The CacheControl Property

The CacheControl property is used to determine whether a **proxy server** can cache the output generated by ASP. Most businesses and organizations use proxy servers as a gateway between the user's workstations and the Internet. Proxy servers are responsible for separating the enterprise network from the outside networks, via a firewall, while remaining invisible to the user. They can be used to control security, administration and (in some cases) caching – the process of storing a web page locally, thus avoiding the need to repeatedly download pages that are used more than once.

Not all proxy servers can cache information; and even those that can cache don't have caching turned on by default. Microsoft Proxy Server does support caching. What happens if a proxy server supports caching? When it receives a request for a web page, it checks its internal cache for the web page – if the page isn't cached, it will forward the request out onto the Internet.

If a proxy server is permitted to cache a page, then the proxy server's other users can access the page more quickly – because the page will be returned by the proxy server (there's no need to contact the web site). Moreover, if your web page doesn't change very often, you can reduce the load on your web server by allowing proxies to cache the page.

The syntax for doing this is:

```
Response.CacheControl = cacheControlHeader
```

where `cacheControlHeader` can be either `Public` or `Private`. If the cache control header is `Public`, proxy servers will cache the output generated by ASP, otherwise they won't. The default value for this property is `Private`.

The Charset Property

The `Charset` property appends the name of the character set to the content-type header in the `Response` object. The default is the US ASCII character set. The syntax is:

```
Response.Charset(CharsetName)
```

where `CharsetName` is a string that specifies a character set for the page.

The `Charset` property is used to solve internationalization problems that can occur if the client browser doesn't recognize the character set used in the output HTML stream. By specifying the right character set, we can tell the client browser to use the appropriate code page. If the ASP page does not include the `Response.Charset` property, the content-type header will be:

```
content-type:text/html
```

Suppose our `.asp` file includes the following statement:

```
Response.Charset("windows-1251")    ' Set the content type to
                                    ' the Cyrillic Alphabet
```

Then the content-type header will be:

```
content-type:text/html; charset=windows-1251
```

Note that the server does *not* check to see whether the string contained in the `Charset` property represents a valid character set. Moreover, if a single page contains multiple `Response.Charset` statements, the character set will be set to the value specified by the last `Response.Charset` statement in the page.

The ContentType Property

The ContentType property sets the **HTTP content type** for the response. The HTTP content type specifies the type of the media sent to the client browser – such as text, graphics, Word documents, or Excel spreadsheets. The syntax is:

```
Response.ContentType = ContentType
```

where ContentType is a string describing the content or MIME (Multipurpose Internet Media Extensions) type.

The usual format for the ContentType string is type/subtype, where type is the general content category and subtype is the specific content type. The default value is text/HTML. Here's an example of how to set the ContentType property:

```
Response.ContentType = "application/msword"
```

The most common use of this property is in conjunction with database applications, where we store graphics in BLOB (binary large object) fields and need to show an image. In this case, we set the content type to image/GIF or image/JPEG, depending on how the data is stored inside the database. For an example, see the section on the Response.BinaryWrite method in this chapter.

For the list of the common content types, refer to Appendix G.

The Expires Property

If you've permitted your page to be cached (e.g. using CacheControl), the Expires property controls the period of time between when the page is cached and when it will expire. The syntax is:

```
Response.Expires = number
```

where number sets the time (in minutes) before the page expires. This property works by setting the Expires header in HTTP. If the Expires header is not set, the browser instead uses the Last Modified header to expire pages in the cache. The Last Modified header simply contains the date that the page was last altered:

```
Last-modified: Thu, 10 Dec 1998 03:19:41 GMT
```

The Expires header contains the same type of information about the expiry date:

```
Expires: Fri, 11 Dec 1998 12:00:00 GMT
```

These headers can be viewed by looking at the properties of cached files (look in C:\Windows\Temporary Internet Files on Windows 95, for example).

> We've already noted in this chapter that proxy servers can also cache pages. However, there is often limited space for such information on the proxy server – therefore the proxy will expire cached pages based on the amount of inactivity. Some proxy servers (including Microsoft Proxy Server) use the `Response.Expires` property to expire old ASP pages in the cache. This is not a general rule for all proxy servers – if you're in doubt about your proxy server's procedure for expiring cached pages, you should check the local documentation.

If the user calls a page, and then returns to the same page at some later time (*before* the page expires), he gets the cached version of the page. If the user returns to the page *after* it has expired, the browser will load a fresh copy from the server. Here's how to set the `Expires` property to four hours from now:

```
Response.Expires = 240        ' in minutes (240 mins = 4 hours)
```

If you want your cached page to expire immediately, set the `Response.Expires` property to 0. When local time on client and server machines is different (e.g. the machines are located indifferent tine zones), setting `Response.Expires` might not be enough – you can make absolutely sure by setting `Response.Expires` to a large negative value, like –1000 (or by using the `Response.ExpiresAbsolute` property, described below).

If the `Response.Expires` statement is used more that once in the page, the shortest expiration time is used.

The ExpiresAbsolute Property

If we allow a page to be cached on the client-aide, we can use the `ExpiresAbsolute` property to set a specific time at which the page will expire from the cache. We can set a date, or a time, or both:

```
Response.ExpiresAbsolute = [date][time]
```

Here, `date` specifies the date on which the page will expire, and `time` specifies the time at which the page will expire. This value is converted to UTC before an `Expires` header is sent.

If the user returns to the same page before the specified date/time, the cached version of the page is displayed. If we specify the `date` only (i.e. the `time` portion is omitted), the page expires at midnight on the specified date. If we specify the `time` only (i.e. the `date` portion is omitted), the page expires at the specified time on the day that the script is run.

Here's an example:

```
Response.ExpiresAbsolute = #1/1/2000 00:00:00#.
```

If the `Response.ExpiresAbsolute` statement is used more that once in the page, the earliest expiration date or time is used.

The IsClientConnected Property

This read-only property indicates whether the client is still connected to the server, or has disconnected since the last `Response.Write` call. The syntax is:

```
[boolConnected = ]Response.IsClientConnected()
```

The `Response.IsClientConnected` property is returns a Boolean – it takes the value `true` if the client is still connected, `false` otherwise.

We use `Response.IsClientConnected` to check whether client is stil connected to the server. For example, if the client requests some operation that takes some time to complete (e.g. a SQL-request to a large database), it's worth checking that the client is still connected before you allocate resources to the operation:

```
If Response.IsClientConnected Then
    ' Perform some time-consuming operations here...
End If
```

It's also worth checking that the client is still there at the end of the operation, before sending the results of the operation across the network. As we mentioned above, it's usually wise to use buffering to split output of long operations smaller chunks – if the client's screen shows signs of life, then he's less likely to break the connection and surf elsewhere.

The PICS Property

To restrict the distribution of certain kinds of materials over the Internet, a set of technical specifications (called PICS – Platform for Internet Control Selection) was proposed in 1995. PICS provides a way to implement client-side control over Internet content. The idea behind PICS is that every site has an associated label – the PICS label. The PICS label is the digital equivalent to the film classification labels found on video tapes and in the cinema, in the USA and other countries.

You can obtain a label from one of the two self-rating authorities that give them out (RSACi and SafeSurf), by going to their web sites (http://www.rsac.org/ratingsv01.html and http://www.classify.org/safesurf/) and filling out a questionnaire about the type of material contained on your site. They'll send you a label for each page you completed a questionnaire for (or if every page has the same sort of content, you'll just get a single label for your site). PICS labels are then placed in the META tag.

When a client browser requests your web page, it examines the PICS label and decides (according to rules set by the parent or administrator) whether to allow the user to see the content.

In Internet Explorer, the user can set ratings via View | Internet Options, selecting the Content tab and clicking the Enable button in the Content Advisor section. Contents can be rated in four categories – language, nudity, sex and violence –each category can be rated from level 0 to level 4.

Using the `PICS` property, we can add a value of the `PICSLabel` field to the response header. The syntax is:

```
Response.PICS(PICSLabel)
```

where `PICSLabel` is a string containing a properly-formatted `PICS` label. The value specified by `PICSLabel` will be appended to the `PICS` label field in the response header. This header is usually presented in the HTML document itself, inside `<META>` tags within the `<HEAD>` section:

```
<META http-equiv="PICS-Label" content='(PICS-1.1
"http://www.rsac.org/ratingsv01.html" l gen true comment "RSACi North America
Server" " for "http://www.foobar.org" on "1996.04.16T08:15-0500" r (n 3 s 3 v
3 l 2))'>
```

You can use `PICS` property if you need to supply `PICS` label dynamically for the current page:

```
<%
Response.PICS("(PICS-1.1 <http://www.rsac.org/ratingv01.html> labels on " &
chr(34) & "1997.01.05T08:15-0500" & chr(34) & " until" & chr(34) &
"1999.12.31T23:59-0000" & chr(34) & " ratings (v 0 s 0 1 0 n 0))")
%>
<%
'   ... other ASP code here
%>
<HTML>
</HTML>
```

This adds the following header:

```
PICS-label:(PICS-1.1 <http://www.rsac.org/ratingv01.html> labels on
"1997.01.05T08:15-0500" until "1999.12.31T23:59-0000" ratings (v 0 s 0 1 0 n
0))
```

In addition to obtaining a PICS label from RSACi or SafeSurf, you can also create a PICS label manually. To do this, you need to understand the PICS specification found at `http://www.w3.org/PICS`. The syntax for PICS is fairly complex; it's a lot easier to use the established services to create an appropriate label.

The `PICS` property will insert *any* string into the header – there's no check to confirm that the string supplied is a valid `PICS` label. If a single page contains multiple `Response.PICS` tags, each successive instance will replace the `PICS` label set by the previous one. As a result, the `PICS` label will be set to the value specified by the last instance of `Response.PICS` in the page. Because `PICS` labels contain quotes, you must replace each quote with `" & chr(34) & "`.

You can find the full version of the RSAC PICS label in RSAC web site, `http://www.rsac.org`. *Note that PICS specification goes beyond the ratings supplied by the RSACi and can be used to describe any content of the Internet. However, current browsers only support RSACi-based filtering.*

The Status Property

The Status property specifies the status string returned by the server. You're probably already familiar with status strings – they're what you see when you click on a link and you get an error (instead of being directed to another page). Status strings are also generated when the link is valid. The syntax for returning a status string is:

```
Response.Status = StatusDescription
```

where StatusDescription is a string containing a three-digit number (that indicates a status code), and a brief explanation of that code.

The status string determines the status code that has special meaning for the client browser. Each code has a unique number. For an error-free document response this will be 200 OK. No doubt 404 (*Document not found*) will be a familiar (if unwelcome) status message. As another example, the Response.Redirect method sends a header of value 302 to the browser:

```
HTTP/1.0 302 Object Moved
Location URL
```

The first digit of the code represents the type of response, as shown in this table. You'll find a list of them in Appendix D.

First Digit	Type of response
1	Information
2	Success
3	Redirection
4	Client Error
5	Server Error

We can use the Status property of the Response object to set the status code. For example, to request authentication, we can use the following script:

```
<%
' Security using IIS authentication
If (Len(Request.ServerVariables("LOGON_USER")) = 0 ) Then
    Response.Status = "401 Unauthorized"
    Response.Write "<HTML><BODY>" &_
            "<B>Error: Access is denied.</B><P></BODY></HTML>"
    Response.End
End If

' Logged user - proceed here. Check password and so on...
%>
```

We have covered all properties of the Response object. Now it's time to talk about the Response object methods.

Response Object Methods

In this section we will take a look at the methods of the `Response` object.

The AddHeader Method

The `AddHeader` method is used to add an HTTP header with a specified value that can be used to invoke some functions of the client browser. The syntax for this method is:

```
Response.AddHeader strName, strValue
```

Name	Type	Description
strName	String	The name of the new header variable
strValue	String	The value stored in the new header variable

In the following example, we add the new HTTP header `New-Header`, with the value `New Header Value`:

```
Response.AddHeader "New-Header", "New Header Value"
```

The client-side software should be able to recognize the new HTTP header attached to the response, and take appropriate actions upon receiving it. For example, we can use the `AddHeader` method to set cookie values, like this:

```
Response.AddHeader "Set-Cookie", "Name=FIRST=Alex&LAST=Fedorov"
```

You can use the `Response.AddHeader` method to add (or modify) any HTTP header sent to the client. Note that:

❑ Once a header has been added, it cannot be removed

❑ The `strName` parameter should not contain any underscore (_) characters

❑ The `AddHeader` method should be called before any output statements – you can't add to the header after the HTTP header has been sent to the browser. Alternatively you can set the `Buffer` property to `true`. In the latter case, this call to the `AddHeader` method should precede any calls to the `Flush` method.

Here is an example of how to use the `AddHeader` method without using the `Buffer` property:

```
<%
   Response.AddHeader "Set-Cookie", "Name=FIRST=Alex&LAST=Fedorov"
%>
<HTML>
   ' The rest of the page goes here
</HTML>
```

If we need to call the `AddHeader` method *after* HTML code has been written, we should set the `Buffer` property to `True`:

```
<% Response.Buffer = True %>
<HTML>
   ' HTML code here...
<%
   Response. AddHeader "Set-Cookie", "Name=FIRST=Alex&LAST=Fedorov"
%>
   ' More code here
<%
   Response.Flush
%>
</HTML>
```

The syntax of the `Set-Cookie` response header is as follows:

```
Set-Cookie: NAME=VALUE; expires=DATE; path=PATH; domain=DOMAIN
```

This allows you to set other properties as well, such as the expiry date.

The AppendToLog Method

The `AppendToLog` method is used to add a text string to the web server's log file. The syntax is:

```
Response.AppendToLog strText
```

Name	Type	Description
strText	String	The text that is to be appended to the log file; must not contain commas, and mustn't exceed 80 characters in length

Here's an example of how it's used:

```
<%
   Response.AppendToLog("This should go to the Web Server's Log File.")
   Response.Write("Done...")
%>
```

The log entry in IIS should look something like this:

```
127.0.0.1 - - [09/Nov/1998:18:47:54 +0300] "GET /aspref/ch03/log_demo.ASP?This should
go to the Web Server's Log File. HTTP/1.1" 200 177
```

The web server should be properly configured so that it is able to maintain the log file. Refer to the web server's documentation for additional information.

The BinaryWrite Method

The `BinaryWrite` method writes the specified data to the client without any character conversion.

```
Response.BinaryWrite varData
```

Name	Type	Description
varData	Variant	The data that is to be written to the client

This method is useful for writing non-string information, such as binary data required by a custom application. As we have mentioned above, we can use the `BinaryWrite` method to output graphics stored on the server in the database. Here is an example of how we can do so:

```
<%@ LANGUAGE=VBSCRIPT %>
<%
' Clear out the existing HTTP header information
Response.Expires = 0
Response.Buffer = True
Response.Clear

' Change the HTTP header to reflect that an image is being passed
Response.ContentType = "image/gif"

' Open a database
Set Conn = Server.CreateObject("ADODB.Connection")

' Here we assume that we have System Data Source by the name of GRAPH
Conn.Open "GRAPH", "", ""
Set RecSet = Conn.Execute("SELECT bookcover FROM logos WHERE
                                     book_id =          '2459'")
Response.BinaryWrite RecSet("bookcover")
Response.End
%>
```

The Clear Method

The `Clear` method erases any buffered HTML output. It takes no parameters, and so its syntax is simply:

```
Response.Clear
```

The `Clear` method only erases the response body and not response headers. You can use this method to handle error cases. This method will only erase information that has been added to HTML output since the last call to the `Response.Flush` method. If there were no such call, then the `Clear` method will erase all information added to HTML output since the beginning of the page (except the headers).

> If you attempt to use the `Clear` method to clear a non-empty buffer, and `Response.Buffer` has not been set to `true`, then a run-time error occurs.

The End Method

The `End` method causes the web server to stop processing the script and return the current buffer. The remaining contents of the file are not processed. Again, there are no parameters involved so the syntax is simple:

```
Response.End
```

If `Response.Buffer` has been set to `true`, then `Response.End` will flush the buffer. If you do not want output to be returned to the user, you can use the `Clear` method first to clear the buffer:

```
<% Response.Buffer = true %>
..' some code...
<%
   Response.Clear
   Response.End
%>
```

The Flush Method

The `Flush` method sends buffered output immediately. It's another parameter-less function:

```
Response.Flush
```

Note that after sending the output, the `Flush` method continues to process the remaining script. One of the examples for the `Flush` method is to use it to display partial results of long output.

> The `Flush` **method will cause a run-time error if** `Response.Buffer` **has not been set to** `true`.

The Redirect Method

The `Redirect` method can be used to redirect the client browser from the current page to a different page. The syntax is:

```
Response.Redirect strURL
```

Name	Type	Description
strURL	String	The address of the web page in the form of the Uniform Resource Locator.

This is useful for situations where you provide a `Default.asp` page that loads the first page of an application. It's also regularly used in situations where you carry out some authentication or comparison test in a page and want to redirect certain visitors to another page. For example:

```
<%
   'check if query string contains the password 'OpenSesame'
   If Request.QueryString("password") = "OpenSesame" Then
      Response.Redirect "enter.asp"
   Else
      Response.Write "Sorry, you must provide the password"
   End If
%>
```

What many people don't realize is that the redirection is not accomplished entirely on the server – the browser is also involved in the process. When the server executes the `Redirect` method, it sends a set of HTTP headers to the browser – these HTTP headers indicate that the object has moved. More specifically, it's a **302 Object Moved** status message followed by the **LOCATION** header that indicates the new location. The browser uses this status message and header to load the new page.

Note that some older browsers don't support the `Redirect` *method.*

So, it's the *browser* that loads the new page (i.e. it's not the server that sends the new page to replace the existing page). This also explains why you have to redirect the browser *before* sending any other HTML output back to the browser. Once any non-header output has been sent, you can't send any more HTTP headers.

Problems with Proxies

If the client is connected to your server directly, through their ISP or a direct Internet connection, this process works well and appears to be seamless. The user just sees their browser load the new page automatically. However, it doesn't always work quite so seamlessly when your visitor is the other side of a firewall or proxy server. In this case, it's the proxy server that receives the **Object Moved** status message, and not the browser. Many proxy server/browser combinations will create a page that indicates to the user that the object has moved, and then wait for them to click on a link in this page to load the page from the new location.

This is particularly the case when the browser is Internet Explorer 4 (or later), and is almost always observed with Microsoft Proxy Server – even if no packet filtering or security is established. The simple page has a heading saying just **Object Moved**, and a line of text indicating that 'the page you requested can be found here.'

To minimize the appearance of this page, you should always buffer output when using `Response.Redirect`. In general, the following code will reduce the number of occurrences of the **Object Moved** message:

```
<%
  Response.Buffer = True
'check if query string contains the password 'OpenSesame'
If Request.QueryString("password") = "OpenSesame" Then
   Response.Redirect "enter.asp"
     Respose.Flush
     Response.End
Else
   Response.Write "Sorry, you must provide the password"
     Respose.Flush
End If
%>
```

The Write Method

The `Write` method is used to send a specified string to the client. The syntax is:

```
Response.Write varText
```

Name	Type	Description
varText	Variant	The data that is to be sent to the browser

The varText parameter can consist of any data type, including characters, strings and integers. The only restriction is that varText cannot contain the ASP script terminator (the %> combination) – if you need to output this combination, use the escape sequence %\>. It is the responsibility of the web server to translate this escape sequence to the set of appropriate characters – this will be done when the web server processes the script.

There are plenty of examples using the Write method in this book – it's a very commonly-used method. Here's a simple one:

```
<%
   Response.Write("Hello, Web Surfer!")
%>
```

Since the calculated value of varText is inserted to the HTML stream that the browser receives, we can use HTML tags within the string:

```
<%
   Response.Write("Hello, <B>Web Surfer!</B>")
%>
```

Note that the <% = %> syntax is a useful subsitute for the Response.Write method syntax (Chapter 1 has more information on this short cut):

```
<% ="Hello, <B>Web Surfer!</B>"%>
```

We can also use variables and the results of calculated expressions. For example, if we have a 1-dimensional array called arrExample containing six numerical values, we can output these values by iterating through them like this:

```
<%
   For intCounter = 1 to 6
      Response.Write("The number is: " & arrExample(intCounter) & "<BR>")
   Next
%>
```

In this example, we're also concatenating various elements of output (the string "The number is: ", the array element, and the HTML <BR> tag) within the parameter using the & symbol.

We can create formatted output – for example, using tables:

```
<%
   Response.Write("<TABLE BORDER>")
   Response.Write("<TR><TD>Step</TD><TD>Sum</TD></TR>")
   For intCounter = 1 to 6
      Response.Write("<TR>")
      Response.Write("<TD>" & intCounter & "</TD>")
      Response.Write("<TD>" & arrExample(intCounter) & "</TD></TR>")
   Next
   Response.Write("</TABLE>")
%>
```

This gives the following output:

Summary

In this chapter we have discussed the collections, properties and methods of the Response object that – coupled with the Request object – serve as the main pipe to make client-server interactions between the client browser and the web server. Here is what we have learned:

❑ We can use the Cookies collection to store information on the client-side

❑ We can use several properties of the Response object, namely CacheControl, Charset, ContentType, Expires, ExpiresAbsolute, PICS and Status to change the values of the HTTP header. Also for this purposes we can use the AddHeader method

❑ The Redirect method can be useful when we need to instruct the browser to connect to a different URL

❑ Using the Buffer property and the Clear, End, Flush method we can control the buffering of the page and its content

❑ Two methods – BinaryWrite and Write – allow us to insert non-textual and textual information into a page

❑ We can check is the client is still connected by using the IsClientConnected method

❑ To write to the server's log file we can use the AppendToLog method

The next two chapters, are dedicated to the other objects of the Active Server Pages object model – Server, Application, and Session.

4

The Application and Session Objects

Using Active Server Pages, we have seen how information can be sent from the client to the server, and how the server can create a page dynamically and return it to the client. In these interactions, the request and the response existed by themselves. So far, we haven't seen any mechanism that allows us to tie two (or more) pages together.

Until recently, existing web technologies demanded that if you wanted to pass information from one page to another, you had to use cookies or hidden form fields. Active Server Pages gives you a simpler, more robust, more flexible way to do this: the Application and Session objects.

In this chapter, we will look at these objects and the power and flexibility that they add to ASP. In fact, we will now be able to start referring to our web site as an **application** – instead of thinking of it as just a group of pages. Specifically, we will be examining:

- ❏ The Application object, which allows us to tie together all of the pages of a single web site into a consistent web application.
- ❏ The Session object, which allows us to treat a user's interaction with the web site as a continuous action, rather than as a disconnected series of page requests.

You can use the Application object to share information among all users of a given application. Each Application object can have many *sessions*. You can use the Session object to store temporary context information needed for a particular user session. Variables stored in the Session object are not discarded when the user jumps between pages in the application. These variables persist for the duration of the session.

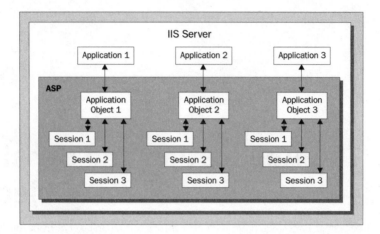

In the diagram, the applications at the top refer to the collections of web pages and objects defined on the server as virtual directories. The sessions represent individual client sessions using the application. The first time a client asks for an .asp page from your server, a session is established for that client. Any number of sessions can be hosted by any one application –the only limit is the memory resources of your server.

> You should be wary of placing too much information in your Session object. For example, if you store arrayed recordsets in the Session object, and at some point you attract a large number of consecutive users to your site, then your server *could* run out of memory resources – because you have to allocate memory for each session. Use the Session object as sparingly as possible.

The Application Object

One of the features of an application is that you can store information that is available to *all* the clients that are accessing the application. This information is stored in what is known as an **application-scope** variable.

In ASP scripts, you can create new variables just by naming them for use (unless you have added the Option Explicit statement to the file). For application-level variables, it is *essential* that you explicitly declare them *before* they are used.

To initialize variables in the Application object, you store the information about them in a text file named global.asa. Each application can have only one global.asa, and it's placed in the root virtual directory. We will cover the items that can be placed in global.asa later in this chapter.

The interface of the `Application` object looks like this:

APPLICATION	
Collections	
Contents	StaticObjects
Properties	
Methods	
Lock	Unlock
Events	
OnStart	OnEnd

Application Object Collections

The `Application` object has two collections – `Contents` and `StaticObjects`. These collections allow us to browse through objects and variables created at the `Application` scope.

The Contents Collection

The `Contents` collection contains all of the items that have been added to the `Application` through script commands.

```
[varValue = ]Application.Contents(key)
[varValue = ]Application(key)
```

Parameter	Type	Description
key	String	Specifies the name of the item to be retrieved

You use the `Contents` collection to get a list of items with application scope or to set a value for a particular application-level variable.

You can iterate through the `Contents` collection the same way you would for any collection, with a `For...Each` statement. An example of this is:

```
<%
  For Each key in Application.Contents
    Response.Write (key)
  Next
%>
```

Just as with a normal collection, you can retrieve the number of elements in the collection by using the `Count` property:

```
<%= intNoOfElts = Application.Contents.Count %>
```

We can also create instances of objects that will have *global* scope. For example:

```
Set Applicaton("objASPEXT") = _
              Server.CreateObject("ASPEXT.BrowserType")
```

The preferred method for creating application-scope objects is through the use of the <OBJECT> tag. We'll look at this when we talk about the global.asa file in more detail, later in this chapter.

The StaticObjects Collection

The StaticObjects collection contains all of the objects created with the <OBJECT> tags within the scope of the Application object.

[objAppObj =]Application.StaticObjects(key)

Parameter	Type	Description
key	String	Specifies the name of the item to be retrieved

Application Object Methods

As we've already seen, the Application object allows us to store information that is globally used among all application users. This information could include object reference variables and other values that all application users require access to. However, there is a problem: because they are shared, we can come up against concurrency problems. Consider the following example:

```
Application("NumberOfSales") = Application("NumberOfSales") + 1
```

We could use this line of code in an ASP file, to count the number of users who had ordered goods from our site. It maintains the count in an Application variable, called NumberOfSales. The problem is this: if two users access this variable at the same time then corruption is likely to occur, because the single Application object has global scope and is visible to all.

User A reads the value of NumberOfSales at the same time as user B. Both instances of the ASP page get the same value, they both increment it, and they both store it back in the Application object. The net result is that the global variable is only incremented *once*. If both writes occurred at the same moment, it might even corrupt the variable altogether. Let's have a look at the solution.

The Lock Method

The Lock method prevents other clients from modifying Application object properties.

Application.Lock

We use the Lock method to lock the variables stored in the scope of the Application object. While they are locked, *only* the client who called the Lock method will be able to alter or access the Application object variables. If another client is accessing an ASP page, and needs to access an application-level variable that is locked, that client's request will be forced to wait until the variable is unlocked.

To unlock the `Application` object variables, the ASP page should explicitly call the `Unlock` method, described below. If we do not call the `Unlock` method, the server will unlock the locked `Application` object when the Active Server Page times out.

```
<%
  Application.Lock
  Application("SomeGlobalVar") = Application("SomeGlobalVar") + 1
  Application.Unlock
%>
```

The Unlock Method

The `Unlock` method unlocks the `Application` object properties, thus allowing other clients to modify them.

```
Application.Unlock
```

We should use the `Unlock` method to unlock the variables stored in the `Application` object after it has been locked using the `Lock` method. It is best to unlock the `Application` object explicitly, as soon as possible after the `Lock` method was called. Think of the `Application` object as a very scarce resource. When your page has locked the `Application` object, no other client accessing the web application can access any part of the `Application` object. This means that all the other clients will sit and wait for you to release it. If your ASP pages lock the `Application` object for any longer than necessary, your site will simply appear to be very slow – this will generally decrease the usability of the site.

Application Object Events

The `Application` object has two events that set the Active Server Pages application lifetime. The `onStart` event occurs when the application starts, and the `onEnd` event occurs when an application finishes.

Event Handler Syntax

If we need to write some code that executes when our application starts or finishes, we need to put this code into an appropriate **event handler**. Event handlers should be placed in the `global.asa` file. Here is the skeleton example of the two event handlers for the `Application` object:

```
<SCRIPT LANGUAGE = "VBScript" RUNAT="Server">
  Sub Application_OnStart
    ' The code here will be executed when the application starts
  End Sub

  Sub Application_OnEnd
    ' The code here will be executed when the application ends
  End Sub
</SCRIPT>
```

We will examine the `global.asa` file later in this chapter – after we have looked at the `Session` object.

The Session Object

There is one `Application` object for each application on the web server. Every client accessing that application can get a reference to it. Each of these clients is called a **session**. Therefore, each of them has a reference to a unique `Session` object. The `Session` object will allow you to:

❑ Be notified when a user session begins, so that you can take appropriate actions for a new client.

❑ Be notified when a client has ended their session. This can be caused by a timeout, or by an explicit method called `Abandon`.

❑ Store information that can be accessed by the client throughout the session.

The `Session` object is the most powerful object for creating applications using Active Server Pages. It solves a problem that has existed in creating web-based applications – namely, that the connection between the client and the server is **stateless**. When a client requests a page, the web server itself has no mechanism for tying this request back to previous requests by the same client. This means that each request that one client makes of a web server is treated independently from the rest. While this allows for a very efficient and fast web server, it makes writing applications nearly impossible – and that's why the `Session` object is such a valuable tool.

The interface of the `Session` object looks like this:

SESSION	
Collections	
Contents	StaticObjects
Properties	
CodePage	SessionID
LCID	Timeout
Methods	
Abandon	
Events	
OnStart	OnEnd

Session Object Collections

The `Session` object has two collections – `Contents` and `StaticObjects`. These are similar to the collections of the same name in the `Application` object – except that the `Session` object collections have session scope (while `Application` object collections have global scope).

The Contents Collection

The `Contents` collection contains all the variables established for a session without using the `<OBJECT>` tag. The `Contents` collection is used to determine the value of a specific session level variable, or to iterate through the collection and retrieve a list of all items in the session.

```
[varValue = ]Session.Contents(key)
[varValue = ]Session(key)
```

Parameter	Type	Description
key	String	Specifies the name of the item to be retrieved

For example, you can store a value into a session-level variable:

```
Session.Contents("VisitorID") = Request("VisitorID")
```

Since `Contents` is the default property for the `Session` object, this is sometimes shortened to:

```
Session("VisitorID") = Request("VisitorID")
```

Once this value is stored in a session-level variable, it will be accessible from any ASP page in the application that is accessed during the duration of the session. We will see later in this chapter how to set the duration of the session. Now, from another page in the web application, you can retrieve this value and use it in that page:

```
Response.Write "The Visitor ID Is " & Session("VisitorID")
```

You can iterate through the `Session.Contents` collection with the following code:

```
<%
  Dim SessProp
  For Each SessProp in Session.Contents
    Response.Write("Session " & SessProp & _
                   " = " & Session(SessProp) & "<BR>")
  Next
%>
```

This code will produce a list of names and values of all the `Session` variables.

The StaticObjects Collection

The `StaticObjects` collection contains all of the objects created with the `<OBJECT>` tag within the scope of the `Session` object. These objects are usually created in the `global.asa` file.

```
[objAppObj = ]Session.StaticObjects(key)
```

Parameter	Type	Description
key	String	Specifies the name of the item to retrieve

The following code iterates through the keys of the `StaticObjects` collection.

```
Dim Item
For Each Item in Session.StaticObjects
  Response.Write(Item & " = " & Session.StaticObjects (Item) _
                 & "<BR>")
Next
```

Session Object Properties

The Session object has four properties that are discussed below.

The CodePage Property

A code page is a character set that can include numbers, punctuation marks, and other glyphs. Different languages and locales may use different code pages. For example, most Western European languages use code page 1251; in Russia, code page 866 is used for DOS and 1251 for Windows. (There's a list of the common code page numbers in Appendix G.)

A code page can be represented in a table as a mapping of characters to single-byte or multi-byte values. Many code pages share the first half of the ASCII character set for characters in the range 0x00 - 0x7F.

```
Session.CodePage = intCodepage
<%@CODEPAGE = intCodepage %>
[intValue = ]Session.CodePage
```

Parameter	Type	Description
intCodepage	Unsigned Integer	A valid codepage for the system that is running the ASP scripting engine

As the Active Server Pages engine processes the content and script on the page, it uses the code page we have specified to determine how to convert characters from our script's character set into Unicode, which is a double-byte fixed-width character encoding standard used internally by the ASP engine.

When you temporarily change a code page for a portion of your script, you should ultimately restore it to its original value. For example:

```
<%
    Session("CurrentCP") = Session.CodePage
    Session.CodePage = 1252
    ' Other code here...
    Session.CodePage = Session("CurrentCP")
%>
```

The LCID Property

The LCID property specifies the locale identifier – a standard international abbreviation that uniquely identifies one of the system-defined locales.

```
Session.LCID = intLocaleID
[intID = ]Session.LCID
```

Parameter	Type	Description
iLocaleID	Integer	A valid locale identifier.

The locale identifier is a set of user-defined preference information, related to the user's language. The locale determines how dates and times are formatted, how items are sorted alphabetically, and how strings are compared. The *locale identifier* (LCID) is a 32-bit value that uniquely defines a locale. The ASP engine uses the default locale of the web server, unless you specify a different locale for a particular script.

Here's a simple demonstration of the effects of different LCIDs. The code required to produce this page is shown below. For a list of all predefined LCIDs, refer to Appendix G.

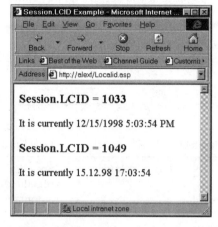

```
<%
  ' Set LCID for Standard US English (0x409)
  Session.LCID = 1033
%>
<H3>Session.LCID = <% =Session.LCID %> </H3>
It is currently <% =Now () %>
<BR>

<%
  ' Set LCID for Russian (0x419)
  Session.LCID = 1049
%>
<H3>Session.LCID = <% =Session.LCID %> </H3>
It is currently <% =Now() %>
```

The SessionID Property

The `SessionID` property stores the session identification for the current session.

```
[intSessionID = ]Session.SessionID
```

The `SessionID` property is a unique identifier that is generated by the server when the `Session` object is created, and is used to keep track of the sessions. The value of the `SessionID` property is read-only. The `SessionID` is a long integer value that may look like this:

```
875239632
```

It is important to understand how the `SessionID` value is created by the server. For the duration of the time that the server is running, it will guarantee that all session IDs are unique. This will ensure that no user coming into the site will be able to access the session information of another user.

However, the server will only guarantee this as long as it is running. If the server is rebooted, or if the Web Publishing service is stopped and restarted, then the server will no longer track those session IDs that have already been created. This means that you should never store the value of the session ID in any type of permanent storage (such as a database). Likewise, you should never use the session ID as a primary key in a database table. If you need temporary storage locations associated with a session, then use the capabilities of the session-level variables that we looked at earlier.

The Timeout Property

The Timeout property specifies the timeout period for this Session.

```
Session.Timeout = intMinutes
[intTimeout = ]Session.Timeout
```

Parameter	Type	Description
intMinutes	Integer	Specifies the number of minutes that a session can remain idle before the server terminates it automatically.

The default value for the Session.Timeout property is 20 minutes, but we can alter this on a per-session basis by changing the value of this property. If the user does not refresh or request a page within the timeout period, the session ends.

You should exercise caution when setting timeout values. If you set Timeout too short, the server will terminate user sessions too quickly. For example, if you rely on session variables to process user data and the user has not been able to complete the processing of an identification form, the loss of session variables will cause all sorts of problems.

Setting Session.Timeout too long also has its problems. All session variables are stored in the server's memory. Unless you decide to use IsClientConnected a lot (which is cumbersome if you use it in every .asp page), you'll probably have quite a few user sessions eating up server memory resources, if sessions last for too long a time. This is particularly critical if you store database query results in session-level arrays. These results can hold a lot of data sometimes, and having multiple unused sessions still open, with large amounts of data stored in them, could reduce the efficiency of your server.

The best strategy is to analyze each application, by conducting average user browsing time tests, and then set the session timeout to a more appropriate value where needed. Generally, the 20-minute timeout is a good compromise for most applications. So use that as a starting point, and begin tweaking from there.

Session Object Methods

The Session object has only one method – the Abandon method described below.

The Abandon Method

The Abandon method destroys all the objects stored in a Session object and releases their server resources. If you do not call the Abandon method in a script, the server destroys the session objects when the session times out.

```
Session.Abandon
```

If, when a user finishes browsing a certain page, you know that they don't need any more session variables, you can call the Abandon method to release server memory resources associated with that session. Bear in mind that if you set certain useful session variable values, like UserName, these values will be lost. On the other hand, if you are programming web games, which use server memory resources heavily, you might be better off explicitly ending the session and having the user log in for another game.

We can use the Abandon method during development, when testing Session variables. If you create a page named abandon.asp, as described below, you can call it when needed:

```
<%
   Session.Abandon
   Response.Redirect "default.asp"
%>
```

In this page, we first call the Abandon method of the Session object. This releases all of the session-level variables. Next, the Redirect method of the Response object is used to send the browser to the starting page of the application. In this example, that page is named default.asp.

Session Object Events

There are two events that mark the beginning and end of the Session object's lifetime. The onStart is fired when the server creates a new session and the OnEnd is fired when the session is abandoned or times out. Just like the event handlers for the Application object events, these events are handled in the global.asa file, which we will look at next.

The global.asa File

We can store objects and variables in an application-level scope – now we need a file to store these declarations. This file is called global.asa. Each web application can have only one global.asa, and it's placed in the virtual directory's root. In global.asa, you can include event handler scripts and declare objects that will have Session or Application scope. You can also initialize and store application-level variables and objects used by the application. The file has no display component, since it's not displayed to users.

Understanding the Structure of global.asa

If you are using VBScript, `global.asa` can contain only four event handling subroutines:

```
Application_OnStart
Application_OnEnd
Session_OnStart
Session_OnEnd
```

An example of the most basic `global.asa` file would be:

```
<SCRIPT LANGUAGE="VBScript" RUNAT="Server">

Sub Application_OnStart
'...your VBScript code here
End Sub

Sub Application_OnEnd
'...your VBScript code here
End Sub

Sub Session_OnStart
'...your VBScript code here
End Sub

Sub Session_OnEnd
'...your VBScript code here
End Sub
</SCRIPT>
```

Notice that we have to use the `<SCRIPT>` tag at the top of the page. Also (as previously mentioned), there are no `<%...%>` blocks, because in `global.asa` all of the ASP script needs to be enclosed in the `<SCRIPT>` block. All four of the event handling scripts must be defined within this `<SCRIPT>` block. Since these scripts will be running on the server (not the client), we have also included the RUNAT directive inside of the SCRIPT element.

Application_OnStart

This event handler is run **once**, when the application starts. The application starts when the first visitor to the application calls the first `.asp` page. Any application initialization steps, that need to be run before anyone can access the application, should be placed in this procedure. For example, you could store the database login information in an application-level variable, so that all pages have easy access to it.

If you want to initialize an application-scoped variable in `Application_OnStart`, you'd use:

```
Sub Application_OnStart
  Application("YourVariable") = "SomeValue"
End Sub
```

Once this event handler is complete, `Session_OnStart` runs.

Application_OnEnd

This event handler runs when the server is stopped or the web application is unloaded. You can stop the server from the Personal Web Manager application. From this screen, you can press the **Stop** button to stop the server.

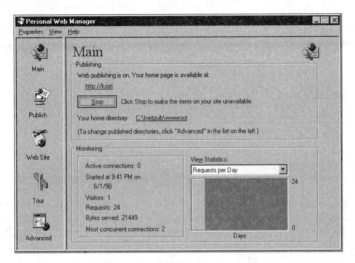

If you are using Windows NT, then you have another option for forcing an application to end. (You can still stop the web server, which will cause the application to end. In fact, it will cause all applications currently running on your web server to end.) If you have created an application that will run in its own memory space, you can also explicitly unload it by using the Microsoft Management Console. In the properties dialog box for each web application, there is an Unload button. By pressing this button, the `Application_OnEnd` event will be fired, and then the application will be unloaded.

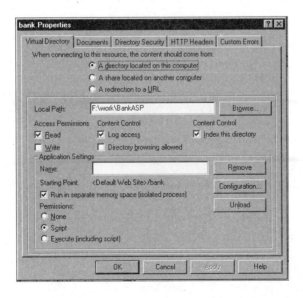

`Application_OnEnd` scripts are used for "cleaning up" settings after the application stops. For example, you might want to insert code to delete unneeded database records, or write essential information to text files. However, the `Application_OnEnd` event will only ever be fired during a graceful shutdown. This will only occur if one the earlier mentioned steps is followed, or if the server is shutdown properly. In the event of a server failure, `Application_OnEnd` will not be fired. In other words, you shouldn't rely on this event to perform your housekeeping. The `Session_OnEnd` is fired with more regularity, and therefore is a better location for application-level housekeeping chores.

Session_OnStart

`Session_OnStart` is called every time a new user begins a session with the web site. If you want to initialize a session-scoped variable in `Session_OnStart`, you'd use:

```
Sub Session_OnStart
   Session("YourVariable") = "SomeValue"
End Sub
```

One basic difference between application-level and session-level variables is that you can create session-level variables any time (from `global.asa` or from any `.asp` page), while you can only initialize application variables in `global.asa` – although you can change application-level variable values from any `.asp` page. The reason for this is that `Application_OnStart` only runs *once* – when the application starts – so you can't add any variables unless you stop and restart the application.

For example, let's say you want to track the number of visitors *currently* accessing your site. (This is different from a traditional counter, which tracks total numbers of visitors.) To do this, you would have an application-level variable that tracks the current number of users. Of course, this is equal to the number of sessions that are currently active. Every time a new session starts, we would add one to that number – this can be done in the `Session_OnStart` routine. We will take a look at an example of this in just a bit.

Session_OnEnd

`Session_OnEnd` is called whenever a session terminates. This can happen if the session times out, or if it is explicitly abandoned. In `Session_OnEnd`, you might want to transfer temporary session variables to databases, or set application-level variables to another value. For example, if you are tracking the number of users currently visiting a site in an application-level variable, then you would subtract one from this number every time `Session_OnEnd` was run:

```
SUB Session_OnEnd
   Application.lock
   Application("Active")= Application("Active") - 1
   Application.unlock
END SUB
```

Declaring Objects in global.asa

You can declare application-scoped objects in `global.asa`. This will allow you to create one instance of an object and then use it on any page and in every session that accesses your web application. To declare an object in `global.asa`:

```
<OBJECT RUNAT=Server SCOPE=Scope ID=Application PROGID="progID">
</OBJECT>
```

Or if you are using the CLASSID of the object:

```
<OBJECT RUNAT=Server SCOPE=Scope ID=Application CLASSID="ClassID">
</OBJECT>
```

You can also declare session-scoped objects in global.asa:

```
<OBJECT RUNAT=Server SCOPE=Scope ID=Session PROGID="progID">
</OBJECT>
```

```
<OBJECT RUNAT=Server SCOPE=Scope ID=Session CLASSID="ClassID">
</OBJECT>
```

You can use either ProgID or ClassID, but not both.

Some Warnings on Declaring Objects in global.asa

You should be careful about creating components in application scope. Some components are not designed to be given application scope. This is to do with the threading model of the component. There are four types of threading models for components in Windows:

- ❑ **Single-threaded**: Bad all round for use in ASP.
- ❑ **Apartment-threaded**: Fine for storage in page scope, performance hit when stored at session or application scope.
- ❑ **Free-threaded**: Sounds good, but bad all round for use in ASP.
- ❑ **Both-threaded**: Best overall threading model for all scopes. Only acceptable threading model for application and session scope.

If you are not sure if an object can be used in application or session scope, then you should err on the side of caution and find another place to store the object.

Objects declared in global.asa are not created until the server processes a script that calls the object. This saves resources by only creating objects that are actually used.

Using Type Libraries in global.asa

When you are using components in your Active Server Pages, such as the ADO libraries, you often have to pass constants to methods. These constants have a name (for example, adopenForwardOnly) which represents some numeric value (in this case, 0). When we use the method we can pass either the numeric value or the name of the constant.

There are two ways that your ASP script can identify the named constant. First, you can include a file in your ASP script that contains the name and value of the constant. Generally, this file will include the name and values of *all* the constants for a particular library – e.g. for ADO, this file is called `adovbs.inc`. Since ASP is processed as a script language, the more data that each page has to read, the slower the performance of your page.

Second – and a great way to improve your performance – is to use a type library. A type library is a file that contains information about the objects, types, and constants supported by an ActiveX component. But these are already in a binary format, so the ASP script engine does not have to recompile them every time. This will make it possible to refer to the data types declared in the type libraries from any script within the application.

To declare a type library, use the `<METADATA>` tag in the `global.asa` file for your application. For example, to declare the ADO type library, use the following statements:

```
<!--METADATA TYPE="typelib" FILE = "c:\program files\common
files\system\ado\msado15.dll" -->
```

Then, you can then use ADO constants in any script in the same application as the `global.asa` file without having to include the `adovbs.inc` file – thus avoiding the associated performance effects.

Using global.asa

In this example, we will see how application and session level variables can be used to track a web site's visitors. We will be using the `global.asa` file to manage all of the counting.

Here is the `global.asa` file that will perform the tracking routines:

```
<SCRIPT LANGUAGE=VBScript RUNAT=Server>
Sub Application_OnStart
  Application("visits") = 0
  Application("Active")= 0
End Sub

Sub Application_OnEnd

End Sub

Sub Session_OnStart
  Session.Timeout = 1
  Session("Start")=Now
  Application.lock
    Application("visits")= Application("visits") + 1
    intTotal_visitors = Application("visits")
  Application.unlock
  Session("VisitorID") = intTotal_visitors

  Application.lock
    Application("Active")= Application("Active") + 1
  Application.unlock
End Sub
```

```
Sub Session_OnEnd
  Application.lock
    Application("Active")= Application("Active") - 1
  Application.unlock
End Sub
</SCRIPT>
```

In order to use this application, we will need an ASP script that is running inside the application. In this example, the page will be used to display the total number of visitors and the number currently accessing the site:

```
<HTML>
<HEAD>
  <TITLE>Retrieving Variables Set in Global.asa</TITLE>
</HEAD>

<BODY>
<P>
There have been <B><%=Session("VisitorID")%></B> total visits to this site.
<BR>You are one of <B> <%=Application("Active")%></B> active visitors.
<BR>Your session started at <%= Session("Start") %>

</BODY>
</HTML>
```

How It Works

In this application, we use application-level variables to track the number of users that are currently looking at a site, and the total number that have accessed it.

In the first event handler of the global.asa file, we will be working with the Application_OnStart method, that is called whenever the application is started:

```
<SCRIPT LANGUAGE=VBScript RUNAT=Server>
Sub Application_OnStart
  Application("visits") = 0
  Application("Active")= 0
End Sub
```

There are two variables that we will need to maintain throughout the life of the application. The visits variable will hold the total number of visits since the application was started. The Active variable will hold the number of current user sessions in the application.

We will not be doing any processing when the application is ended, so we just add the Application_OnEnd event handler as a placeholder:

```
Sub Application_OnEnd

End Sub
```

When a session is started, we will perform some processing in the Session_OnStart event handler. To make our example work faster, we set the Timeout value of the Session object to 1 minute:

```
Sub Session_OnStart
  Session.Timeout = 1
  Session("Start")=Now
```

In a real application, you would very rarely have your Timeout value set so low. We will also store the starting date and time for this session into a session-level variable, Start.

We will need to find out the total number of users who have visited the site since the application was started. This information is stored in an application-level variable, visits:

```
Application.lock
    Application("visits")= Application("visits") + 1
    intTotal_visitors = Application("visits")
Application.unlock
Session("VisitorID") = intTotal_visitors
```

In order to change an application-level variable, we need to first Lock the Application object. We can then increment the value stored in the visits variable by one. This new value will represent the total number of visitors, including the one currently starting. The incremented value is returned to the same application-level variable. When we've made all the changes that we need to, we will call Unlock to free up the AppIon object.

Finally, we will update the current number of active users by one. This information is stored the application-level variable, Active:

```
    Application.lock
        Application("Active")= Application("Active") + 1
    Application.unlock
End Sub
```

When the user leaves the site and their session times out, the Session_OnEnd event handler will be called:

```
Sub Session_OnEnd
    Application.lock
        Application("Active")= Application("Active") - 1
    Application.unlock
End Sub
```

The important thing here is that the number of active users must be decremented by one. Since this information is stored at the application-level, you will need to Lock the Application object when making the change, and the Unlock the object as soon as possible after you've made the necessary changes.

In our test page, we display the total number of visits to this site since the application was started. We also show the number of active visitors, as well as the time at which the current session commenced. Note that we are interacting with an application-level variable, but we don't need to Lock and Unlock the Application object at this stage, because we're only want to *read* the data.

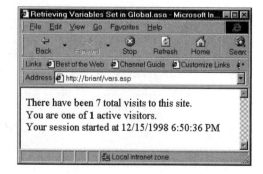

Summary

The world of web-based applications is made possible by Active Server Pages and the `Application` and `Session` objects. These powerful objects allow you transform a web site from a series of linked pages to an actual application by creating a means to hold user information from page to page. In this chapter, we have looked at:

❑ How the `Application` object can be used to store information that can be accessed by all users accessing a web site.

❑ The powerful `Session` object, which allows us to treat a user's interaction with the web site as a continuous action, rather than just a disconnected series of page requests.

❑ What the `global.asa` file is used for, and how it helps us interact with the beginning and the end of sessions and applications.

Now that we are on our way towards building web-based applications, we will look at the remaining object in the ASP object model – the `Server` object.

5

The Server Object

In this short chapter we will move on to cover the Server object. The Server object is a low-level object that provides some basic properties and methods that can be used in almost every Active Server Page. This object will allow you to do things like:

- ❑ Set the length of time for which a script can run before an error occurs
- ❑ Take a user-supplied string and encode it into HTML format
- ❑ Convert a virtual path to a physical path on the server
- ❑ Take a user-supplied string and encode it into the proper format for a URL string
- ❑ Create an instance of an Active Server component

The interface of the Server object looks like this. These methods and properties don't directly affect the appearance of the page on the browser, but they do provide valuable support in creating Active Server Pages.

SERVER	
Collections	
Properties	
ScriptTimeout	
Methods	
CreateObject	URLEncode
HTMLEncode	URLPathEncode
MapPath	
Events	

Server Object Properties

The Server object has only one property – the ScriptTimeout property, described below.

The ScriptTimeOut Property

The ScriptTimeout property specifies the maximum amount of time that a script can run before it is terminated. This will prevent bugs (such as infinite loops) from causing the server process to hang indefinitely. The ScriptTimeout property is a read/write property. Its default value is 90 seconds.

```
Server.ScriptTimeOut = intSeconds
[intTimeoutVal = ]Server.ScriptTimeOut
```

Parameter	Type	Description
intSeconds	Integer	Maximum number of seconds that a script can run. When this period has elapsed, the script is terminated by the server

Server Object Methods

The CreateObject Method

The CreateObject method is used to create an instance of an Active Server component.

```
objCompRef = Server.CreateObject(progID)
```

Parameter	Type	Description
progID	String or GUID	Specifies the type of object to create. The format for progID is ComponentName[.Class]

For example, we use the CreateObject method to create instances of the server components supplied by Microsoft along with ASP:

```
Set objBrowser = Server.CreateObject("MSWC.BrowserType")
Response.Write("Hello, " & objBrowser.Browser & " user!")
```

The progID in this example is MSWC.BrowserType. All objects that come as part of the Microsoft Internet Information Server have MSWC (MicroSoft Web Component) in the Vendor part of the progID.

The CreateObject method is also used to create instances of the ADO database access objects:

```
Set objConn = Server.CreateObject("ADODB.Connection")
objConn.Open "driver={SQL Server}; server=srv; uid=sa; pwd=; database=pubs"
```

We will look at ADO in more detail in Chapter 8.

Lastly, the CreateObject method is used to create instances of custom Active Server components. These are components that are acquired from a third party, or that you've developed yourself. In either case, the method for creating an instance of them is the same:

```
Set objCustomASC = Server.CreateObject("MyComponentName.MyClass")
objCustomASC.methodCall
```

Objects created with the `Server.CreateObject` method are visible only to the script that is on the page where the object was created. We call this the **page scope**. Page-scoped objects are automatically destroyed by the server when at the end of the current page (although destroying the object formally using `Set objName = Nothing` is a good habit – it's a safer way to ensure that the server's resources are released). As we described in Chapter 4, we use the `Application` and `Session` objects to store instances with global scope or with session scope.

The HTMLEncode Method

The `HTMLEncode` method applies HTML encoding to the string supplied as its parameter.

`[strEncoded = ]Server.HTMLEncode(strText)`

Parameter	Type	Description
strText	String	Specifies the string to be encoded

HTML Encoding ensures that the string supplied will appear in a web page in the exact format that it is stored. Why is this necessary? Suppose you're passing a string to the browser for display. If your string contains any character-strings that look like HTML tags, then the browser *interprets* them as HTML tags – for example, of your string contains the substring <B> then the browser will display all subsequent text in bold.

This may be the effect that you are looking for; but if you are writing HTML documentation (or anything else that requires the tags themselves to be visible in HTML), then you have a problem. By HTML-encoding the string, the parts of the string that *look* like HTML will be converted such that they will appear properly in the page. In the case of the <B> tag, the HTML encoded version would look like `&lt;B&gt;`. You'll find an example that uses the `HTMLEncode` method towards the end of Chapter 6.

The MapPath Method

The `MapPath` method is used to provide file location information for use in our scripts. The `MapPath` method takes a virtual path and converts it to a physical path.

`[strPhysPath = ]Server.MapPath(strPath)`

Parameter	Type	Description
strPath	String	Specifies the relative or virtual path to be mapped to a physical directory

If *strPath* starts with a forward slash (/) or with a backward slash (\), the `MapPath` method returns a path as if *strPath* is a full virtual path. If *strPath* doesn't start with a slash, the `MapPath` method returns a path relative to the directory of the script file being processed. The `MapPath` method is also seen in action in Chapter 6.

The URLEncode Method

The URLEncode method takes a string of information and converts it into URL-encoded form. This method is used mostly for converting URLs into acceptable characters for browsers (hence the name URLEncode). However, the method works for *any* string, which makes it a very useful function, especially when dealing with e-mail addresses.

```
[strEncodedString = ]Server.URLEncode(strURL)
```

Parameter	Type	Description
strURL	String	Specifies the string to encode

Using the Server Object

The Server object is a utility object, and you'll be seeing it action throughout many of the examples in the book. In particular, you'll see a lot of the CreateObject method in the examples of Chapters 7 and 8; you'll find the MapPath method utilized in the FileSystemObject example of Chapter 6, and you'll see URLEncode and HTMLEncode in the TextStream example, also in Chapter 6.

Summary

In this short chapter we have discussed the remaining object from the Active Server Pages object model. The Server object is a utility object that provides methods which are necessary in many web pages:

❑ A method to create instances of the server-side components
❑ The ability to set a global script timeout value
❑ Methods to encode strings based on HTML or URL formatting rules
❑ A method to translate a virtual directory name to its physical path on the hard drive

In the next chapter we will look at the objects that are part of the Scripting Library. While not exclusively for the use of ASP developers, they provide a great deal of functionality to make developer's lives easier.

The Built-in Scripting Objects

In Chapters 2–5, we examined the objects that comprise the Active Server Pages object model. In this chapter we will take a look at the built-in scripting objects that are available for ASP developers. These objects are not part of the ASP object model itself, but they are available to the scripting programs that run on the server. These objects are:

- ❏ The Dictionary object
- ❏ The FileSystemObject object and its subordinate objects:

  The Drive object and Drives collection

  The File object and Files collection

  The Folder object and Folders collection

- ❏ The TextStream object

These objects and collections are part of the **Microsoft Scripting Runtime**. This is a special dynamic link library (DLL), implemented in a file called scrrun.dll. This file is supplied as part of Internet Information Server for Windows NT Server 4.0, and as part of Personal Web Server for both Windows NT Workstation 4.0 and Windows 9x.

The Dictionary Object

The Dictionary object is used to store and access data, represented in the form of **name/value pairs**. In a name/value pair, the **name** (or **key**) is used to uniquely identify the **value** (or **item**). Since the key uniquely identifies one and only one value, there can only be one entry in the object with the specified key. The key can take the form of anything except an array; in most cases, we use an integer or string key.

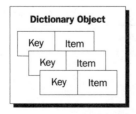

Before we can use a `Dictionary` object, we have to create it:

```
Set objDict = CreateObject("Scripting.Dictionary")
```

This line creates an empty dictionary called `objDict`, in which we can store key/item pairs. Here's the full interface for the `Dictionary` object:

THE DICTIONARY OBJECT	
Collections	
Items	Keys
Properties	
CompareMode	Item
Count	Key
Methods	
Add	Keys
Exists	Remove
Items	RemoveAll
Events	

Dictionary Object Properties

The properties of the `Dictionary` object allow us to obtain the number of key/item pairs in the `Dictionary`, to get or set the value of the item associated with a key, to set the new value of the key, and to change the comparison mode for the keys.

The CompareMode Property

We use the `CompareMode` property to set and to return the string comparison mode for the keys. The string comparison mode determines how keys are matched when doing searches, or when looking up a key. You can either treat the keys as being case-sensitive or as being case-insensitive.

The `CompareMode` property can only be set on a dictionary that doesn't contain any entries. This property is currently supported only in VBScript – it's not supported in JScript. You will need to explicitly create these constants in VBScript if you wish to use the named values. The default value is `vbBinaryCompare`.

```
objDict.CompareMode = comparison_mode
```

Name	Type	Description
comparison_mode	CompareMethod	The comparison mode.
		`VbBinaryCompare = 0`
		`VbTextCompare = 1`

The Count Property

The Count property returns the number of key/item pairs in the Dictionary. This property is read-only.

```
lCount = objDict.Count
```

The Item Property

The Item property is used to set or to retrieve the value of the item for the specified key and dictionary:

```
objDict.Item(keyvalue)[ = itemvalue]
```

Name	Type	Description
keyvalue	Variant	The value of the key associated with the item being retrieved or set
itemvalue	Variant	Optional value – when used, this sets the value of the item associated with the key keyvalue

The Key Property

The Key property is used to reset the key value of an existing key/item pair, or to generate a new key/item pair (with an empty item).

```
objDict.Key(keyvalue) = newkeyvalue
```

Name	Type	Description
keyvalue	Variant	The current key value (the value of this is to be reset by this command)
newkeyvalue	Variant	The new value for the key

Dictionary Object Methods

The Dictionary object contains methods for adding, removing and retrieving key/item pairs. There's also a method that allows us to check whether a specified key exists.

The Add Method

The Add method adds a key/item pair to the specified Dictionary object.

```
objDict.Add keyvalue, itemvalue
```

Name	Type	Description
keyvalue	Variant	The value of the key in the new key/item pair
itemvalue	Variant	The value of the item in the new key/item pair

The Exists Method

We use the Exists method to check whether a specified key already exists in the specified dictionary. The Exists method returns true if the specified key exists in the dictionary, and false otherwise.

[bExists =]objDict.Exists(*keyvalue*)

Name	Type	Description
keyvalue	Variant	The key that is to be searched for

The Items Method

The Items method returns an array that contains all the items in the specified dictionary.

[arItems =]objDict.Items

The Keys Method

The Keys method returns an array that contains all the keys in the Dictionary.

[arKeys =]objDict.Keys

The Remove Method

The Remove method is used to remove a single key/item pair from the dictionary.

objDict.Remove *keyvalue*

Name	Type	Description
keyvalue	Variant	The 'key' part of the key/item pair to be removed from the dictionary

The RemoveAll Method

Finally, the RemoveAll method clears the dictionary by removing *all* key/value pairs.

objDict.RemoveAll

Dictionary Example

Let's take a look at a simple example that will show you how to use the Dictionary object. When you view this page in your browser, you won't see a very exciting display, since all the cool stuff is going on in the code behind the scenes.

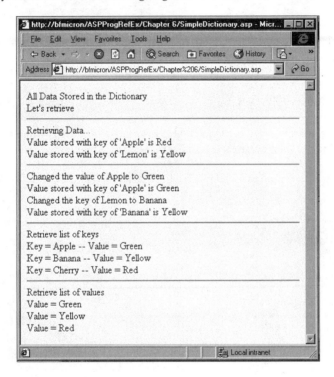

How It Works

The goal of this example is to show how to create a Dictionary object, then add some information to it, retrieve and change that information. Finally, we will see how to look at the contents of the dictionary as an array. The first step is to create the instance of the Scripting.Dictionary object and set the comparison mode for the dictionary:

```
dim objDictionary
Set objDictionary = CreateObject("Scripting.Dictionary")
ObjDictionary.Comparemode = 0 ' Use binary comparison
```

This is done using the VBScript CreateObject method. Note that to create an instance of a scripting object we use the CreateObject method of the appropriate script, and not the CreateObject method of the Server object, as we did for the ASP intrinsic objects. Next, we will use two different methods to add name/value pairs to this new dictionary object. The first method passes the name/value pair directly as parameters to the Add method:

```
objDictionary.Add "Apple", "Red"
objDictionary.Add "Lemon", "Yellow"
```

The second stores values as variables, and then passes those variables as parameters to the Add method:

```
dim strKey
dim strValue
strKey = "Cherry"
strValue = "Red"
objDictionary.Add strKey, strValue
```

With the information stored in the Dictionary object, we can use the Item property to retrieve a value for a particular key:

```
Response.Write "Retrieving Data..."
strValue = objDictionary.Item("Apple")
Response.Write "<BR>Value stored with key of 'Apple' is " & strValue
```

In this example, we are retrieving the value that is associated with the key named "Apple". This value can then be displayed in the browser by using Response.Write.

We can also pass the key value to a variable, and then use that variable with the Item property:

```
strKey = "Lemon"
strValue = objDictionary.Item(strKey)
Response.Write "<BR>Value stored with key of '" & _
                        strKey & "' is " & strValue
```

We can also store new information in the Dictionary object with the Item and Key properties:

```
if objDictionary.Exists("Apple") then
    objDictionary.Item("Apple") = "Green"
    Response.Write "Changed the value of Apple to Green"
    Response.Write "<BR>Value stored with key of 'Apple' is " _
                                    objDictionary.Item("Apple")
end if
```

Here, we use the Exists method to see if the key that we are interested in exists: this prevents an error message from being generated if the key does not exist. The new value associated with the key named "Apple" is then assigned using the Item method. In the Response.Write line, we use the Item property again – this time to retrieve the item value for printing to the screen. So you can see that the Item property is dual-purpose – it can be used to retrieve an item value from the dictionary as well as change an existing value.

In addition to changing the value associated with a key, you can change the key itself:

```
if objDictionary.Exists("Lemon") then
    objDictionary.Key("Lemon") = "Banana"
    Response.Write "<BR>Changed the key of Lemon to Banana"
    Response.Write "<BR>Value stored with key of 'Banana' is " & _
                                    objDictionary.Item("Banana")
end if
```

Again, you should always use the `Exists` method to ensure that the key exists within the dictionary. Then you can change the key using the `Keys` property (just as we changed item values using the `Item` property). Once the key is changed, the item can no longer be retrieved using the old key. You should take care when renaming keys to ensure that you will remember what the new key is – or else you won't be able to access the item.

Finally, we can use the `Items` and `Keys` methods to retrieve a set of the items or keys in the dictionary and store them in an array:

```
Response.Write "Retrieve list of keys"
dim arKeys, i
arKeys = objDictionary.keys
for i = 0 to objDictionary.Count -1
  Response.Write "<BR>Key = " & arKeys(i) & _
           " -- Value = " & objDictionary.Item(arKeys(i))
next
```

The `Keys` method returns a reference to an array that contains all of the keys in the dictionary. The `Items` method returns a reference to an array that contains all of the item values in the dictionary. Once the information is in the array, we can use a `For...Next` loop to iterate through each key. We will use the `Count` property of the dictionary object to determine how many entries there are in the dictionary. The array that is returned is zero-based, so the for loop will need to go from 0 to the value of the `Count` property minus 1.

Dictionary Object Persistence

The `Dictionary` object allows us to store information in the web server's memory. By storing the reference to the `Dictionary` object into a session variable, we can make this information available between pages in a web application.

> In order to store the `Scripting.Dictionary` object in a session variable, the object needs to be marked as a Both-threaded object. With the release of the Windows NT Option Pack, this was the case. However, with the subsequent release of Visual Studio 6, this object became marked as Apartment-threaded, which will cause major problems if stored in the `Session` object. Hopefully, Microsoft will notice the error in their ways and correct this. In the meantime, if you have upgraded to VS6, there is no way to store the `Scripting.Dictionary` object in the `Session` object.

The FileSystemObject Object

When our ASP server is handling requests from its clients, there are two types of pages it can return. As we have seen in this book, we can use the scripting power of ASP to dynamically create pages on-the-fly and send them back to the client. We can also serve static pages that are stored on the web server itself. But up until this point, we as web application developers had to know which files were stored in what place on what drive.

With the `FileSystemObject`, we can use our code to access the file system of the web server itself. This will allow us to:

❑ Get and manipulate information about all of the drives in the server. These can be physical drives or remote drives that the web server is connected to
❑ Get and manipulate information about all of the folders and sub-folders on a drive
❑ Get and manipulate information about all of the files inside of a folder

With this information, there is a very broad range of things that we can do with the file system. Aside from setting security information, just about anything that you can do with the file system using Windows Explorer or File Manager can also be done using the `FileSystemObject`.

By combining the file and folder manipulation capabilites of the `FileSystemObject`, with the web server configuration functionality of ADSI (which you will see in chapter 8), you can build your own web-based server management tool. The advantage of a web-based management tool is that it frees you from having to be at the server console to perform basic management functions such as copying files, moving folders, and creating virtual web directories.

Here's the full interface for the
`FileSystemObject` object:

THE FILESYSTEMOBJECT OBJECT

Collections
Drives

Properties

Methods

BuildPath	GetDrive
CopyFile	GetDriveName
CopyFolder	GetExtensionName
CreateFolder	GetFile
CreateTextFile	GetFileName
DeleteFile	GetFolder
DeleteFolder	GetParentFolderName
DriveExists	GetSpecialFolder
FileExists	GetTempName
FolderExists	MoveFile
GetAbsolutePathName	MoveFolder
GetBaseName	OpenTextFile

Events

To get access to the properties and methods of the `FileSystemObject` object, we need to create an instance of the object:

```
Set objFSO = CreateObject ("Scripting.FileSystemObject")
```

This creates a new `FileSystemObject` object, called `objFSO`.

The following diagram illustrates the relationship between the properties and methods of the FileSystemObject object and other objects and collections:

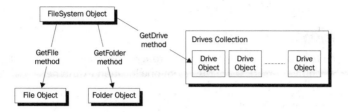

FileSystemObject Object Properties

The FileSystemObject object has one property – Drives.

The Drives Property

The Drives property returns a Drives collection – this consists of all the Drive objects available on the computer. Naturally, this is a read-only property (it would be an interesting feat if we could use Active Server Pages to create new drives in our server...)

[*collDrives* =]*objFSO*.Drives

FileSystemObject Object Methods

The FileSystemObject object has 24 methods that perform various tasks on the file system.

The BuildPath Method

The BuildPath method appends a name to an existing path.

[*strFullPath* =]*objFSO*.BuildPath(*path*, *name*)

Name	Type	Description
path	Variant	Existing path to which name is appended. Can be absolute or relative. This path does not necessarily have to exist.
name	Variant	Name being appended to the existing path.

The resulting string is a concatenation of path and name, with a backslash (\) inserted between them. Note that BuildPath doesn't create directories and folders – it just produces "well-formatted" path names.

The Copy... and Move... Methods

This group of methods provides the functionality with which to move and copy existing files and folders within the file system.

The CopyFile and MoveFile Methods

The `CopyFile` method copies one or more files from one location to another. The `MoveFile` method moves one or more files from one location to another.

```
objFSO.CopyFile source, destination[, overwrite]
objFSO.MoveFile source, destination
```

Name	Type	Description
source	Variant	The file(s) to be moved or copied (including the path). Can specify multiple files by using wildcards within the filename
destination	Variant	The new location for the file(s) specified in source. Can't contain wildcards
overwrite	Boolean (optional)	If true, then CopyFile is permitted to overwrite existing files in the destination; if false, existing files in the destination cannot be overwritten. The default value is false

If you try to move or copy a *source* file that doesn't exist, you'll get an error message. It's best to use the `FileExists` method with `CopyFile` and `MoveFile` to avoid such errors – see later in this chapter.

Also, note that the permissions on the destination will overrule the value of the *overwrite* parameter. Thus, if the destination has the read-only attribute set, then the `CopyFile` method will fail – even if the *overwrite* parameter is set to `true`.

The CopyFolder and MoveFolder Methods

The `CopyFolder` method copies a folder and all of its contents, including files and subfolders, from source to destination. The `MoveFolder` method is used to move one or more folders from one location to another.

```
objFSO.CopyFolder source, destination[, overwrite]
objFSO.MoveFolder source, destination
```

Name	Type	Description
source	Variant	The folder(s) to be moved or copied (including the path). Can specify multiple folders by using wildcards
destination	Variant	The new location for the folders specified in source. Can't contain wildcards
overwrite	Boolean (optional)	If true, then CopyFolder is permitted to overwrite existing folders in the destination; if false, existing folders in the destination cannot be overwritten. The default value is false

Again, if you specify non-existent folders in the source parameter then you'll generate an error – you can use the FolderExists method (see later in this chapter) to avoid these errors.

The Create... Methods

The CreateFolder Method

The CreateFolder method is used to create a folder, and returns a Folder object.

objFSO.CreateFolder "foldername"

Name	Type	Description
foldername	Variant	The name of the folder to be created

If the value of foldername is the name of an existing folder, you'll generate an error. You can use the FolderExists method of the FileSystemObject object to check for existing folders *before* you create a folder:

The CreateTextFile Method

The CreateTextFile method creates a specified text file. It returns a TextStream object. that we can then use to write to the newly created text file.

objFSO.CreateTextFile filename[, overwrite[, unicode]]

Name	Type	Description
filename	Variant	The name of the file to be created
overwrite	Boolean (optional)	If `true`, then `CreateTextFile` is permitted to overwrite an existing file; if `false`, existing folders cannot be overwritten. Default value is `true`
unicode	Boolean (optional)	If `true`, the new text file is created as a Unicode file; if `false`, it's created as an ASCII file. Default value is `false`

The DeleteFile and DeleteFolder Methods

The `DeleteFile` method deletes a specified file. The `DeleteFolder` method deletes a specified folder and all files and subfolders within it.

```
objFSO.DeleteFile file[, force]
objFSO.DeleteFolder folder[, force]
```

Name	Type	Description
file	Variant	The name of the file to be deleted. Multiple files can be specified using wildcards
folder	Variant	The name of the folder to be deleted. Multiple folders can be specified using wildcards
force	Boolean (optional)	If `true`, then the method is permitted to delete files with read-only attributes. Default value is `false`

If you try to delete a read-only file using `DeleteFile`, but the *force* parameter is `false` (the default), you'll generate an error (this is not the case with `DeleteFolder`). You'll also get an error message from either method if you try to specify a non-existent file or folder in the *file* or *folder* parameter.

> Note that the `DeleteFolder` method will delete your folder and all of its contents, including subfolders, without warning! When implementing the `DeleteFolder` method, it's a good idea to check the folder first for files and subfolders contained within. Use the `FileExists` and `FolderExists` methods.

The ...Exists Methods

Many of the other methods of the `FileSystemObject` object are responsible for moving items around, and for creating and deleting items. To keep the code clean, it's a good idea to keep tabs on whether the item you're dealing with actually exists – it can make a big difference to the outcome of the command! For example, attempting to delete a non-existent file using `DeleteFile` will generate an error – using `CreateFolder` to create an existing folder will also land you in hot water.

The solution is to use these methods in conjunction with the `...Exists` methods. For example, here's a simple way to avoid an error when using `DeleteFile`:

```
If objFSO.FileExists("d:\mydocs\mytext.txt") Then
    objFSO.DeleteFile "d:\mydocs\mytext.txt"
    Response.Write("File deleted")
Else
    Response.Write("Error. File does not exist")
End If
```

Here's how to avoid an error when using `CreateFolder`:

```
If Not objFSO.FolderExists("d:\mydocs\") Then
    objFSO.CreateFolder "d:\mydocs\"
    Response.Write("Folder created")
Else
    Response.Write("Error. Folder does not exists")
End If
```

Now let's quickly check through the details of these three methods.

The DriveExists Method

The `DriveExists` method allows us to check whether a specified drive exists, returning the Boolean value `true` if the drive is exists, and `false` otherwise.

[bExists =]objFSO.`DriveExists(`*drive*`)`

Name	Type	Description
drive	Variant	A drive letter or complete path specification

The FileExists Method

The `FileExists` method allows us to check whether a specified file exists, returning a Boolean – `true` if the file is found, and `false` otherwise.

[bExists =]objFSO.`FileExists(`*file*`)`

Name	Type	Description
file	Variant	The name of the desired file, including the complete path to the file (the complete path isn't necessary if you're searching for the file in the current directory)

The FolderExists Method

The `FolderExists` method is very similar to the `FileExists` method. On specifying a folder, the methods returns a Boolean – `true` if the folder is found, and `false` otherwise. If you mistakenly pass a file name as the parameter, then it will return `false` as well.

[bExists =]objFSO.FolderExists(folder)

Name	Type	Description
folder	Variant	The name of the desired folder, including the complete path to the folder (the complete path is unnecessary if the folder is a subfolder of the current folder)

The Get... Methods

The following methods return an object that represents the drive, file or folder specified. In each case, an error will result if the item specified in the parameter in non-existent – so it's a good idea to check first using the `. . .Exists` methods.

The GetDrive Method

The `GetDrive` method returns a `Drive` object for the specified drive or path.

[objDrive =]objFSO.GetDrive(drive)

Name	Type	Description
drive	Variant	The name of the drive or path

The GetFile Method

The `GetFile` method returns the `File` object for the specified file name.

[objFile =]objFSO.GetFile(filename)

Name	Type	Description
filename	Variant	The path for a file

The GetFolder Method

The `GetFolder` method returns a `Folder` object for folder specified in the `folder` parameter:

[objFolder =]objFSO.GetFolder(folder)

Name	Type	Description
folder	Variant	The path for a folder

The GetSpecialFolder Method

The GetSpecialFolder method returns the path to one of the special folders –
\Windows, \System or \TMP.

[*strFolder* =]*objFSO*.GetSpecialFolder(*folder*)

Name	Type	Description
folder	Variant	Specifies the special folder required

The Get...Name Methods

In addition to the Get... functions listed above, there's a whole bunch of methods
that are essentially string-manipulation functions. There are two special ones –
GetAbsolutePathName and GetTempName – and a group of five functions that
simply extract different parts of a file path. All of these methods deal in hypothetical
filenames and paths – that is, none of the methods in this section support any
mechanism to verify that the parameter represents an existing file. It's up to you to
make the necessary checks.

The GetAbsolutePathName Method

The GetAbsolutePathName method returns a complete path for the specified path
string.

[*strPath* =]*objFSO*.GetAbsolutePathName(*path*)

Name	Type	Description
path	Variant	Path string to be completed

The GetTempName Method

The GetTempName method is a random filename generator. Specifically, it generates a
filename for a temporary file.

[*strFileName* =]*objFSO*.GetTempName

The Others

Each of the remaining methods (listed here) takes a single parameter – a filename
including its full path – and returns the relevant part of that path.

```
[strDriveName = ]objFSO.GetDriveName(path)
[strFileName = ]objFSO.GetFileName(path)
[strBaseName = ]objFSO.GetBaseName(path)
[strExtName = ]objFSO.GetExtensionName(path)
[strFolderName = ]objFSO.GetParentFolderName(path)
```

Name	Type	Description
path	Variant	The path for a file or folder

The OpenTextFile Method

Finally, the OpenTextFile method opens the file specified in filename parameter and returns an instance of the TextStream object for that file. This instance can then be used to read from or append to the file.

```
[objTextStream = ]
    objFSO.OpenTextFile(filename[, iomode[, create[, format]]])
```

Name	Type	Description
filename	Variant	The name of the file to be opened
iomode	Integer (optional)	Constant that indicates the mode of opening. ForReading = 8 (default) ForAppending = 1
create	Boolean (optional)	If the file specified in filename doesn't already exist, then this dictates whether a new file can be created (true) or not (false). The default value is false
format	Integer (optional)	Constant that indicates the format of the opened file. If this parameter is omitted, the file will be opened in ASCII format TristateTrue = -2 TristateFalse = -1 TristateUseDefault = 0 (default)

116

FileSystemObject Object Collections

The Drives Collection

The `Drives` collection is the read-only collection of all disk drives available on the system. This collection can be obtained through the `Drives` property of the `FileSystemObject` object. The `Drives` collection has a property – the `Count` property – which contains the number of disk drives installed on the system and available through the network:

[colDrives = *]objFSO*.Drives

Later in the chapter, we'll look at an example that shows much of the functionality of the `FileSystemObject` object. First, we'll walk through the `Drive`, `Folder` and `File` objects and the `Files` and `Folders` collections.

The Drive Object

The `Drive` object provides access to the various properties of the local or remote disk drive. There are two ways to get an instance of the `Drive` object. You can use the `GetDrive` method of the `FileSystemObject` object to get the `Drive` object for the particular drive:

```
Set objFSO = CreateObject("Scripting.FileSystemObject")
Set objDrv = objFSO.GetDrive("C")
```

Alternatively, you can iterate through the `Drives` collection of the `FileSystemObject` object – this contains the `Drive` objects for all the drives available in the system.

Here's the `Drive` object's interface:

THE DRIVE OBJECT	
Collections	
Properties	
AvailableSpace	Path
DriveLetter	RootFolder
DriveType	SerialNumber
FileSystem	ShareName
FreeSpace	TotalSize
IsReady	VolumeName
Methods	
Events	

Drive Object Properties

All properties of the Drive object (apart from VolumeName) are read-only. They are able to read the state of the file system, but obviously you can't arbitrarily change these states.

The IsReady property is particularly useful – you should use it as a check that the drive is ready for use, before making use of other properties and methods.

The AvailableSpace Property

The AvailableSpace property returns the amount of space available of the specified local or remote disk drive.

[lSpace =]objDrv.AvailableSpace

The DriveLetter Property

The DriveLetter property contains the drive letter for the specified local or remote disk drive.

[strLetter =]objDrv.DriveLetter

The DriveType Property

The DriveType property indicates the type of the drive.

[iType =]objDrv.DriveType

The DriveType property returns an integer. The integer value returned corresponds to the following constants:

DriveTypeConst
0 = Unknown
1 = Removable
2 = Fixed
3 = Network
4 = CD-ROM
5 = RAM Disk

These constants will need to be defined in your scripting code. The value returned by the DriveType property will just be the integer value

The FileSystem Property

The FileSystem property returns the file system type that's in use on the specified drive.

118

[*strFileSystem* =]*objDrv*.FileSystem

This property returns a string, and takes one of the values FAT, FAT32, NTFS or CDFS.

The FreeSpace Property

The FreeSpace property is the amount of free space available to a user on the specified local or remote drive.

[*lFreeSpace* =]*objDrv*.FreeSpace

The IsReady Property

The IsReady property is a Boolean whose value is true if the specified drive is available for use, and false otherwise.

[*bReady* =]*objDrv*.IsReady

The Path Property

The Path property returns a string that specifies the path to the specified local or remote drive.

[*strPath* =]*objDrv*.Path

The RootFolder Property

The RootFolder property contains a Folder object that represents the root folder of the specified local or remote drive.

[*objFolder* =]*objDrv*.RootFolder

The SerialNumber Property

The SerialNumber property returns the decimal serial number for the specified local or remote drive. This number can be used to uniquely identify a disk volume.

[*dSerial* =]*objDrv*.SerialNumber

The ShareName Property

The ShareName property returns the network name (in UNC format) for the remote disk drive. You'll only ever want to use this property if you're working with a remote drive (in which case, the value of the DriveType property is 3).

[*strShareName* =]*objDrv*.ShareName

The TotalSize Property

The TotalSize property specifies the total space of the specified (local or remote) drive. The value returned is in bytes.

[*lBytes* =]*objDrv*.TotalSize

The VolumeName Property

The VolumeName property returns a string containing the volume name for the specified local drive. VolumeName is the only read/write property of the Drive object – so you can also use it to set the name of the drive volume.

```
objDrv.VolumeName[ = strNewName]
[strVolume = ]objDrv.VolumeName
```

Name	Type	Description
strNewName	Variant (optional)	Specifies the new volume name

The File Object

We use instances of the File object to represent files within the file system. We can obtain an instance of the File object via the GetFile method of the FileSystemObject object. Here is the example of how to do this:

```
Set objFile = objFSO.GetFile("c:\autoexec.bat")
```

Here's the interface for the File object:

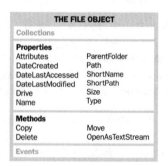

File Object Properties

The Attributes Property

The Attributes property is used to set or to get the attributes of the file.

```
objFile.Attributes[ = varNewAttributes]
[varAttributes = ]objFile.Attributes
```

Name	Type	Description
varNewAttributes	Variant (optional)	Bitwise combination of file attributes

The Attributes property is a bitwise combination, which takes some logical combination of the following values:

Name	Value	Description	Read/Write attribute
Normal	0	Normal file	N/A
ReadOnly	1	Read-only file	Read/write
Hidden	2	Hidden file	Read/write
System	4	System file	Read/write
Volume	8	Disk drive volume label	Read-only
Directory	16	Folder or directory	Read-only
Archive	32	File has changed since last backup	Read/write
Alias	64	Link or shortcut	Read-only
Compressed	128	Compressed file	Read-only

Thus, for example, it's easy to check whether the file you're using is a read-only file:

```
' Check that file is not read-only
If NOT (objFile.Attributes AND 1) Then
    ' ... write to the file
Else
    ' ... create new file for writing
End If
```

The DateCreated Property

The DateCreated property returns the date and time that the file was created. This value is read-only.

[*strDate* =]*objFile*.DateCreated

The DateLastAccessed Property

Each file's DateLastAccessed property contains the date and time at which the file was last accessed. This value is read-only.

[*strDate* =]*objFile*.DateLastAccessed

The DateLastModified Property

A file's DateLastModified property contains the date and time at which the file was last modified. This value is read-only.

[*strDate* =]*objFile*.DateLastModified

The Drive Property

The Drive property returns the drive letter of the drive on which the file currenly lives. If you move the file to another location on a different drive (e.g. using the Move method) then the value of the Drive property changes to reflect this. This property is read-only.

[*strDrive* =]*objFile*.Drive

The Name Property

A file's Name property contains the file's filename. This is a read/write property.

[*strName* =]*objFile*.Name
objFile.Name[= *varNewName*]

Name	Type	Description
varNewName	Variant	The new filename for objFile

The ParentFolder Property

The ParentFolder property contains a Folder object that represents the parent folder of *objFile*. This value is read-only.

[*objFolder* =]*objFile*.ParentFolder

The Path Property

The Path property returns the path to the file.

[*strPath* =]*objFile*.Path

The ShortName Property

The ShortName property returns the short version of file name. The short name is computed by the operating system and is composed of 8 characters plus a 3-character suffix. Thus, if objFile represents a file called Employees.html, then objFile.ShortName contains the truncated string Employ~1.htm.

[*strFileName* =]*objFile*.ShortName

The ShortPath Property

The ShortPath property returns the short version of file path. Thus, if *objFile* represents the file C:\MyBusiness\Employees.html, then *objFile*.ShortPath contains the truncated string C:\MyBusi~1\Employ~1.htm.

[*strPath* =]*objFile*.ShortPath

The Size Property

The Size property returns the size of the file, in bytes.

```
[lSize = ]objFile.Size
```

The Type Property

The Type property returns a string that contains the file type description. This is stored in the registry and is the value that appears in the Type column of Windows Explorer. This is a read-only property.

```
[strType = ]objFile.Type
```

File Object Methods

There are four methods here. As is often the case, the functionality provided by these methods can also be found in the FileSystemObject objects CopyFile, DeleteFile, MoveFile and OpenTextFile. Of course, which you choose to use depends on the context of your code – there's no point using up resources on multiple File, Folder and FileSystemObject objects if you can code your application cleanly with a single object.

The Copy Method

The Copy method creates an identical copy of the file and places it in the location specified by the *destination* parameter.

```
objFile.Copy destination[, overwrite]
```

Name	Type	Description
destination	Variant	The location for the copy of the existing file. Wildcards are not allowed
overwrite	Boolean (optional)	If true, existing files with the same name as *destination* will be overwritten. If false, existing files are protected from overwrite. The default value is false.

For example, we can place a copy of the file Employees.html in the temp folder, like this:

```
Set objFSO = CreateObject ("Scripting.FileSystemObject")
Set objFile = objFSO.GetFile("C:\mybusiness\employees.html")
objFile.Copy "C:\temp\copy_of_employees.html"
```

Note that, after execution of the Copy method, the File object objFile still refers to the *original* version – not the copy.

The Delete Method

When you call a file's `Delete` method, the file will be deleted from the file system.

`objFile.Delete [force]`

Name	Type	Description
force	Boolean (optional)	Determines whether a read-only file can be deleted. If `false`, and `objFile` is read-only, the file will be unable to delete itself using the `Delete` method. The default value is `false`.

The Move Method

The `Move` method moves the file from its current location to the location specified by the `destination` parameter. Properties like `Name`, `ParentDirectory` and `Drive` are updated to reflect the new location of the file.

`objFile.Move destination`

Name	Type	Description
destination	Variant	The new location for the file.

Unlike the `Copy` method, there is no optional `overwrite` parameter. If `destination` specifies the location of an existing file, you'll generate an error. Your code will be cleaner if you check for existing files (using the `FileSystemObject.FileExists` method) before using the `Move` method – look before you leap!

The OpenAsTextStream Method

The `OpenAsTextStream` method is used to open the specified file. This method returns an instance of a `TextStream` object that can be used for future file manipulations – to read from, to write to or append to the file.

`[objTS = ]objFile.OpenAsTextStream [iomode [, format]]`

Name	Type	Description
iomode	Variant (optional)	Indicates input/output mode Values: `forReading`, `forWriting`, `forAppending`
format	Variant (optional)	Indicates the format of the opened file Values: `TristateTrue`, `TristateFalse`, `TristateUseDefault`

The permitted constants for the *iomode* and *format* parameters are the same as those outlined for the FileSystemObject.OpenTextFile method (see earlier in this chapter).

The Files Collection

The Files collection is a standard collection that contains a set of File objects. The collection is usually stored as a property of another object, such as a Folder object. In this case, the collection would contain a File object that corresponds to each file in the directory.

As a collection, the Files collection can be treated in the same way that you treat other collections. That is, if you want to see every element in the collection, you can use the For...Each statement. The collection also has a Count property, which indicates the number of elements in the collection, as well as an Item property, which will let you refer to a specific element of the collection.

The Folder Object

We can represent any folder (or directory) of our file system by creating an instance of the Folder object. With this instance, we can access all the properties of the folder, and execute methods relating to the folder.

There are two ways to obtain an instance of the Folder object. You can do it through the ParentFolder property of the File object, by using the SubFolders property of another Folder object, or through the GetFolder method or the FileSystemObject.

This is how the Folder object's interface looks:

THE FOLDER OBJECT	
Collections	
Files	SubFolders
Properties	
Attributes	Name
DateCreated	ParentFolder
DateLastAccessed	Path
DateLastModified	ShortName
Drive	ShortPath
IsRootFolder	Size
Methods	
Copy	Delete
CreateTextFile	Move
Events	

Folder Object Properties

Many of the properties of the Folder object are similar the properties of the File object. If you think about this, it makes a lot of sense – there are many aspects of files and folders which can obviously be handled in the same way (e.g. parent directory, path, date of creation properties; creation, deletion methods; etc). Of course, folders and files are not exactly the same, so there are also differences between the interfaces of the Folder and File objects.

The following diagram shows which properties are common to both the `Folder` and `File` object, and which are unique to just one of those objects:

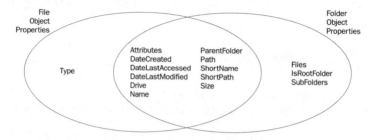

> We'll just cover those properties that are unique to the `Folder` object here. For information on the others, refer to the section on `File` object properties above – syntax and usage is comparable.

The Files Property

The `Files` property contains a reference to a `Files` collection, which consists of all `File` objects contained in the specified folder. This is a read-only property.

```
[colFiles = ]objFolder.Files
```

The IsRootFolder Property

A folder's `IsRootFolder` property contains a Boolean value: `true` if the folder is the root folder, and `false` otherwise. This is a read-only property.

```
[bIsRoot = ]objFolder.IsRootFolder
```

The SubFolders Property

A `SubFolders` property of a folder contains a `Folders` collection (that is, a collection of `Folder` objects). This `Folders` collection represents the subfolders within the folder. This is a read-only property.

```
[colFolders = ]objFolder.SubFolders
```

Folder Object Methods

The `Folder` object features four methods. Again, three of these methods – `Copy`, `Delete`, `Move` – are also the methods of the `File` object:

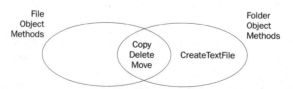

The remaining method, CreateTextFile, is similar to a method of the same name, to be found in the FileSystemObject object. For information on these methods, refer to the sections above – syntax and usage is comparable.

The Folders Collection

A Folders collection contains a set of Folder objects. You can use a Folders collection to represent any set of folders you like. For example, when we use an instance of the Folder object to represent a folder, its SubFolders property is a Folders collection that consists of all the subfolders of the folder.

Folders Collection Properties

The Count Property

The Folders collection has a single property, called Count, which returns an integer value that tells us the number of Folder objects in the collection. This is a read-only property.

[*lCount* =]*objFolders*.Count

Folders Collection Methods

The AddFolders Method

The AddFolders method adds a new Folder to a Folders collection. An error will occur if the folder being added already exists.

objFolders.AddFolders *folderName*

Name	Type	Description
foldername	Variant	The name of the folder to be added to Folders

Using the FileSystemObject Object

In this example, we will see how the FileSystemObject and its subordinate objects can be used to display information about the file stored on the web server.

> *One drawback of IIS3 and PWS is that you cannot turn on directory browsing on a directory by directory basis. Instead, you have a stark choice: you can turn it on globally (for the whole site), or you can prohibit all directories from being browsed.*

This example will use the FileSystemObject object to display the contents of a directory. It will also show you how to retrieve information about a particular file. Here's what you see when you display this page in your browser:

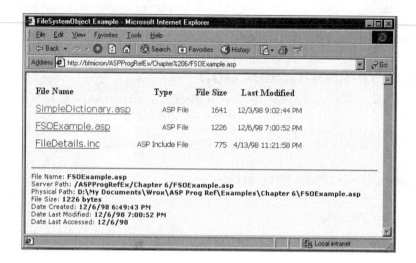

How It Works

We'll walk through the key parts of this code. In fact, there are two files involved in creating this page. The first, `FSOExample.asp`, generates the directory listing. (We'll come to the second, `FileDetails.inc`, shortly.)

In this example, we use the `FileSystemObject` to display the contents of the directory that the ASP file is in. The first step is to determine the path to the current file:

```
<%
    dim strPathInfo, strPhysicalPath
    strPathInfo = Request.ServerVariables("PATH_INFO")
    strPhysicalPath = Server.MapPath(strPathInfo)
```

When working with a web server, there are two file spaces that we need to deal with: the virtual space and the physical space. The virtual space is represented by the virtual directory, where the browser perceives the file to be. The physical space indicates the actual location of the file on the server's hard drive. For the `FileSystemObject` to work, it needs to know the physical space.

The first step is to determine the virtual location of the file by examining the `PATH_INFO` server variable. To convert that from virtual space to physical space, we will use the `MapPath` method of the `Server` object. Once we have the physical location of the current file, we can begin our work with the `FileSystemObject`:

```
Dim objFSO, objFile, objFileItem, objFolder, objFolderContents
Set objFSO = CreateObject("Scripting.FileSystemObject")
Set objFile = objFSO.GetFile(strPhysicalPath)
```

The first step here is to create an instance of the `FileSystemObject`. This is done using the `CreateObject` method. Notice that this is not the `CreateObject` method of the `Server` object. Since the `FileSystemObject` is part of the Scripting Libraries (and not part of ASP), we use the VBScript `CreateObject` method instead.

With the object created, we can then get a reference to a `File` object that represents the current file. Passing the path the current file that we derived earlier to the `GetFile` method of the `FileSystemObject` object does this. This will return a reference to a `File` object.

In this example, we're interested in the files that are in the same directory as the current file – so we want to get a collection that refers to these files. The first step to achieving this is to get the `ParentFolder` property of the current `File` object. This will hold a reference to a `Folder` object that represents the current directory:

```
Set objFolder = objFile.ParentFolder
```

Once we have the reference to this `Folder` object, we can look at its `Files` property. This property actually refers to a collection of `File` objects. Each element in that collection corresponds to a single file in the directory:

```
Set objFolderContents = objFolder.Files
%>
```

We now have something that represents all of the files that we are interested in.

To display each file in this directory, we need to look at each `File` object in the `Files` collection individually. The best way to do this by using a `For Each...Next` statement. This statement will loop through the collection and return us a reference for each `File` object it contains. With each of these `File` objects, we can display the information that we are interested in. The key parts are shaded:

```
<TABLE cellpadding=5>
  <TR align=center><TH align=left>File Name</TH><TH>Type</TH>
                   <TH>File Size</TH><TH>Last Modified</TH></TR>
<%
  For Each objFileItem in objFolderContents
%>
  <TR><TD align=left>
    <A HREF="<%= objFileItem.Name %>"><FONT FACE="Verdana" SIZE="3">
    <%= objFileItem.Name %></A></FONT></TD>
    <TD align=right><FONT FACE="Tahoma" SIZE="2" COLOR="DarkGreen">
    <%= objFileItem.type %></FONT></TD>
    <TD align=right><FONT FACE="Tahoma" SIZE="2" COLOR="DarkGreen">
    <%= objFileItem.size %></FONT></TD>
    <TD align=right><FONT FACE="Tahoma" SIZE="2" COLOR="DarkGreen">
    <%= objFileItem.DateLastModified %></FONT></TD>
  </TR>
<%
  Next
%>
</TABLE>
```

Here, we create a table that displays the name, type, size, and last modified date of each file in the directory. Displaying this information is as simple as retrieving the property value and then sending to the output stream by using the `<%= ... %>` shortcut to the `Response.Write` method.

Next, we show some additional information about the file that we are currently displaying. Since this is a helpful routine that could be used in any number of files, we want a way to easily reuse it. One way to package code is to put it into a **server-side include** file. Then, to display the information in any file, all you need to add is one line of code:

```
<!-- #include file="FileDetails.inc" -->
```

This server-side include file contains some of the same steps as the directory display page. We will use the same procedure to determine the physical path to the file currently being displayed.

One thing that we need to be careful about is that the variables used in a server-side include will exist in the same namespace as the variables in the page. This means that if you choose common names for your variables in a server-side include file, there is a chance that their names could conflict with variables in the page itself. To greatly lessen the chance of this happening, the variable names in the server-side include file will be "mangled" such as to be relatively unique to the include file itself:

```
<%
   dim strFDPathInfo, strFDPhysicalPath
   strFDPathInfo = Request.ServerVariables("PATH_INFO")
   strFDPhysicalPath = Server.MapPath(strFDPathInfo)

   Dim objFDFSO, objFDFile
   Set objFDFSO = CreateObject("Scripting.FileSystemObject")
   Set objFDFile = objFDFSO.GetFile(strFDPhysicalPath)
%>
```

You can see that the code is almost exactly the same – the variable names have been changed to protect the innocent. Once we have retrieved a reference to a `File` object that represents the current file, we can use its methods to display information about the file:

```
File Name: <B><%= objFDFile.Name %></B><BR>
Server Path: <B><%= Request.ServerVariables("PATH_INFO") %></B><BR>
Physical Path: <B><%= objFDFile.Path %></B><BR>
File Size: <B><%= objFDFile.size %> bytes</B><BR>
Date Created: <B><%= objFDFile.DateCreated %></B><BR>
Date Last Modified: <B><%= objFDFile.DateLastModified %></B><BR>
Date Last Accessed: <B><%= objFDFile.DateLastAccessed %></B><BR>
```

You can see that in addition to displaying information derived from the `File` object, we are also displaying information about the file that exists in the `ServerVariables` collection of the `Request` object.

This example shows just a few ways that the `FileSystemObject` and its subordinate objects can be used to display information about the files and the file system on the web server. Next, we will look at an object that can be used to peer inside of files themselves – the `TextStream` object.

The TextStream Object

The `TextStream` object allows you to access the contents of a file stored on the web server. It's applicable to any file whose contents are in text-readable form – so you can use the `TextStream` object to get sequential access to files of type `.txt`, `.html`, `.asp` and so on.

How do we access an instance of the `TextStream` object? We can use the `CreateTextFile` or `OpenTextFile` methods of the `FileSystemObject` object; alternatively, we can use the `OpenAsTextStream` method of the `File` object:

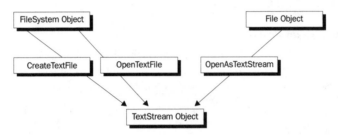

For example:

```
Set objFSO  = CreateObject("Scripting.FileSystemObject")
Set objText = objFSO.CreateTextFile("d:\temp\mytext.txt", true)
' Here we can perform manipulations with the newly created text file
objText.Close
```

The `CreateTextFile` (with the *overwrite* parameter set to `true`) opens the file `d:\temp\mytext.txt`. If no such file exists, but the path exists, then a new file is created.

Here's the full interface of the `TextStream` object:

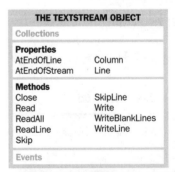

THE TEXTSTREAM OBJECT	
Collections	
Properties	
AtEndOfLine	Column
AtEndOfStream	Line
Methods	
Close	SkipLine
Read	Write
ReadAll	WriteBlankLines
ReadLine	WriteLine
Skip	
Events	

File Pointers

A key concept to understand, before looking at the properties and methods, is that of a **file pointer**. With each `TextStream` instance, there is an internal pointer that points to a specific point in the file. When the stream is first opened, the file pointer points to the first character in the file. As you manipulate the `TextStream` using the methods and properties, this pointer will move around, to represent different points in the file.

TextStream Object Properties

The TextStream object provides us with four properties that are discussed below. These four properties are all read-only.

The AtEndOfLine Property

A text stream's AtEndOfLine property is a Boolean value. If the file pointer is positioned immediately before the file's end-of-line marker, then this value is true; otherwise, it's false.

[bEOL =]objText.AtEndOfLine

The AtEndOfStream Property

A text stream's AtEndOfstream property is also a Boolean. If the file pointer is positioned at the end of a file, then this value is true; otherwise, it's false.

[bEOS =]objText.AtEndOfStream

The Column Property

The Column property contains an integer, which represents the current position of the file pointer (within the current line). This property can be used to jump to a particular column in a line. Column 1 represents the first character in each line.

[iCol =]objText.Column

The Line Property

The Line property is similar to the Column property: it contains an integer value representing the current line number.

[iLine =]objText.Line

TextStream Object Methods

The Close Method

The Close method closes a text file that is currently open. After closing a file, you can no longer use the properties and methods of the TextStream object that referred to it.

objText.Close

The Read Method

The Read method reads a specified number of characters from the text file. Note that we need to have opened the file in read mode in order to use any of the read methods – if you open the file for writing and attempt to use a read method, you will generate a Bad File Mode error.

[*strText* =]*objText*.Read(*characters*)

Name	Type	Description
characters	Integer	The number of characters to read from the file

The ReadAll Method

The ReadAll method reads an entire text file into one string.

[*strText* =]*objText*.ReadAll

The ReadLine Method

The ReadLine method reads a single line (excluding the newline character) from the file.

[*strText* =]*objText*.ReadLine

The Skip Method

The Skip method will move the file pointer a specified number of characters in the file. This can be a positive or negative number.

objText.Skip(*characters*)

Name	Type	Description
characters	Integer	The number of characters to be skipped

The SkipLine Method

The SkipLine method moves the file pointer from its current position to the beginning of the next line.

objText.SkipLine

The Write Method

The Write method writes a given string to the text file. Where the text is written is based on the input/output mode that you selected when opening the file. If you selected ForAppending, the text will be added to the end of the file. If you chose ForWriting, the first write to the file will be at the beginning of the file and any subsequent writes will be appended to it.

objText.Write *string*

Name	Type	Description
string	String	The text that is to be added to the file

133

The WriteBlankLines Method

The `WriteBlankLines` method writes a specified number of consecutive newline characters to the text file.

`objText.WriteBlankLines ilines`

Name	Type	Description
ilines	Integer	The number of consecutive newline characters to be written to the file

The WriteLine Method

The `WriteLine` method writes a specified string to the text file and then writes a newline character to the file following it.

`objText.WriteLine string`

Name	Type	Description
string	String	The text that is to be added to the file

Using the TextStream Object

In this example, we will use the `TextStream` object to enhance the way that ASP files can be when trying to teach people about your code. One of the best ways to learn how to program on the web is to look at people's source code. You can learn many HTML tricks by looking at the source code of your favorite pages.

How can you use this same approach to learn the insides of ASP? With ASP, the source is interpreted on the server, and all the client sees is the completed HTML. In this example, we will create an ASP script that displays the source of any of the ASP files on your server. The file name will be passed in as a URL parameter. We will also show how to link it to an existing ASP page.

When you view the example from earlier in the chapter, you will now see a new entry at the bottom of the page.

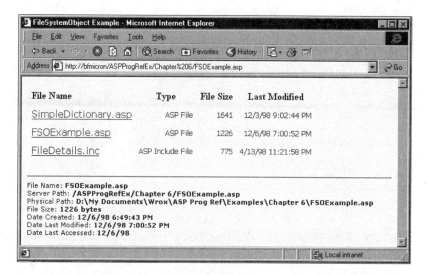

When you click on this hyperlink, you will see:

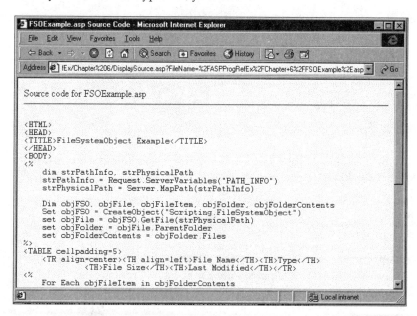

How It Works

We've used `FSOExample.asp` (from earlier in this chapter) as the starting point for this example – we could have used any ASP page. In order to make the ASP code of the page available to the user, we've added the following single line of code:

```
<A HREF="DisplaySource.asp?FileName=<%=
Server.URLEncode(Request.ServerVariables("PATH_INFO")) %>">Click here to see
ASP source</A>
```

This hyperlink will request the page `DisplaySource.asp`. This line will look for `DisplaySource.asp` in the same directory as the current ASP file (generally, you need to reference `DisplaySource.asp` via a relative filepath). One parameter, called `FileName`, will be passed in the `QueryString`. This will contain the virtual path to the file, as contained in the `PATH_INFO` server variable.

Since this information is going to be passed on the URL string, we will need to ensure that it is properly formatted. We *could* go through and replace each spaces with "%20" – but an easier way is to employ some method that does all this for us. Luckily, the `URLEncode` method of the `Server` object will make sure that the string is properly formatted to be a URL. When the user clicks on this hyperlink, the `DisplaySource.asp` page is displayed.

Let's walk through the code sections of `DisplaySource.asp`. We'll be using some methods of the `TextStream` object that require parameters. Rather than just passing the numerical value, we'll be create constants that represent the possible values:

```
<%
Const ForReading = 1, ForWriting = 2, ForAppending = 3
Const TristateUseDefault = -2, TristateTrue = -1, TristateFalse = 0
```

You will see later how this makes the code more readable. Also, in order to create a `TextStream` object, we need to start with a valid `File` object for the file we are interested in. To get this, we substitute the value passed in on the URL line:

```
dim strPathInfo, strPhysicalPath
strPathInfo = Request.QueryString("FileName")
strPhysicalPath = Server.MapPath(strPathInfo)
Dim objFSO, objFile
Set objFSO = CreateObject("Scripting.FileSystemObject")
set objFile = objFSO.GetFile(strPhysicalPath)
%>
```

Once we have the valid `File` object, the next step is to open that file as a text file. To do this, we use the `OpenAsTextStream` method of the `File` object:

```
<%
Dim objFileTextStream
set objFileTextStream = objFile.OpenAsTextStream(ForReading, _
                                        TristateUseDefault)
```

This method will return a reference to a `TextStream` object that contains the contents of the file. Since we are not interested in modifying the file, we will open it `ForReading` only. You should usually open the file in the default format mode, unless you are absolutely sure that the contents are not of the default type.

Once the file is open, we can begin reading the information from the file. There are plenty of different methods that allow us to do this in different ways. For example, we could read the file all at once, using `ReadAll` – it's the easiest to implement, but it doesn't work too well for large files. Instead, we'll read it line-by-line, using the `ReadLine` method.

We need some indication as to when we've run out of file to read. The `TextStream` object provides the `AtEndOfStream` property, which returns `true` when the file pointer is at the end of the file:

```
dim strLine, strFileLine
Do While objFileTextStream.AtEndOfStream <> True
   strFileLine = objFileTextStream.ReadLine
```

If we simply use `Response.Write strFileLine` now, we'll probably get some messy results – first we need to handle any special characters in the string. This is particularly relevant in this case, because we're trying to display HTML and ASP code – the HTML tags are a particular problem. When a client displays an HTML page, it looks for HTML tags (bounded by < >) and uses them as formatting instructions. We need to format these symbols so that they'll be interpreted as text characters instead. The `Server` object's `HTMLEncode` method does just that. We'll also use the `Replace` method to replace tab characters with ` ` (explicit space characters), to retain the tab formatting in the original file:

```
strLine = Server.HTMLEncode(strFileLine)
strLine = Replace (strLine, Chr(9), "    ")
```

Now that the whole line is properly formatted, we can output it to the client using the `Response.Write` method. Since the client will ignore any carriage returns in the text file, we need to add our own line break to the displayed source code:

```
   Response.Write strLine
   Response.Write "<BR>" + vbCrLf
Loop
objFileTextStream.Close
%>
```

`DisplaySource.asp` can be referenced from any ASP page on your web server, so you can see that it makes it very easy to add documentation to your pages for other developers to see how you actually created the page. And since the documentation is generated from the actual page itself, you never have to worry about the documentation becoming out of sync with the real code.

Summary

In this chapter, we have looked at the Scripting Objects and how they can be used inside of Active Server Pages. The Scripting Objects are part of the VBScript library, and are useful as a set of helper routines for developing web applications.

The Scripting Objects consist of:

❑ The `Dictionary` object, which allows us to store and retrieve information in a flexible key/item data structure.

❑ The `FileSystemObject` object, which provides access to the physical file system of the web server.

❑ The `TextStream` object, which gives you access to the contents of text files stored on the web server.

These objects extend the reach of your web applications beyond the objects that exist inside of the ASP object model. They allow you to categorize and store information more efficiently, and manipulate the physical file system of the server itself.

In the next chapter we will talk about **Active Server Components** – ActiveX components that provide a particular piece of functionality for use in your ASP code.

Active Server Components

In this chapter we will talk about **Active Server Components** – ActiveX components (or COM objects) that are designed to be executed on the server. The main characteristic of the Active Server Components is that they are non-visual, in that they don't have a graphical user interface. Users can only interact with Active Server components programmatically, through the COM interfaces that they expose. There are hundreds of components available for use in Active Server Pages programs – both from Microsoft and many third-party companies. These components cover various tasks, such as communications, e-commerce, tools and so on. Also you can write your own components, fine-tuned to the particular tasks of your business. We will look here at the principal components available for ASP developers. Details of the interfaces for these components can be found in Appendix F.

Creating an Instance of the Component

Before we can use methods and properties of the Active Server Components we need to create an instance of the component. There are two ways we can do this:

- ❑ with the CreateObject method of the Server object
- ❑ with the <OBJECT> tag.

The main difference between the two methods is that the instance of the component will be created immediately with the CreateObject method while in the second case (using the <OBJECT> tag) an instance will be created only when the component is first referenced. Note however that if the component is in an MTS package, MTS will provide just in time initialization.

Using the CreateObject Method

This method should be familiar from Chapter 5. Here's how we create an instance of the AdRotator component (we'll look at this component in detail a bit further on):

```
Set MyAd = Server.CreateObject("MSWC.AdRotator")
```

We can now use the variable name MyAd to reference our AdRotator instance in our code, and use the AdRotator's methods and properties. For example, an ad may or may not provide a link to another page, specified with the Clickable property. We could reference this property as follows:

```
If MyAd.Clickable=FALSE then
    Response.Write("This ad is not a link")
End If
```

The AdRotator component is one of the components supplied with Internet Information Server or Personal Web Server – these components are installed automatically with all the appropriate software. There may be some cases, especially with third-party components that are not properly installed, when the component can't be found or the wrong identifier is used. This is one of the causes of the following error message (other causes may be incorrect permissions or parameters):

```
Server object error 'ASP 0177 : 800401f3'
Server.CreateObject Failed
/aspref/comp.asp, line 2
```

We should wrap the call to the CreateObject method with the following code, in order to verify that we can find and identify the component:

```
On Error Resume Next
Set MyAd = Server.CreateObject("MSWC.AdRotator")

If IsObject(MyAd) Then
  'Use the component
Else
  Response.Write("ERROR. Can't access component")
  'Other actions here...
End If
```

In the code above IsObject returns true if the object has been created successfully. Note that IsObject is a standard VBScript function and it returns true if the supplied parameter is a valid reference to an object

Using an <OBJECT> Tag

To create an instance of an Active Server component with the <OBJECT> HTML tag we need to use the server-side version of the tag, by specifying RUNAT=Server. We also need to provide an identifier with which we can refer to our component instance, and either a PROGID or a CLASSID to specify the component we want to use. Here is how we create an Ad Rotator instance using the <OBJECT> tag:

```
<OBJECT RUNAT=Server ID=MyAd PROGID="MSWC.AdRotator">
</OBJECT>
```

We can now use the AdRotator's properties and methods through MyAd in the same way as we did in the CreateObject example.

There is one further attribute that we can set when we create the server instance with an <OBJECT> tag. The SCOPE attribute can be used to define the scope of an instance of the component, and has three possible values: PAGE (the default value), SESSION and APPLICATION. This enables us to create a component instance in the global.asa file and set it to have either session or application scope. This code in global.asa:

```
<OBJECT RUNAT=Server SCOPE=Session ID=MyInfo PROGID="MSWC.MyInfo">
</OBJECT>
```

creates an instance of the MyInfo component with session scope.

Note that if you use the SESSION or APPLICATION values of the SCOPE attribute outside the global.asa file, you will receive the following error message:

```
Active Server Pages error 'ASP 0121'
Invalid Scope in object tag
/obj.asp, line 1
The object instance 'MyInfo' cannot have Application or Session
scope. To create the object instance with Session or Application
scope, place the Object tag in the Global.asa file.
```

We originally said if we used an <OBJECT> tag, a component instance would only be created the first time that we needed it. However, if we use the object tag in global.asa the component instance will be created as soon as the application is started, which means we might be using unnecessary resources. We can also give application or session scope to a component instance created with the CreateObject method, by assigning that instance to a session or application variable.

Now we are ready to take a look at the components available for us as Active Server Pages developers. We will start with several standard components.

The Standard Components

Microsoft provide several components with Internet Information Server 4.0 and the IIS Resource Kit. Microsoft components are also available from the Microsoft downloads site (see Appendix G for URLs). We will cover probably the most important of these, the **ActiveX Data Objects** (ADO), and the **Collaborative Data Objects** (CDO) in the following chapters. Here we'll look briefly at the standard Microsoft components available, and focus in on three of the most interesting and commonly used – the **Ad Rotator** component, the **Browser Capabilities** component and the **Content Linking** component. Here is a summary of the remaining standard components and their uses:

❑ The **Content Rotator** component displays a different "content" item each time the page is accessed or refreshed. Each "content" item is made up of HTML and text, and they are defined in the Content Schedule File. This file is a formatted text file; for each entry there is an initial line of %%Priority, where Priority is a value specifying the number of times that entry will be shown, relative to other entries in the file. This initial line is followed by the content that you want to appear on the page. We will see a very similar component when we look in detail at the Ad Rotator Component a little further on.

❑   The **Page Counter** component stores the number of times that your page has been requested in the `Hit Count Data` file. You can retrieve this value for any page where the component has been instantiated using the `Hits` method. This method returns total hits for the current page by default, but it also has an optional parameter with which you can specify the virtual path to another page.

❑   The **Permission Checker** component allows us to check a user's permissions with the `HasAccess` method before we allow them access to another page or file, according to the method of authentication set in IIS. The authentication methods are `anonymous` (no password is required), `basic` (the user will be prompted for a login name and password) and `Windows NT Challenge/Response` (only supported by IE Browsers).

❑   We can use the **Counters** component to count any value on an ASP page, from anywhere within our ASP application. We only need to create one instance of it (in fact if you are using PWS you will already have an instance), and then we can use this instance to create as many counters as we want, with the `Set` method: `myInstance.Set(CounterName, CounterValue)`. The value of the counter is stored in the `Counters.txt` file, and can be incremented, read or removed with the appropriate `Counters` component method.

❑   The **Status**, **Load Balancer** and **Tracer** components collect server, performance and ASP profile information respectively. The **Status** component is only available with PWS for Macs.

❑   The **MyInfo** component uses a file, `MyInfo.xml`, to store pieces of personal information labeled with a descriptive tag – for example `<Title>MyPage</>`. You can use an instance of the MyInfo component to access information in this file, for example `MyInstance.Title`, or to add new data, for example `MyInstance.XmasGreeting = "Happy Christmas"`.

❑   The **Tools** component features five miscellaneous methods, two of which are only available for Macs. The most useful method of this component (available for all platforms) is probably the `FileExists` method, which takes a parameter of a file name and returns true if it exists.

❑   The **Registry Access** component provides access to the registry on a local or remote computer and can be used to retrieve, set, add, delete, modify and copy registry keys and names values.

❑   The **ASP to HTML** (ASP2HTML) component is a Java component exposing several methods that can be used to connect to the given URL, get the contents of the HTML document, save it to a local file, extract its title, creation date and other information.

❑ The **Document Summary Information** component is useful when you need to display properties of a document, such as "Author", "Title", "Date Created" or "Subject" found in the most Microsoft Office documents. This component can work with a single document or with a directory of documents.

❑ The **HTML Table Formatter** component is used when you need to automatically convert data from an ADO data source into an HTML table.

The Ad Rotator Component

The Ad Rotator component can be used to display different advertisements on our pages, each time the page is referenced from a browser. This component automatically rotates advertisements according to a specified schedule, stored in the **rotator schedule file.** The ads are rotated on the server when another client requests the page, or the client refreshes the page. We can also specify redirection to another URL when the ad is clicked, using the **redirection file**. To use the Ad Rotator component we need to create a schedule file, and make sure that we have set all the properties of the Ad Rotator that we require.

Creating a Schedule File

The Ad Rotator component obtains all the information it needs from the rotator schedule file. This is a specially formatted text file that consists of two sections, separated by a line containing a single asterisk. The first section (optional) contains values that will apply to all advertisements; the second section has values specific to each advertisement.

Below is an example of a simple rotator schedule file with three ads:

```
REDIRECT /ads-demo/redirect.asp
WIDTH 440
HEIGHT 60
BORDER 1
*
http://www.somesite.com/ads/site-ad.gif
http://www.somesite.com/
Christmas Shopping Time! Hurry!
20
http://www.newshop.com/ads/shop-ad.gif
http://www.newshop.com/shopping-cart/default.asp
Best prices in town
20
http://www.wrox.co.uk/graph/new/wroxlogo.gif
http:// www.wrox.co.uk/
Best programmer's books
20
```

In the first section we set the default values for the attributes that apply to all advertisement images in the schedule. If we skip this section our rotator schedule file should still start with a single asterisk in the first line. Here is the list of attributes available in the first section.

Name	Type	Description
REDIRECT	URL	Specifies the virtual path and name of the DLL, CGI application or ASP file that will implement redirection to the URL specified with AdHomePageURL below when the advertisement is clicked. This can be either the full URL (for example, http://localhost/ads-demo/redirect.asp), or the path relative to the virtual directory (for example, /ads-demo/redirect.asp)
WIDTH	Number	Specifies the width of the advertisement. Default value is 440 pixels
HEIGHT	Number	Specifies the height of the advertisement. Default value is 60
BORDER	Number	Specifies the width of the border around the advertisement. Default value is 1 pixel

The second section contains details of the individual advertisements. For each advertisement we should supply the following attributes:

Name	Type	Description
AdURL	URL	The location of the advertisement image file. This should be a virtual path and file name. This can be a graphics file in JPG or GIF format.
AdHomePageURL	URL	The URL to which the client will be redirected, usually the advertiser's home page. If there is no URL supplied, place the hyphen (-) symbol here
AltText	String	Alternative text for browsers that do not support graphics
Impressions	Number	A number between 0 and 4,294,967,295 that indicates the relative weight of the advertisement. The higher the impressions value for the advertisement, the more frequently it will appear on the page

In the example rotator schedule file above we have three advertisements that have the same value for the impressions parameter, meaning that each advertisement is equally likely to appear.

The Redirection File

As we've just seen, we can specify a file in the REDIRECT property of the rotator schedule file, which will handle redirection to the URL specified with the adHomePageURL property. We can use the following line of code for the redirection:

```
Response.Redirect(Request.QueryString("url"))
```

For more information on the Response *object, refer to Chapter 3.*

Redirecting the client is the simplest thing we can do here. We can add code to the redirection file that will perform other useful functions, before we redirect the client. For instance, we might want to record statistics, such as the number of users who have jumped from our page to the home page of one or other advertiser. We have the URL value passed as part of the query string to tell us which ad the user has chosen, and we can either store this information in a file, using the TextStream object discussed in Chapter 5, or write the statistics to a database using ADO. This would allow us to gauge the success of an ad, or prove to the advertisers that our site is attracting potential customers for them, and bill the advertisers accordingly.

Ad Rotator Properties

There are three properties of the Ad Rotator component that we can use from our scripting programs:

The Border Property

The Border property sets the size of the border around the advertisement. The default value can be set in the header of the rotator schedule file and changed with this property. The value of 0 indicates that there should be no border around the advertisement. The larger the value, the greater the thickness of the border. For example:

```
Set MyAd = Server.CreateObject("MSWC.AdRotator")
MyAd.Border = 3    'This sets the size of the border 3 pixels wide
```

The Clickable Property

The Clickable property enables us to specify whether the advertisements are displayed as hyperlinks. This is the default (the URL is defined by the adHomePageURL attribute in the rotator schedule file), but if you don't need this functionality, you can assign the value false to this property. For example:

```
Set MyAd = Server.CreateObject("MSWC.AdRotator")
MyAd.Clickable = False    ' Show ads as static graphics
```

The TargetFrame Property

The `TargetFrame` property allows us to set the name of the frame into which the hyperlink (the one that is defined by the `adHomePageURL` attribute in the rotator schedule file) from the banner will be loaded. This property works the same way as the `TARGET` attribute of the HTML anchor (`<A>`) element. The value of this parameter can be the name of any frame within the page, or one of the following predefined HTML frame identifiers such as `_top`, `_new`, `_child`, `_self`, `_parent`, or `_blank`. The default value of the TargetFrame property is NO FRAME.

Ad Rotator Methods

The `Ad Rotator` component has only one method – `GetAdvertisement`. This method gets details of the next advertisement from the rotator schedule file and formats it as HTML. It retrieves the next scheduled advertisement each time the script is invoked – either when a user opens the ASP file or refreshes it. The `GetAdvertisement` method has the following syntax:

MyAd.GetAdvertisement(*Path*)

Name	Type	Description
path	String	The location of the rotator schedule file relative to the virtual directory

The `GetAdvertisement` method returns the HTML formatted string that can be used to display the advertisement in the current page. We can call the method as follows:

```
Set MyAd = Server.CreateObject("MSWC.AdRotator")
Response.Write(MyAd.GetAdvertisement("/new-ads/schedule.txt"))
```

In this example we assume that the schedule file called `schedule.txt` is stored in the `/new-ads/` folder within the current folder where our application runs. The output of this call will be a section of HTML text for the new advertisement to be displayed, which should look something like this:

```
<A
HREF="redirect.asp?url=http://www.somesite.com/&image=http://www.somesite.com
/ads/site-ad.gif">
<IMG SRC="http://www.somesite.com/ads/site-ad.gif" ALT="Christmas Shopping
Time! Hurry!" WIDTH=440 HEIGHT=60 BORDER=1>
</A>
```

The Browser Capabilities Component

The **Browser Capabilities** component can be used to obtain information about the client's web browser. We can use it to check, for example, that a client's browser supports a particular feature, before we generate client-side logic (HTML or scripting) which requires that feature.

This component consists of a single DLL, browscap.dll, and a text file browscap.ini that should reside in the same directory as the DLL. The component takes the browser name and version information from the HTTP_User_Agent variable sent by the browser, and compares its contents with the entries in the browscap.ini file. If a match is found, the Browser Capabilities component makes available the appropriate properties for that browser. If no match is found, the values for the default browser are returned, unless there is no default browser defined in the browscap.ini file, when all the properties will be set to the value "UNKNOWN".

The BROWSCAP.INI File

Let's look at the format of the browscap.ini file. As we have already said, this is a text file so we are able to browse through it and even edit its contents and update it when new versions of browsers appear. Here is a simple browscap.ini file, with cut-down entries for two browsers, IE 2.0 and Mozilla 1.22, and a default browser:

```
;Browsers - last updated xx/yy/zz;;;

[IE 2.0]
browser=IE
version=2.0

[Mozilla/1.22 (compatible; MSIE 2.0; Mac_PowerPC)]
parent=IE 2.0
platform=MacPPC


;Default Browser

[Default Browser Capability Settings]
browser=Default
Version=0.0
```

Our example browscap.ini file begins with a comment – one or more lines that start with a semicolon (;). Comments are ignored by the Browser Capabilities component and can be placed anywhere in the file.

The beginning of an entry for a particular browser is marked by the [HTTPUserAgentHeader] line – such as [IE 2.0] in the example above. This is the value that the Browser Capabilities component compares with the HTTP_USER_AGENT entry of the Request.ServerVariables collection (discussed in the Chapter 2), and it should be unique for each browser. The asterisk ("*") character can be used to replace one or more characters if needed.

Next come browser properties. Each line should start with an alpha character and should not be longer than 255 characters. There is no limit on the number of lines for a browser. All of the properties for the particular browser are available as properties of the Browser Capabilities component. Some of the most significant are listed in the following table.

Property	Description
ActiveXControls	Specifies whether the browser supports ActiveX controls
backgroundsounds	Specifies whether the browser supports background sounds
beta	Specifies whether the browser is beta software
browser	Specifies the name of the browser
cdf	Specifies whether the browser supports the Channel Definition Format (CDF) for webcasting
cookies	Specifies whether the browser supports cookies
frames	Specifies whether the browser supports frames
javaapplets	Specifies whether the browser supports Java applets
javascript	Specifies whether the browser supports JavaScript or JScript
platform	Specifies the platform that the browser runs on
tables	Specifies whether the browser supports tables
vbscript	Specifies whether the browser supports VBScript
version	Specifies the version number of the browser

The [parent=browserDefinition] line indicates that the browser "inherits" all the characteristics of its "parent" browser. In our example file above the entry for Mozilla 1.22 specifies that it will have all the same properties as IE 2.0, in addition to any other properties subsequently listed.

The [Default Browser Capability Settings] section defines the properties of the "default browser" – the one that will be used if the Browser Capabilities component can't find any match for the HTTP header in other sections.

An uptodate version of the BROWSCAP file is maintained by Juan T. Llibre at http://www.aspalliance.com/juan/browscap.ini.asp. You can get the file itself at http://www.aspalliance.com/juan/browscap.zip.

Using the Browser Capabilities Component

As you may already guess, the Browser Capabilities component can be very useful in situations when we use Active Server Pages to dynamically generate HTML contents for the client browser. Knowing what the client browser can do and what features it supports allows us not to send Java applets to the Mozilla 1.0 browsers, ActiveX components to the Sun platforms and use VBScript code with Netscape Navigator. Even more, we can simply redirect our clients to the appropriate versions of our pages. The first thing we should do before we start using the Browser Capabilities component is to create an instance of it:

```
Set BroCaps = Server.CreateObject("MSWC.BrowserType")
```

This creates an instance of the component available at our current page. To make an instance available to all pages of our application we can use the <OBJECT> tag in the global.asa file:

```
<OBJECT RUNAT=Server SCOPE=Session ID=BroCaps
 PROGID="MSWC.BrowserType">
</OBJECT>
```

After we have done this we can refer to the properties of the client browser through the newly created instance. For example we can check if the client supports VBScript:

```
If BroCaps.vbscript Then
  Response.Write("VBScript supported. " &_
   "You will be redirected to a different version of the site")
  Response.Redirect("\new\dhtml.asp")
Else
  Response.Write("VBScript is not supported. " &_
   You will be redirected to the plain HTML version of the site")
  Response.Redirect("\old\plain.asp")
End If
```

The Content Linking Component

The **Content Linking** component manages a list of URLs that can be used to create table of contents, navigation links and other structures, which can be represented as a set of related Web pages. This component works with the special file called a **Content Linking List** file (or list file) that is a text file with a special format in it. This file is stored on the web server. Before we can use the Content Linking component we need to create a list file.

The Content Linking List File

For each URL in our list of linked URLs we provide one line of text in the list file. Each line can have three parts, separated from each other by a *TAB* character:

```
Page URL           Description      Comment
```

❑ The **Page URL** part should contain the virtual or relative URL of the file we want to include in our list. These can be not only HTML or ASP files, but also other file types supported by the client browser, i.e., Image files (JPG and GIF), Microsoft Office files (if the client browser is Microsoft Internet Explorer) and so on. Absolute URLs, that start with "http:", "//" or "\\", are not supported. You should also ensure that there are no infinite loops, i.e. the referenced page should not redirect the user back to the list page, etc.

❑ The **Description** part can contain text that gives the textual description for the **Page URL** part

❑ The **Comment** part may contain some explanatory text that is ignored by the component

Here is an example of a list file.

```
0898.asp        Sales for AUGUST
0998.asp        Sales for SEPTEMBER     incomplete
1098.asp        Sales for OCTOBER
1198.asp        Sales for NOVEMBER
Home.asp        This month so far       last updated xx/yy/zz
```

After the list file is created we can display it in our page and use the Content Linking component's methods to manage it.

Using the Content Linking Component

As usual, before we can use the Content Linking component we should create an instance of it, e.g.

```
Set objLinkList = Server.CreateObject("MSWC.NextLink")
```

Now we can refer to the Content Linking component through the objLinkList object, and use its methods.

The Content Linking component provides us with eight methods that can be used to return URLs from the list and return line number information. All methods of the Content Linking component have one parameter in common, which points to the list file we want to use. For example, if our listfile containing links to weekly sales reports, saleslinks.txt, is in the current directory, all we need to specify is the filename:

```
NumWeeks = objLinkList.GetListCount("saleslinks.txt")
```

If necessary the value of this parameter could also be a relative path, e.g. "sales\saleslinks.txt", or a virtual path, e.g. "/sales/saleslinks.txt". Once we have created an instance of the Content Linking component we can use it with different list files.

Let's look at a couple of examples in which we'll use all eight methods. Firstly, say we wanted to iterate through the list file and print out all the links on the screen, so that the user has a menu from which they can choose which month of sales data they would like to view. We can use the GetListCount method to return the number of lines, and therefore the number of links, in the list file. Starting at 1 (the first line in the listfile), we can access each line of the listfile in turn, using the GetNthDescription and GetNthURL methods. These two methods have an extra numeric parameter that allows us to specify a line number in the listfile. We can set the value of this parameter to the current line number, print out an HTML anchor, and then go round the loop again incrementing the line number. The code looks like this:

```
<H1>Sales Figures</H1>
<%
 Set objLinkList = Server.CreateObject("MSWC.NextLink")
 ListFile = "saleslinks.txt"
 NumLinks = objLinkList.GetListCount(ListFile)
 For I = 1 to NumLinks
  URL = objLinkList.GetNthURL(ListFile, I)
  Txt = objLinkList.GetNthDescription(ListFile, I)
%>
 <A HREF=" <% =URL%>"><% =Txt %> </A><BR>
<%
 Next
%>
```

This will produce the following page

The method GetListIndex will return the line number in the listfile of the page we are currently on (if our current page is not included in the listfile, the return value is 0). We could use the value of our current position to replace the value 1 in the code above, if for example we only wanted to display the remaining links ahead of us.

Let's look at another example. We have two methods which enable us to get the details of the next entry in the list – GetNextURL and GetNextDescription – and two which return the same information for the previous entry – GetPreviousURL and GetPreviousDescription. We can use these methods to implement navigational links to the next and previous months so that we don't have to display all the links as a table of contents on every page. We can use the GetNextIndex method that we mentioned above to check that there is a previous or next link, relative to our current position in the list, before we try and display it. Using the same example, we could create an extra ASP file that looks like this:

```
<%
Set objLinkList = Server.CreateObject("MSWC.NextLink")
ListFile = "saleslinks.txt"
If (objLinkList.GetListIndex (ListFile) > 1) Then
   URL = objLinkList.GetPreviousURL(ListFile)
   Txt = "Compare with previous month: " &
                              objLinkList.GetPreviousDescription(ListFile)
%>
   <A HREF="<%= URL%>"><%= Txt%></A>
   <P>
<%
End If

If (objLinkList.GetListIndex(ListFile) < objLinkList.GetListCount(ListFile))
                                                                       Then
   URL = objLinkList.GetNextURL (ListFile)
   Txt = "Compare with following month: " &
                                objLinkList.GetNextDescription(ListFile)
%>
   <A HREF="<%= URL%>"><%= Txt%></A>
<% End If %>
```

We can include this ASP code in every file listed in our listfile saleslist.txt, so that no matter which page we are on we will always have a link to the next and previous month's sales figures. Probably the easiest way to do this, particularly in terms of maintenance, is to use the #include syntax shown below. If our Next/Previous Links code is stored in an ASP file ex2.asp, we would add the following to the files 0998.asp, 1098.asp and so on:

```
<!--#include file="ex2.asp" -->
```

The page containing figures for September could look something like this:

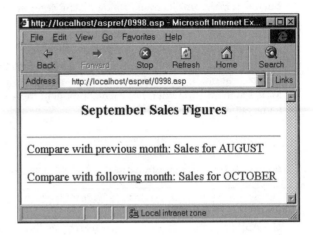

This is only a very simple example to demonstrate some of the many possibilities of the Content Linking component – it is a very powerful tool which makes it easy to build a navigational structure into your web pages.

Third-Party Server Components

As we have mentioned at the beginning of this chapter, Active Server Components are based on the popular Microsoft COM technology, so it is not surprising that there are hundreds of third-party server components available. Rather than provide you with page after page descriptions of Active Server Components available, we have decided to give you several URLs that can be useful in your future investigations on this topic.

Definitely, one of the best sources of information on third-party components (and on Active Server Pages as well) is the **15Seconds** site maintained by Wayne Berry. The component's section is a programmer's reference to components that can be added to Active Server Pages. For the first time 15Seconds has started documenting those components for programmers. As part of the documentation there is a detailed description of each method and property for the components featured here. The component's catalog can be viewed by Prog Id or by Vendors. In the comparison section 15Seconds has compared component products that have similar features. Several companies and individuals have produced COM objects with similar functionality and varying price ranges. To choose efficiently a product that meets your development requirements 15Seconds has broken down the products by feature and compared them side by side. Look at

```
http://www.15seconds.com/component/default.htm
```

The Active Server Pages site contains its own huge list of components that are grouped in the following categories: Free components, Commerce/Shopping Carts, Database, E-mail, File Upload/Download and Management, Networking, Reports/Graphics and Other.

Look at `http://www.activeserverpages.com/components/`

Microsoft maintains its own catalog of ASP components that can be found at

```
http://www.microsoft.com/workshop/server/components/catalog.asp
```

ASP Site has a huge list of components, divided into the following categories: Authentication, Banner Advertisement, Database, File Manipulation, Graphics/Charts, Mail, Payment and Other. For each component there is a short description, vendor name and URL. You can find this list at

```
http://www.aspsite.com/resources/components.asp
```

A list of several free components can be found at

```
http://www.softwing.com/iisdev/components.asp
```

The ASPxtras site provides its own searchable list of the components. Look at

```
http://www.aspxtras.com/ProductList.asp?Type=AXDLL
```

The **Software Artisans** company has created several commercial components – **SA-FileUpload**, that allows files to be uploaded to a web site via a browser, **SA-Check**, that checks form data for validity before accepting from users and **SA-Session**, that can used by web farms to share sessions between multiple users. You can find them at `http://www.softartisans.com/`.

Stephen Genusa maintains **The ASP Developer's Site** (`http://www.genusa.com/asp/`), and has developed a number of Active Server Components that are available for purchase or evaluation at

```
http://www.serverobjects.com/products.htm
```

With such a list of links to check, you stand a good chance of finding one or more ASP components that can solve your particular problem. If not, you can write your own component – something we'll cover in the next section.

Creating Your Own Components

As we have seen above, there are hundreds of commercial, shareware and free components that cover everything from trivial utilities to full-blown e-commerce payment solutions and can be used in your Active Server Pages programs. But sometimes you may need to perform some special tasks, and for this you'll need to write your own server component. This task is not as hard as it may sound. Server components are based on standards such as COM and can be implemented with any tool that supports the creation of COM objects. This can be Microsoft Visual Basic, Microsoft Visual C++ or any other C++ compiler that supports COM-technologies, Visual J++ and Inprise's Borland Delphi. The latest generation of these development tools insulate the developer from the complexities of COM and allow the developer to concentrate on the business rules rather than COM plumbing. The topic of creating COM objects with any of the tools mentioned above deserves its own book and we will not get into great detail on how to create server components. Rather we will outline some common tasks needed for Visual Basic and Borland Delphi – the two of the simplest RAD tools available.

Using Visual Basic

You can create Active Server Components using Microsoft Visual Basic version 5.0 and higher. Starting from version 5 Visual Basic has the ability to create both in-process and out-of-process ActiveX Servers that can be used with Active Server Pages.

First, start Visual Basic and select the ActiveX DLL in the New Project window. This will create an empty project called `Project1` with one class module – `Class1`. Rename your project `ASPDemo`, and your class module `Demo`. In the source for the class module write the following code:

```
Public Function Hello()
Hello = "Hello from VB/ASP"
End Function
```

Save your project using the File|Save Project command from the File menu – this should create four files, namely:

```
DEMO       CLS
ASPDEMO    VBP
ASPDEMO    LIB
ASPDEMO    EXP
```

After that choose the File|Make ASPDemo.DLL command from the File menu. This will produce the `aspdemo.dll` file.

The `aspdemo.dll` is now your newly created Active Server Component. We can test it now.

Create the following file and save it as `test.asp` in the virtual root of your web server:

```
<%
 Set Demo = Server.CreateObject("ASPDemo.Demo")
 Response.Write(Demo.Hello)
%>
```

Note how project name and class name is mapped to the PROGID *of the component – it's the* ProjectName.ClassName *syntax.*

Now launch your web browser and enter the URL `http://localhost/demo.asp`:

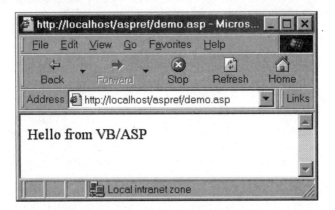

This may not look particularly impressive, but we have in fact managed to create an Active Server Component in less than five minutes!

Accessing the ASP Object Model

The example above can be used as the skeleton for simple or complex ASP components that, for example, access Win32 API functions, or make calculations based on business rules. It would be great if we could access the ASP Object model from our component and have available the context of what happens on the server and the information that users supply to us. To do this we need to extend our component and add some extra code to it. Before we do that let's look at what happens when the server creates an instance of our component.

When the server creates an instance of our component it looks at the component's
IDispatch interface (the one that is the heart and soul of Automation technology) for
two methods – OnStartPage and OnEndPage. If these methods are found, the server
will invoke the OnStartPage method *before* the component is used and the
OnEndPage method *after* the ASP page is complete. Note that the abovementioned
methods are called for all components on the page except the ones with application
scope. This gives us a way to create and initialize variables, and to read initial
information from files, the registry and so on when our component is created. We can
also save the information we need to a file or the registry at the end of the component
instance's life.

We also receive the ScriptingContext interface from the server, as discussed in
Chapter 1. Through this, we can access the methods and properties of the intrinsic ASP
Objects.

We have briefly covered some theory, now it's time to write some code. You can
continue to extend the component implemented above, or start a new project. The first
thing we should do is to include a reference to the ASP Object library – this will give
our code access to the objects in ASP Object model. To do so run the Project I
References command, and in the Available References listbox check the line that
reads Microsoft Active Server Pages Object Library.

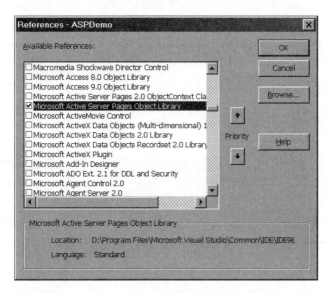

Click the OK button and return to the code editor. Now we need to implement the
OnStartPage and OnEndPage methods. Here is the code:

```
'
' Variables to store ASP Objects
'
Private ScrContext As ScriptingContext
Private ASPApp     As Application
Private ASPReq     As Request
Private ASPRes     As Response
Private ASPServ    As Server
Private ASPSess    As Session
```

```
' The OnStartPage method will be called when our
' component is created by the server
'
Public Sub OnStartPage(ScriptingContext As ScriptingContext)
  Set ScrContext = ScriptingContext
  Set ASPApp    = ScrContext.Application
  Set ASPReq    = ScrContext.Request
  Set ASPResp   = ScrContext.Response
  Set ASPServ   = ScrContext.Server
  Set ASPSess   = ScrContext.Session
End Sub
'
' The OnEndPage method will be called when our
' component will be destroyed by the server
'
Public Sub OnEndPage()
Set ScrContext = Nothing
  Set ASPApp    = Nothing
  Set ASPReq    = Nothing
  Set ASPResp   = Nothing
  Set ASPServ   = Nothing
  Set ASPSess   = Nothing
End Sub
```

Now we have full access to the ASP object model and can use the properties and methods of any object. For example, instead of implementing the Hello procedure, as we have done earlier, we can call the Response.Write method to output the fully HTML-formatted string:

```
' In the component's code
' we use Response.Write method:
'
ASPResp.Write "<B>ASP Demo</B> - Demo object was <i>just created...</i>"
```

We create an instance of our component with the following statement:

```
<%
  Set Demo = Server.CreateObject("ASPDemo.Demo")
%>
```

and after accessing the page we see the result:

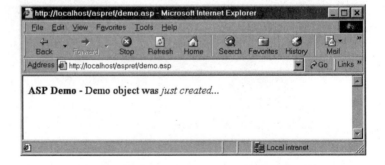

It should be clear that the example above only serves a demonstration purpose – we could also use Win32 API functions, collections or properties of ASP objects, or even drive some Automation Servers, such as Microsoft Word or Microsoft Excel. Anyway, the code provided in this section can be used over and over again as it forms the base of any ASP Component, created with the help of Visual Basic.

A Note on the Threading Model

At the project name node in the project window press the right mouse key and choose the Project Properties menu item (ASPDemo Properties in our case). In the dialog box that will appear, you can set the threading model for the component – either Apartment- or Single-threaded.

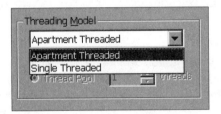

The Apartment threading model is the one to choose here. The advantage of Apartment over Single threading is that with Apartment threading a method of the component can execute in its own thread – the thread runs in an apartment for that instance of the component. If you choose Single Threaded, all methods will execute on the same, single thread, and consequently can only execute in sequence. The Apartment threading model is much the faster option.

There are four threading models in total, but Apartment and Single are the only ones available in Visual Basic. If you create components in Visual J++ or C++ you can additionally choose from Free threading or Both threading, and your preference here should be to make your components Both threaded. All Free threaded objects are created in one multi-threaded apartment (MTA). This can mean very quick execution of calls between components that are both running in the MTA, but will be slower if you need to make calls to a component running in a different apartment (a single-threaded apartment of the type described in the Apartment threading model), as the call will have to be made via a proxy. If you choose Both threading you have the best of both the Apartment and the Free threading worlds – an component that is Both threaded can use the Apartment or the Free threading model as appropriate. Whether the object that is creating the component is running in a single-threaded apartment or the MTA, the component will be created in the same apartment as the object.

So in this example we will create an Apartment-threaded component. However, note that Apartment threaded objects **should not** be given session or application scope. When an Apartment threaded session or application object is being accessed it will be locked down to a single thread – all calls will be dealt with in sequence. This will cause a significant decrease in server performance. This problem is avoided with objects that are Both threaded.

Using Borland Delphi

We can use Borland Delphi version 3 and 4 to create Active Server Components. We will use version 4 for this example – it provides more reliable support for COM development and greater flexibility to work with type libraries and interfaces.

First, start Delphi 4 and close all files using the File I Close All command from the File menu. Choose the File I New command, and in the New Items panel select the ActiveX tab and the ActiveX Library icon inside it.This will produce the skeleton project for the ActiveX library.

Once again, choose the File I New command and this time select the Automation Object icon at the ActiveX tab. This will bring up the Automation Object Wizard. Enter the class name for your component, for example, D4ASP. Leave all other fields as is, and press the OK button.

Now you face the Type Library Editor. Select the ID4ASP Interface and press the New Property button. Give the property name HTMLHello and set its type to WideString. Now switch to the source code for your automation object and enter the following code in the function TD4ASP.Get_HTMLHello: WideString:

```
Get_HTMLHello := '<B>Hello from <I>Delphi/ASP</I></B>';
```

Your code now should look like this:

```
function TD4ASP.Get_HTMLHello: WideString;
begin
 Get_HTMLHello := '<B>Hello <I>from Delphi/ASP</I></B>';
end;
```

Compile your project with the Project I Compile command and choose the Run I Register ActiveX Server command. It should tell you that ActiveX registered OK.

Create the following file, d4test.asp, in the virtual root of your web server:

```
<%
 Set Demo = Server.CreateObject("D4ASP.D4ASP")
 Response.Write(Demo.Hello)
%>
```

Now launch your web browser and type http://localhost/ d4demo.asp:

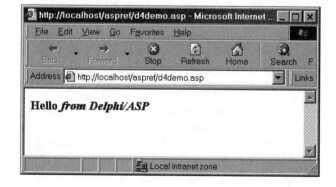

As you can see, it takes more time to create an Active Server Component with Delphi, but it provides more flexibility for experienced programmers – for example you can access the type library directly from the development environment and work with COM interfaces.

At the Microsoft downloads site you can find **Developer Samples 2.0**. This contains two Active Server Pages components, each implemented in five different environments: Microsoft Visual C++ using the Microsoft Active Template Library (ATL), Microsoft Visual C++ using Microsoft Foundation Classes, Microsoft Visual J++, Microsoft Visual Basic Version 4, and Microsoft Visual Basic Version 5. These components, unlike the others listed above, are useful only to developers.

When developing Active Server Components on PWS we recommend that where possible you use separate computers with a Web server installed, as every time you implement the new and improved (i.e. bug fixed) version of your component you will need to stop and start your Web server. Under IIS you can just unload the Web application. If you are not using MTS, it is also important to make sure that you "process isolate" your development environment and those web applications that are not robust – so that any misbehaving component does not kill the main web server. If the web application is isolated, and the component crashes, only the secondary process is killed – the main web server will still be alive and kicking. Any subsequent request for the web application will restart the secondary process. If a component in the main web server process (inetinfo.exe) crashes, then IIS is completely dead.

When your component is ready, put it in a convenient folder, for example, in the \WINNT\SYSTEM32\INETSERV\EXTRA folder under Windows NT, or the \WINDOWS\SYSTEM\INETSERV\EXTRA\ under Windows 95/98, and register it e.g. REGSVR32.EXE MYASP.DLL, where MYASP.DLL is the library that contains your newly created component.

Summary

In this chapter we have looked at what Active Server Components are, studied several standard components that come with Internet Information Server and Personal Web Server, discussed what additional components are available and where to look (and shop) for them, and even managed to look briefly at how to create Active Server Components using Visual Basic and Borland Delphi. Not bad for one chapter!

The next chapter will deal with interfacing with other applications, such as Microsoft Transaction Server (MTS), Microsoft Messaging Queue (MSMQ) that plays a great role in the Windows DNA architecture, CDO to manipulate the SMTP server from Active Server Pages and several others.

8

Database Access with ADO

Since working with databases is such a large part of the ASP Programmer's job, it seems sensible to include a chapter on it here, even though this is an ASP Reference book. What this chapter will give you is an overview to ADO and the most common techniques that you'll need. Bear in mind though, that we can't cover every aspect of ADO here. You can find details of objects, properties and methods for ADO in Appendix C, and for a more in-depth look at the whole of ADO try *ADO 2.0 Programmer's Reference* (ISBN 1-861001-83-5).

Universal Data Access

Universal Data Access (UDA) is the term that Microsoft have given to the way they see data access going, and the stress here is on Universal. In the past we've very much concerned ourselves with relational databases, and whilst these are great, they have their limitations. They are really designed for relational, structured data, and don't handle many of the new types of data that business need to access, such as images, video stream, mail systems, and remote data. UDA defines the idea of data, but doesn't specify what that data is, so we can access any type of data in a consistent manner.

The remote data option is also being driven by the increase in the use of the Web for applications. This has meant we have had to write true client/server systems, often *n*-tier in nature, building in the inherent fallibility of HTTP – that of it's stateless nature. So, if Web applications are being used in a distributed way, then we need to think about data in a distributed way, and this means having data available where it is being used. If a Web application is half a planet away from its data, we really can't expect the user to be pleased if they have to wait every time they want access to that data.

UDA is part of the Distributed interNet Application architecture (DNA) that Microsoft is pushing as the way to develop *n*-tier applications. It is simply based around the three most common layers:

❑ The Presentation layer, which is what the user sees.
❑ The Business layer, which is where the business rules are stored.
❑ The Data layer, which is where the actual data is stored.

Given that these layers could be distributed far from each other, a way of passing data between the two is required – and that's where OLEDB and ADO come in.

OLEDB and ADO

Unlike ODBC, which has served us well for many years, OLEDB is COM based. That means that it forms a core component of existing and future Microsoft products, and can be widely used in a variety of programming languages. It's a set of interfaces designed to replace ODBC, and work in conjunction with the disparate nature of the Web. OLEDB and ADO fit together in a nice way, and even allow for the existence of ODBC:

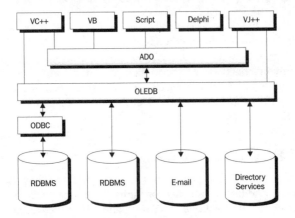

ActiveX Data Objects (ADO) is the COM wrapper around OLEDB. Notice that you can access data stores directly with OLEDB, or use OLEDB to go through ODBC. It is very similar in nature to previous Microsoft data access technologies, such as DAO and RDO, but has a greatly simplified object model.

So, if ADO is just a way to get data, what makes it useful for the ASP programmer? Well, ADO comes with some useful features:

- ❏ Remote Data, giving you the ability to move data between the server and the client.
- ❏ Disconnected data, building on the remote features, allows the data to be disconnected from the server, and reconnected at a later date, with the ability to update data.
- ❏ Persistence, to allow the remote data to be stored locally at the client, without the client being aware that it is a local copy.
- ❏ Hierarchical data, allowing relational data to be dealt with in a single way, rather than multiple calls to the server.
- ❏ Local indexing, to allow remote data to be search more quickly.

These features give you, the ASP Programmer, the ability to write applications that use data in an intelligent and consistent way.

Providers and Consumers

Two fundamental terms are **Providers** and **Consumers**, which simply state who is providing the data, and who is using the data. To access data from a data store from ADO you go through an OLEDB Provider. The following are the OLEDB Providers supplied with ADO 2:

Provider Name	Description
MSDASQL	ODBC, which allows connection to existing ODBC data sources, either via a System DSN or from dynamically provided connection details.
Microsoft.Jet.OLEDB.3.51	Jet, for connecting to Microsoft Access databases.
SQLOLEDB	SQL Server, for connecting to Microsoft SQL Server.
MSDAORA	Oracle, for connecting to Oracle databases.
MSIDXS	Index Server, for connecting to Microsoft Index Server
ADSDSOObject	Active Directory Services, for connecting to Directory Service agents.
MSDataShape	Data Shape, for hierarchical recordsets, where a recordset can contain another recordset.
MSPersist	Persist, for locally saved recordsets.
MSDAOSP	Simple Provider, for creating your own providers for simple text data.

Other vendors of data stores are supplying their own OLEDB providers.

A Consumer is just an application that uses a provider for its source of data. So, in an ASP page, that page is a consumer. The OLEDB specification allows providers to be consumers, thus they can obtain data from another provider, manipulate it in some way, and then supply it. This is exactly what the MSDataShape provider does.

ADO Availability

At the time of writing, ADO is at version 2.0, but if you're using ASP you might be using version 1.5. Here's what the different versions ship with:

Version	Ships with…
1.5	The NT4 Option Pack
2.0	MDAC 2, available from www.microsoft.com/data
	Visual Studio 6.0
2.1	Internet Explorer 5
	Microsoft Office 2000

There is also a fix for 2.0 that comes with NT Service Pack 4

ADO 2.1 will offer some fixes and enhancements, especially in the area of remote data, as well as support for Data Definition Language, allowing data store structures to be created and changed. Support for persisting recordsets to XML is another benefit of 2.1. For the purposes of this chapter we will be using ADO 2.0

ADO Object Model

As mentioned earlier, the ADO object model is simpler than the models for previous technologies. Here's how it looks:

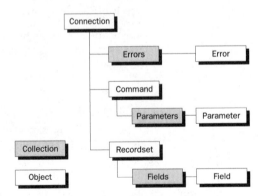

This shows there are three main objects: the Connection, the Command, and the Recordset. Each of these, as well as the Field object, has a collection of Properties:

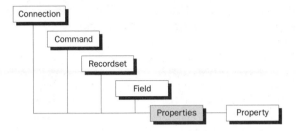

Let's have a quick look at the objects before delving into code.

Connection

The Connection object contains all of the details about a specific connection to a data store, such as data store name, user name, database name, etc. What you supply as part of these connection details varies with the provider.

One of the simplifications that ADO has achieved over its predecessors is the lack of a strict hierarchy. So, whilst it appears as though the Connection is the top dog, you don't need to create a connection object first, before accessing data. You can just access the data (obviously specifying the connection details), and a Connection object will be built for you, behind the scenes. If you are performing a lot of data access, then for efficiency it's best to create an explicit connection, thus saving the time of re-creating on-the-fly every time.

A connection object doesn't just provide the connection to the data store, as it allows execution of queries too. So you've got a flexible approach as to which object you use to obtain data.

Command

The Command object allows the execution of SQL commands, both those that are action based, and those that return results. The main requirement of a Command object is for those queries that require arguments, such as stored procedures with parameters.

Recordset

A Recordset is the container for a set of records, returned from a command. This command could have been created with a Connection object, a Command object, or the Recordset object itself, but if you require data back from the data store, then you must have a Recordset. The Recordset is equivalent to the records returned from running a query, or opening a table.

The Recordset contains methods to allow moving around the records, as well as adding, deleting, and updating the records.

Fields

The Fields are equivalent to the columns in a results set. Each row in the Recordset will contain a Fields collection, containing Field objects. Each Field represents a single value, or possibly another recordset if hierarchical data shaping is being used.

Errors

Errors, or data store information, that occur during the processing of commands are placed in the Errors collection. This gives a central area that can be processed to obtain error details. The Errors collection only belongs to the Connection object, and although we've said that you don't need an explicit Connection object, you always get one behind the scenes via the `ActiveConnection` property, so you can always access the errors.

Parameters

The Parameters collection belongs to a Command object, and contains details of the parameters for a stored procedure, or stored query as they tend to be called in Access. Whilst there are ways to pass parameters into queries without using the Parameters collection, it must be used if output values or return values are required.

Properties

The Properties collection details the dynamic, provider specific properties. One disadvantage of keeping the OLEDB technology small and simple, is that it obviously cannot store many of the details that are specific to Providers. So it provided the Properties collection, which Providers can fill with and specific details they require. This allows providers to be enhanced without OLEDB requiring changing.

Creating Objects

Just like any COM object, ADO objects are created using `Server.CreateObject` method:

```
Set objConn=Server.CreateObject ("ADODB.Recordset")

Set objCmd=Server.CreateObject ("ADODB.Command")

Set objRec=Server.CreateObject ("ADODB.Recordset")
```

Once created these can be used just like any other component.

Constants

ADO uses many constants to describe various options. When using ADO in ASP pages you can use the numbers that these constants represent, which makes your code more difficult to understand, or you can include the constants in your ASP page. There are two ways of doing this.

The first way is to use #INCLUDE, like so:

```
<!-- #INCLUDE FILE="adovbs.inc" -->
```

This file contains all of the constants and their values. It can be found in
C:\Program Files\Common Files\system\ado. There's a version for JScript
too. If using the above format you'll need to copy this file into the same directory as the
ASP page. Or you can use:

```
<!-- #INCLUDE VIRTUAL="include\adovbs.inc" -->
```

This just includes the file from a virtual directory.

A far better solution though, is to reference the type library directly (this can be useful
with any COM component):

```
<!--METADATA TYPE="typelib" FILE="C:\Program Files\Common
Files\system\ado\msado15.dll" -->
```

You can include this command directly at the top of an ASP page, or in the
global.asa file, giving it application scope. Don't be fooled by the name of the DLL
– it has the same name whatever version of ADO.

This is the preferred solution because you are referencing the same data that the
objects themselves use. Using the include file always has the possibility that it might be
out of date, or that someone (heaven forbid) has changed it.

Connection Strings

Connecting to data stores is the first thing that most people do, and for that you need a
connection string. This just includes the details you require to connect to a data store,
and is therefore different for each provider.

Most connection strings need to start with the Provider:

```
Provider=SQLOLEDB
```

If using the OLEDB Provider for ODBC (MSDASQL) you can omit this, since this
provider is the default.

In the following examples everything in round braces is a user definable option.

OLEDB Provider for SQL Server

To connect to SQL Server you need to specify the following:

❑   `Provider=SQLOLEDB`

❑   `Data Source =`(the SQL Server machine name)

❑   `Initial Catalog=`(the name of the database)

❑   `User ID=`(the SQL Server user to connect as)

❑   `Password=`(the password for that user)

For example:

```
Provider=SQLOLEDB; Data Source=Tigger; Initial Catalog=pubs; User Id=sa;
Password=
```

Note – this should all be on one line.

OLEDB Provider for Access

For Access you need the following:

❑   `Provider= Microsoft.Jet.OLEDB.3.51`

❑   `Data Source=`(physical path of mdb file)

❑   `Jet OLEDB:Database Password=`(database password)

❑   `Jet OLEDB:System database=`(physical path of system database)

❑   `User Id=`(user name)

❑   `Password=`(user password)

For example

```
Provider=Microsoft.Jet.OLEDB.3.51; Data Source=C:\temp\pubs.mdb
```

Or with a database password:

```
Driver={Microsoft Access Driver (*.mdb)}; DBQ=C:\temp\pubs.mdb; Jet
OLEDB:Database Password=LetMeIn
```

For a database secured at the user level:

```
Driver={Microsoft Access Driver (*.mdb)}; DBQ=C:\temp\pubs.mdb; Jet
OLEDB:System database=C:\temp\system.mdw; User ID=davids; Password=lobster
```

OLEDB Provider for Oracle

For Oracle you need the following:

❏   `Provider=MSDAORA`
❏   `Data Source=`(Oracle instance)
❏   `User ID=`(the SQL Server user to connect as)
❏   `Password=`(the password for that user)

For example:

```
Provider=MSDAORA; Data Source=2:; User Id=scott; Password=tiger
```

OLEDB Provider for ODBC

OLEDB allows you to connect through ODBC, thus preserving existing data source, or the use of data stores for which there are no native OLEDB drivers. Remember that the OLEDB Provider for ODBC is the default provider, and you therefore do not need to supply the Provider part of the connection string. However, if you do want to supply it, the form is:

```
Provider=MSDASQL
```

There are two ways to create a connection string when using the OLEDB Provider for ODBC.

The first is to use a Data Source Name (DSN), as set up in the Control Panel, under the ODBC applet. This takes the form of:

```
DSN=(data source name)
```

This has the advantage of being able to centrally administer the connection details, but the trouble is that every time a connection is made, the DSN details have to be looked up in the registry. This is therefore slower than the next option.

The second, and more preferable way, is to use a DSN-less connection string. The details for these differ depending upon the ODBC Driver in use:

SQL Server

For SQL Server via ODBC you should use:

❏   `Driver={SQL Server}`
❏   `Server=`(the SQL Server machine name)
❏   `Database=`(the name of the SQL Server database)
❏   `UID=`(the SQL Server user to connect as)
❏   `PWD=`(the password for that user)

For example:

```
Driver={SQL Server}; Server=Tigger; Database=pubs; UID=sa; PWD=
```

Jet

For Access via ODBC you should use:

- ❑ Driver={Microsoft Access Driver (*.mdb)}
- ❑ DBQ=(physical path of mdb file)
- ❑ SystemDB=(physical path of system database)
- ❑ UID=(user name)
- ❑ PWD=(user password)

For example:

```
Driver={Microsoft Access Driver (*.mdb); DBQ=C:\temp\pubs.mdb
```

Oracle

For Oracle via ODBC you should use:

- ❑ Driver={Microsoft ODBC Driver for Oracle
- ❑ Server=(Oracle instance)
- ❑ UID=(the SQL Server user to connect as)
- ❑ PWD=(the password for that user)

For example:

```
Driver={Microsoft ODBC Driver for Oracle; Server=2:; UID=scott; PWD=tiger
```

Oracle Driver Versions

If you are connecting with ODBC then the recommended ODBC driver from Microsoft is: **Microsoft ODBC for Oracle** driver (Msorcl32.dll) version 2.573.2927 (or later). Don't be fooled by the version number. Many of us have the 2.7x.xx version of this driver on our machines, and while it may appear that 2.7x. is later then 2.573., note that the second number (.7x and .573) are the revision numbers. Therefore, the .573 is the newer of the two.

The next chart shows the correct versions of the Oracle software that should be installed:

Oracle Server	7.3.3.0.0	7.3.4.0.0	8.0.3.0.0	8.0.4.0.0
Required Support Files	7.3.3.5.2	7.3.4.2.0	8.0.3.2.3	8.0.4.2.4
SQL*Net	2.3.3.0.4	2.3.4.0.4	N/A	N/A
Net8	N/A	N/A	8.0.3.0.4	8.0.4.0.3

Other

For other ODBC drivers you can look at the Data Source details in the Control Panel applet to find out the Driver name and connection details.

A Word about the Samples

All of the samples in this chapter assume the use of SQL Server and the pubs database. The code should work equally well for other providers. The connection string has been separated out into an include file, which just contains this:

```
<%
strConn="Provider=SQLOLEDB; Data Source=Tigger; Initial Catalog=pubs; User
Id=sa; Password="
%>
```

When running the code samples on your machine you should change the Data Source value from Tigger (my server) to whatever yours is called. The reason for this approach is that it allows a single data store to be used for all samples, so you'll only have to change it once. Therefore all samples will start with:

```
<!-- METADATA TYPE="typelib" FILE="C:\Program Files\Common
Files\system\ado\msado15.dll" -->
<!-- #INCLUDE FILE="DataStore.inc" -->
```

This declares the type library for the ADO constants, and includes the connection string. We won't show these two lines in the samples, although they are in the downloadable code samples for this chapter. When you come to run the code samples you may also need to change the drive letter in the DLL path if your root drive is not C. The DLL shouldn't be in another path, but it might be on a different drive.

If you want to use the samples with Access, then there's a copy of the pubs database in Access format available as part of the samples download. You should change the connection string in DataStore.inc to:

```
<%
strConn="Provider=Microsoft.Het.OLEBD.3.51; Data Source=C:\tmp\pubs.mdb"
%>
```

You will have to enter the path of your database for this. The URL for downloading the code samples for this book is http://webdev.wrox.co.uk/books/2459/.

Accessing a Data Store

Before you can read records you need to connect to a data store, and then create a recordset containing the data you are interested in.

Opening a Connection

To open a connection to a data store you simply use the Open method of the Connection object:

```
Set objConn=Server.CreateObject ("ADODB.Connection")

objConn.Open strConn
```

Where strConn contains the connection details.

Opening a Recordset

Once connected you can then open a Recordset, using the Open method:

```
Set objRec=Server.CreateObject ("ADODB.Recordset")

objRec.Open "authors", objConn, adOpenForwardOnly, _
                     adLockReadOnly, adCmdTable
```

The Open method takes five arguments:

- ❑ Source, identifies the source of the data. This could be a table name, a stored procedure name, a SQL statement, or some provider specific command.
- ❑ ActiveConnection, identifies the connection to use. This can be a connection string or an existing connection object.
- ❑ CursorType, identifies the type of cursor required. This allows us to say whether we only want to move forward through the recordset, or perhaps to move backwards, or see changes in our recordset made by other people.
- ❑ LockType, identifies how we should lock the records.
- ❑ Options, specifies what type of command is being set.

In the above example we are using a cursor type of adOpenForwardOnly, which means that we'll only be able to move forwards through the records. We could use code such as this to fill list boxes, combo boxes, tables and so on. A lock type of adLockReadOnly means that no record locking is to be performed. The options setting of adCmdTable means that Source is the name of a table.

We won't be discussing these arguments in any great detail, since we want to get down to the use of ADO. You'll find them listed in Appendix C.

Reading Records

Now you've seen how to connect, it's time to actually show some real samples, connecting and retrieving data. The following code shows how to connect to a data store and loop through a recordset, printing out the records to the page.

```
<%
    Dim objConn
    Dim objRec

    Set objConn=Server.CreateObject ("ADODB.Connection")
    Set objRec=Server.CreateObject ("ADODB.Recordset")

    objConn.Open strConn

    objRec.Open "authors", objConn, adOpenForwardOnly, _
                            adLockReadOnly, adCmdTable

    While Not objRec.EOF
        Response.Write objRec("au_fname") & " " & _
                        objRec("au_lname") & ", "
            objRec.MoveNext
    Wend

    objRec.Close
    objConn.Close
%>
```

This simply creates two objects, a Connection and Recordset, then opens the connection. Remember that strConn, our connection string, is defined in the include file. The recordset is then opened, and we loop whilst the end of the recordset hasn't yet been reached. EOF is set to True when this happens. Inside the loop we simply print the name, and move onto the next record in the recordset.

This gives a result of:

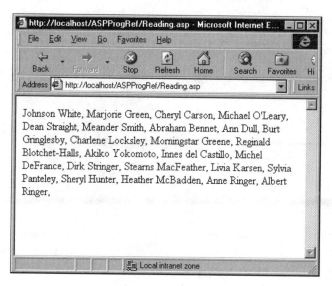

Creating Tables

Creating tables from recordsets is pretty simple, since you don't actually have to loop through every record and field. The Recordset has a method called `GetString`, which returns a recordset as a string. The good thing is that we can specify the field and line delimiters, so we can add HTML tags for table cells and rows. Assuming the recordset has been opened, here's the code:

```
sTable="<TABLE BORDER=1><THEAD><TR>"
For Each objFld In objRec.Fields
    sTable= sTable & "<TD>" & objFld.Name & "</TD>"
Next
sTable= sTable & "</TR></THEAD>" & _
    "<TBODY><TR><TD>" & _
    objRec.GetString (,,"</TD><TD>", "</TD></TR><TR><TD>") & _
    "</TD></TR></TBODY></TABLE>"

Response.Write sTable
```

The third argument of `GetString` is the field separator, so we need to close the current cell and start a new one. The fourth argument is the line separator, so we close the cell, close the line, start a new line, and start a new cell.

Running this code gives you a table containing everything from the recordset.

Creating Combo Boxes

If you're an ASP programmer then you really need to be able to generate HTML elements in response to a database. One feature is the ability to create HTML combo boxes from a recordset. This is simply a matter of building up an HTML string containing a `SELECT` tag and `OPTION` tags. Here's the code:

```
<%
    sQuote=Chr(34)

    Set objConn=Server.CreateObject ("ADODB.Connection")
    Set objRec=Server.CreateObject ("ADODB.Recordset")

    objConn.Open strConn

    objRec.Open "authors", strConn
    While Not objRec.EOF
        sName=objRec("au_lname") & ", " & objRec("au_fname")
        Response.Write "<OPTION ID=" & sQuote & objRec("au_id") & _
            sQuote & " Value=" & sQuote & sName & sQuote & ">"
        Response.Write sName & "</OPTION>"
        objRec.MoveNext
    Wend

    objRec.Close
    objConn.Close
%>
```

This is similar to the very first example, as we've just opened a recordset and are looping through the records. However, instead of just writing out the records, we are constructing an HTML OPTION tag for each record. This results in the following HTML:

```
<SELECT ID="lstAuthors" Name="User">
<OPTION ID="172-32-1176" Value="White, Johnson">White,
Johnson</OPTION>
<OPTION ID="213-46-8915" Value="Green, Marjorie">Green,
Marjorie</OPTION>
<OPTION ID="238-95-7766" Value="Carson, Cheryl">Carson,
Cheryl</OPTION>
. . .
</SELECT>
```

And the following result:

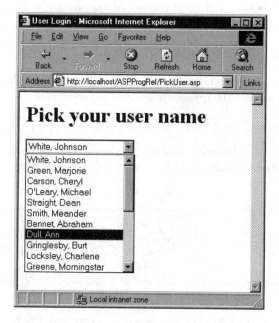

You could even re-write this code using the GetString method shown earlier, which might be even faster.

Creating Option Groups

We can use the same type of procedure to create option groups. For example, suppose we needed a page that showed the fields in a recordset, allowing the user to pick which fields should be displayed:

```
For Each objFld In objRec.Fields
    Response.Write "<INPUT TYPE=" & sQuote & "CHECKBOX" & sQuote & _
        " NAME=" & sQuote & "Field" & sQuote & _
        " VALUE=" & sQuote & objFld.Name & sQuote & _
        ">" & objFld.Name & "<BR>" & sCR
Next
```

Instead of building a SELECT/OPTION list for each record, this builds a CHECKBOX for each field. The HTML it produces is:

```
<INPUT TYPE="CHECKBOX" NAME="Field" VALUE="pub_id">pub_id<BR>
<INPUT TYPE="CHECKBOX" NAME="Field" VALUE="pub_name">pub_name<BR>
<INPUT TYPE="CHECKBOX" NAME="Field" VALUE="city">city<BR>
<INPUT TYPE="CHECKBOX" NAME="Field" VALUE="state">state<BR>
<INPUT TYPE="CHECKBOX" NAME="Field" VALUE="country">country<BR>
```

Adding Records

Reading records is all very well, but if you're building any sort of Web application then you'll probably need to add records to a database. There are two ways to perform this.

Recordset Additions

Recordset additions means using the `AddNew` method of the Recordset object. You can use `AddNew` in two ways. The first is without any arguments:

```
objRec.AddNew
```

This places the record pointer on a new record. You can now set the fields, and then call `Update` to update the data:

```
objRec.AddNew
objRec("pub_id")="9998"
objRec("pub_name")="Wrox Press"
objRec("city")="Chicago"
objRec("state")="IL"
objRec("country")="USA"
objRec.Update
```

The second method is to use the two arrays that `AddNew` optionally takes as arguments. The first identifies the fields, and the second identifies their values:

```
objRec.AddNew Array("pub_id", "pub_name", "city", "state", "country"), _
       Array("9998", "Wrox Press", "Chicago", "IL", "USA")
```

You can easily see how either of these techniques can be linked behind a form to allow the user to enter data:

```
<FORM ID="UserDetails" ACTION="AddUser.asp" METHOD="POST">
<TABLE>
<TR><TD>ID</TD><TD><INPUT TYPE="Text" NAME="pub_id"></TD></TR>
<TR><TD>Name</TD><TD><INPUT TYPE="Text" NAME="pub_name"></TD></TR>
<TR><TD>City</TD><TD><INPUT TYPE="Text" NAME="city"></TD></TR>
<TR><TD>State</TD><TD><INPUT TYPE="Text" NAME="state"></TD></TR>
<TR><TD>Country</TD><TD><INPUT TYPE="Text" NAME="country"></TD></TR>
</TABLE>
<INPUT TYPE="RESET" VALUE="Reset">
<INPUT TYPE="SUBMIT" VALUE="Submit">
</FORM>
```

In the ASP file, `AddUser.asp`, we could have this sort of code, to take the details from the form and add them to the database:

```
objRec.Open "publishers", objConn, adOpenKeyset, adLockOptimistic, _
             adCmdTable

objRec.AddNew
objRec("pub_id")=Request.Form("pub_id")
objRec("pub_name")=Request.Form("pub_name")
objRec("city")=Request.Form("city")
objRec("state")=Request.Form("state")
objRec("country")=Request.Form("country")
objRec.Update

Response.Write "Record added"
```

Notice that we've used a different cursor type and lock type, to ensure that we could add records.

Action Queries

The second method of adding records is by way of an action query, either by passing the values into a stored procedure, or by building a SQL string in the ASP page. This is the preferred method when you don't need to see the data again once it's been added. There's little point in building a recordset if you don't actually need the data. Adding a record via an action query will be quicker because the database is only hit once.

For example, instead of opening a recordset and adding the new record, as shown in the previous example, we could use a Command object to run a query:

```
strQuot=Chr(39)

Set objCmd=Server.CreateObject ("ADODB.Command")

strSQL="INSERT publishers VALUES (" & _
       strQuot & Request.Form("pub_id") & strQuot & ", " & _
       strQuot & Request.Form("pub_name") & strQuot & ", " & _
       strQuot & Request.Form("city") & strQuot & ", " & _
       strQuot & Request.Form("state") & strQuot & ", " & _
       strQuot & Request.Form("country") & strQuot & ")"

objCmd.ActiveConnection=objConn
objCmd.CommandType=adCmdText
objCmd.CommandText=strSQL

objCmd.Execute
```

This just builds a SQL INSERT statement, and uses this as the `CommandText`. We set the `ActiveConnection` to point to the existing connection object, and specify a text command by setting `CommandType` to `adCmdText`. Calling the `Execute` method sends the SQL statement to the provider.

Updating Records

Updating records can be performed in much the same way as adding them, either by using the Update method of a recordset, or by building a SQL statement.

Recordset Updates

To update a record you don't have to tell ADO that you are about to start editing it – you can just change the values directly, and then call Update. For example:

```
objRec("state")="WA"
objRec.Update
```

You could easily build a procedure similar to the one for adding new records, that simply takes the user values from the form, and updates an existing record. Of course you'd have to make sure that you were on the correct record to start with, so your code might look something like this:

```
strQuot=Chr(39)

strSQL="SELECT * FROM publishers WHERE " & _
          "pub_id=" & strQuot & Request.Form("pub_id") & strQuot

objRec.Open strSQL, objConn, adOpenKeyset, adLockOptimistic, _
            adCmdText

objRec("pub_name")=Request.Form("pub_name")
objRec("city")=Request.Form("city")
objRec("state")=Request.Form("state")
objRec("country")=Request.Form("country")
objRec.Update

Response.Write "Record updated"
```

Instead of opening the whole table, we've created a SELECT statement to just find the record we are interested in, so when we open the recordset, there will only be one record. We can then simply update the values.

Action Queries

Like additions, it's often quicker to use an action query to update records. For example, or code might now be:

```
strQuot=Chr(39)

strSQL="UPDATE publishers SET " & _
    "pub_name =" & strQuot & Request.Form("pub_name") & strQuot & ", " & _
    "city=" & strQuot & Request.Form("city")& strQuot & ", " & _
    "state=" & strQuot & Request.Form("state")& strQuot & ", " & _
    "country=" & strQuot & Request.Form("country")& strQuot & _
    "WHERE pub_id=" & strQuot & Request.Form("pub_id") & strQuot
```

This simply builds a SQL UPDATE statement, which can then be run in the same manner as the INSERT statement.

Deleting Records

As with adding and updating you can delete records in two ways.

Recordset Deletion

You can use the `Delete` method of a recordset to delete the current record. For example:

```
objRec.Delete
```

This deletes the current record.

Action Queries

Once again, action queries are often quicker than using the recordset method, since there's less traffic to the server. You could build a SQL statement in a similar way:

```
strQuot=Chr(39)

strSQL="DELETE publishers " & _
       "WHERE pub_id=" & strQuot & Request.Form("pub_id") & strQuot
```

This just sends the command down to the server, where it is quickly deleted.

Stored Procedures

Stored procedures are by far the best way to run action queries, or in place of any SQL statement. A stored procedure is a precompiled SQL statement that is stored on the server. This means that the server knows all about what it is going to do when it runs the procedure, as compared to a SQL statement where it has to work it out every time it receives the statement.

You can use stored procedures in much the same way as a table when opening a recordset, as long as you specify `adCmdStoredProc` for the `Options`:

```
strSQL="stored_proc_name"
objRec.Open strSQL, objConn, adOpenKeyset, adLockOptimistic, _
                 adCmdStoredProc
```

Parameters

One feature of stored procedures is their ability to accept parameters. For example, consider this stored procedure from the pubs database:

```
CREATE PROCEDURE byroyalty
@percentage int
AS
SELECT  au_id
FROM    titleauthor
WHERE   titleauthor.royaltyper=@percentage
```

When running this procedure we have to pass in a value for the `@percentage` parameter, and there are a couple of ways of doing this.

The first involves using the `Execute` method of the Command object, and passing these values in there. For example:

```
objCmd.CommandText="byroyalty"
objCmd.CommandType=adCmdStoredProc
Set objRec=objCmd.Execute (, Array(100))
```

When passing in parameters to a stored procedure in this way they have to be in an array, even if there's only one argument. Therefore we use the `Array` function to convert a single value to an array. Notice that the `Execute` method can be used to return a recordset as well running action queries.

The second method is by far the more complex, as it involves creating Parameters. Here's how the above would look using Parameters:

```
objCmd.CommandText="byroyalty"
objCmd.CommandType=adCmdStoredProc
objCmd.Parameters.Append objCmd.CreateParameter ("@percentage", _
                         adInteger, adParamInput, 8, 100)
Set objRec=objCmd.Execute
```

Using this method you need a Parameter object for each parameter in the stored procedure. You have to specify the name, the type, whether it is being used to pass information into the stored procedure or get information back out, the size, and the value.

This isn't too bad with just one parameter, but with several it gets very complex. If you are only passing values into the procedure, then use the `Array` method – there's almost no difference in speed. However, if your stored procedure has a return value, or output parameters, then you will need to use Parameter objects.

If you are unsure of what values your parameters have you can use the `Refresh` method, to ask the provider to create the Parameters collection for you. For example:

```
objCmd.CommandText="byroyalty"
objCmd.CommandType=adCmdStoredProc
objCmd.Parameters.Refresh
```

However, this means an extra trip to the server, so it is much slower. It is a good method to use when debugging though. You can call `Refresh`, loop through the Parameters to find out what the values should be, write these down, and then remove the `Refresh` and add your own Parameters.

Connection Pooling

Connection pooling is something that a lot of people get confused over, but it's really quite simple. When you open a connection to a data store, ADO first checks the Connection Pool to see if a connection that matches exists already. If it does, then you are given that connection. When you've finished with the connection, and Close it, ADO doesn't destroy the connection, it places it back in the pool, ready to give to another process. If there isn't a connection in the pool, a new one will be created. The connection details (including the user and password) must match exactly for you to be given a connection from the pool.

Why is this a good thing? Because creating a connection is relatively expensive, and it's more efficient to keep a few around in the pool and dish them out when required, rather than creating each one afresh. Connection pooling is switched on by default for OLEDB Providers. For ODBC this can be controlled through the Control Panel applet, but to be honest you're better off leaving it at the default.

Connection & Recordset Caching

Another confusing thing is the talk of recordset and connection caching. The examples you've seen in this chapter all opened a new connection at the start of the page, and then closed the connection at the end of the page. If you are writing a Web application you might thing it would be better to cache the Connection and Recordset objects in Session or Application variables.

Sounds great, but be warned. If you cache any ADO objects in the Session or Application you will lock down your web server to a single thread. This means that your web server will only be processing one request at a time, rather than many if it was multi-threaded. This is very inefficient, performance will drop drastically, and your application simply will not scale.

OK, after that serious warning, there are times when you can do this. If using SQL Server, and only SQL Server, it's possibly to convert ADO into a Both threaded object, which will allow this caching, and some performance gains can be achieved by it. There's a great article by Nancy Cluts of Microsoft, titled 'Got Any Cache?', available on MSDN (http://msdn.microsoft.com/developer/). Read it. Also read the Improving the Performance of Data Access Components in IIS 4.0", also by Microsoft, again under MSDN. This is full of useful performance tips.

Oracle Pitfalls

We've concentrated on SQL Server in this chapter, but one topic that always generates a lot of discussion amongst database people, is the use of Oracle and ADO. Oracle is a great database, and has a large market share, so why is there such a dearth of information available on this subject? Well, no longer, as with this little section we aim to point out a few pitfalls to avoid. For a more in-depth look at Oracle and its use with ADO, take a look at the forthcoming *ADO RDS Programming with ASP* (Wrox Press, ISBN 1861001649).

Stored Procedures

If you are using the OLEDB Provider for ODBC, and Microsoft Driver for Oracle, then you might receive errors if your stored procedure has 10 or more parameters. This is an Oracle problem and can be cured by downloading the Oracle Client software to version 8.0.4.2.0 or higher. The sort of error you can expect is:

```
Access Violation (0xC0000005) in ORA804.DLL @01B20002
```

or

```
Microsoft OLDB Provider for ODBC Drivers error '80040e14'
[Microsoft][ODBC Driver for Oracle]Syntax error or access violation
Spud.asp, line 777.
```

Always set the `CommandType` (or `Options`) to `adCmdStoredProc` when using stored procedures with Oracle, otherwise a large performance hit is taken.

If you revoke access, and re-grant it on a table access by a stored procedure, it's likely you'll receive an error such as:

```
Return: SQL ERROR=-1
szErrorMsg="[Microsoft][ODBC Driver for Oracle]Wrong number of
parameters"
szErrorMsg="[Microsoft][ODBC Driver for Oracle]Syntax error or
access violation"
```

You can cure this by recompiling your stored procedures.

If you have a stored procedure with no parameters, and are using the latest Microsoft ODBC Driver for Oracle, then you might get this error:

```
SYNTAX ERROR OR ACCESS VIOLATION
```

To cure this, just add a dummy parameter to the stored procedure.

The most current set of ODBC drivers for Oracle do not support synonyms when calling stored procedures, although they work when pointing to other Oracle objects.

Updating Records

If using the recordset method of updating records, then your cursor type should be a forward only one, created with `adOpenForwardOnly`. Another cursor type will give:

```
[Microsoft][ODBC Driver for Oracle]Degree of derived table does not
match
```

In-line Comments

Comments that are included in-line in SQL statements are parsed by the ODBC driver. If you receive errors in this area, then upgrade to the latest drivers which cure this problem.

Table Aliases

When using keyset cursors (created with `adOpenKeyset`), a SELECT statement with table aliases will give the following:

```
[Microsoft][ODBC Driver for Oracle]Cannot use Keyset-driven cursor
on join, with union, intersect or minus or on read only results set
```

You can cure this by using a different cursor type.

Authentication

SQL*Net is the service that provides the authentication for logging into Oracle, but this doesn't work so well when using a service, such as IIS, to access your database. The error you'll get is:

```
[Microsoft][ODBC Driver for Oracle][Oracle]ORA-12641:
TNS:authentication service failed to initialize
```

This can be cured by editing the sqlnet.ora file, usually found in the Network/Admin directory, under the Oracle home directory. This is a text file, and you just need to add the following line:

```
SQLNET.AUTHENTICATION_SERVICES=(none)
```

Summary

This chapter has covered a very small area of ADO. There's far more to ADO, including the use of RDS on the client side, but there really isn't room here to cover it in enough detail to do it justice. However, what we've tried to do is cover the most important areas of ADO that you, as an ASP programmer, will use, such as extracting data from data stores, adding new records, and updating existing records.

Extending ASP

In the first eight chapters of this book we've been right through 'pure ASP', seen how server components provide us with unique additional functionality and glanced at the Database capabilities we get from using ADO. There's no denying it's an impressive technology. But the real benefits come from combining ASP with other technologies to utilize and manipulate the many resources that our server has access to. It all stems from the grand masterplan known as Windows DNA.

At the Professional Developers Conference in September 1997, Microsoft unveiled their future strategy with an architectural framework for creating modern, open, scaleable, multi-tier distributed Windows applications using both the Internet and client/server technologies – this is to be known as the Windows Distributed interNet Applications architecture or Windows DNA. This builds on current investments in technologies, hardware, applications and skills.

Microsoft has recognized that developers frequently waste a huge amount of time building infrastructure type software in their applications. The objective of Windows DNA is to lay down the foundations for all this infrastructure type software to be built into the software base of future versions of the operating system. This means that developers can concentrate on innovative application logic rather than worrying about software plumbing.

Many of the services detailed in Windows DNA have been around for a number of years – however Windows DNA is a formalization of the framework and a roadmap for the future. The key to Windows DNA is Windows 2000 (NT 5.0) which is not targeted for delivery until sometime in 1999. However, some of the components – including Internet Information Server 4.0, Microsoft Transaction Server 2.0, ASP 2.0 and Message Queues 1 – are available for use now with Windows NT 4.0 in the Windows NT 4.0 Option Pack.

In this chapter, we will look at those DNA technologies that we can currently incorporate into our pages, and use to enrich page content. Of course, each of the ones we're going to touch on in this chapter could justify a *Programmer's Reference* of its own. But this is a *Programmer's Reference* for ASP – so we'll simply try and give you a feel for each of them. We'll tell you exactly what you'll encounter when you start to use them; give a little bit of sample code; and talk about ways to apply them. Hopefully, when you've finished reading this chapter, you should have a clear idea of which technologies will best help you in your development.

In this chapter we'll be looking at:

- Using RDS to interact with databases through a proxy
- Using ADSI to monitor, control and update your own systems
- Using CDO to interact with e-mail systems
- Using MTS and MSMQ to incorporate transactions and messaging into your applications
- Using Certificate Server to implement a security infrastructure

This chapter does assume a little more knowledge than previous chapters, but if you're about to look into any of the areas covered here, this will give you the necessary foundation.

Localizing Your Data

The key to the Internet is data. Most companies invest very heavily on data systems, and the web has fast become a key technology in data dissemination. It presents us with a uniform interface and (practically) immediate access to the facts we want to know. The World Wide Web as we know it was originally designed for academics to share resources and knowledge. These days there's perhaps a few more pictures, and a lot more commerce, but practically every site still remains dependent on information to fill it and it's from databases we get it raw, so to speak.

Out on the web, many sites are making more and more use of databases and if they're using ASP, then chances are that they're using ADO to do the database work for them. As we saw in the previous chapter, ADO lets us communicate with most types of data source through the use of OLEDB drivers, allowing us to create, alter and delete records with code incorporated into our ASP page.

In such cases, all the client ever receives is the page already filled with data, all processing and accessing of data having already been done on the server. All well and good, but the Internet (and, in the case of intranets, the LAN) is an inherently unstable creature and prone to shutting down. Pages that use a great deal of data also create a great deal of work for the network and if the same data on your page is to be viewed again in a different format, this would require another big round trip to the server and back again to answer the request.

Remote Data Access

The solution to this problem lies in our ability to maintain and manipulate the data we're using on the client-side, accessing the server only when the cached data on the client is insufficient to answer a query asked of it. Let's look at this diagrammatically.

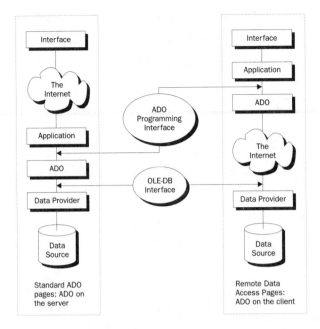

In our discussions on ADO to this point, the actual ADO code to reference the data has been stored, housed and executed on the server. By using Remote Data Access however, we extend our data management applications over the Internet or LAN, thus overcoming the need for lengthy client-server exchanges over the network.

For example, if a user wished to see all the results for the Bears against Giants since 1956, in the standard approach ADO approach (on the left-hand side of the figure above) the entire recordset of results would have to be sent to the client each time it is sorted differently (by Winner, by date, etc). However, by using the Remote Data Access approach (on the right-hand side of the figure above), the recordset is cached locally and can be sorted, filtered and viewed using ADO on the client any number of times, with no further access to the server.

Of course, this approach needs to be balanced against the likelihood that clients will probably want a different recordset each time they access a database and that they may only want to access a few records from the whole. In such cases, the regular ADO approach is likely to be more efficient then sending an entire database down to a client, which would obviously jam up the network. The support for Remote Data Access is also limited. Currently, only Internet Explorer 4 and above have complete support for Remote Data Services, the Microsoft expedient for Remote Data Access.

Remote Data Services

Microsoft's controlling technology for remote data access is currently known as Remote Data Services, or RDS for short. Although it is available for installation as part of the Windows NT Option Pack, this is only version 1.5 of RDS, which has now been superceded by version 2. Version 2 is available as part of the MDAC2.0 SDK which you can download from http://www.microsoft.com/data/mdac2.htm. The full install is 37.8 MB, so make sure you've got plenty of time or patience to download it all. Unlike the Option Pack however, you can choose to download various subcomponents of the SDK by themselves, an option I suggest you choose if you don't want a thousand dollar phone bill. Alternatively, MDAC2.0 is also available as part of Visual Studio 6 and Internet Explorer 5.

How does it work?

Once installed, RDS provides us with three objects – DataFactory, DataSpace and DataControl – that give us all the functionality we need to write some basic pages that cache data remotely on the client.

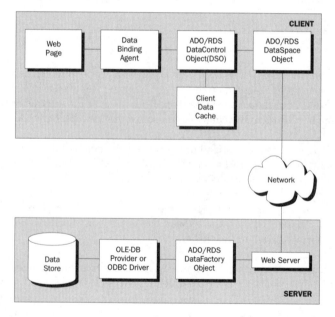

As with standard ADO pages, an OLEDB provider or ODBC driver creates a connection that gives us access to a database. When an RDS instruction comes, that provider or driver sends some (or all) of the database queried to a DataFactory object which takes the data and puts it in a format suitable for transmission across the Internet.

On the receiving end of the Internet, the DataSpace object takes the data from a DataFactory object and translates it back into a format which can be sorted, updated, filtered etc. on the client.

Finally, the `DataControl` object gives the client access to the data now cached on its machine. Web developers at this stage have two options for how they actually wish to display the data on a page. They can either use ADO and script to access the data directly, or bind the data to a custom control that will handle how the data is displayed automatically. Most likely the control will be written in a low-level language that uses the ASP and ADO objects through their COM interfaces just as Active Server Components may do.

The data may also flow from client to server, should the client wish to update the database. If they do, all the updates to the data will be stored within the client-side data cache and sent back in one go. This time, the `DataControl` object puts the code into a transmissible format and sends it over the Internet to the `DataFactory` object, which in turn translates the records back into the correct format for the database and updates it accordingly.

By using RDS,

- ❑ The performance of the web site is increased because data manipulation is no longer handled by the web server
- ❑ The speed with which data can be processed is increased because the program talking to the database is not trying to serve web pages at the same time — it's on the client
- ❑ The user gets a richer web page because the data is being manipulated on the page, therefore there are fewer round trips to the server

By creating an RDS/ADO setup, you also separate the business logic housed in components or web pages on the server from the data handling. For this reason, the business of maintaining and scaling your website will also become easier because in this situation you can concentrate on each of these issues separately.

Where Can I Learn More?

Very little material on RDS is actually available at the moment. The web has some info if you look for it in and around the ASP sites and Microsoft also have an RDS page at `http://www.microsft.com/data/ado/rds` but in terms of printed material there's basically nothing.

There is a two chapter case study in *Professional IE4 Programming* by Mike Barta et al (ISBN 1-861000-70-7) but if you can wait until February '99, then *ADO RDS Programming with ASP* by Johnny Papa et al. (ISBN 1-861001-64-9) will have been published by Wrox Press. This goes into very specific detail about the deployment of an RDS site.

Active Directory Service Interfaces

The web delivers information, pure and simple. By using ADO and RDS we can retrieve information from a database and manipulate it just as we want. But what if we want information on our server's current configuration? How can we access things like:

- ❑ What files are in which directory?
- ❑ What users are in which groups?
- ❑ What print jobs and pending in which print queues?
- ❑ What services are running on which computer?

We're unlikely to be able to get this kind of information from a database! Yet these are the kind of questions that a systems administrator asks every day. In addition, the systems administrator will also need to make changes to these aspects of the system – possibly daily – according to the demands placed on the system.

In order to answer these questions and exact these changes, the administrator needs access to his system's directory services – and for that he needs to be at a terminal on his network. Or, at least, that *used* to be the case. We can now write ASP code that can emulate – and in some cases, offer more functionality than – the suite of tools that we commonly associate with system administration (User Manager, Print Manager and the like). The server's file system manager, Windows Explorer, can be approximated using the `FileSystemObject` scripting object. For the rest, we need to use the **Active Directory Services Interface (ADSI)**.

ADSI allows us to govern the lifecycle of abstract directory objects – things like Computers, Printers and User Groups. In addition, we can also use ADSI to access these objects even if they are located on a different operating system. For example, before ADSI, sharing user information across Windows NT and Novell Netware was pretty much limited to duplicating user information manually on both systems. With ADSI installed, we can update user information from a web page and disseminate it automatically across a multi-operating system network.

How Does ADSI Work?

Setting up ADSI is pretty simple. In order for ADSI ASP pages to work, you simply need to install ADSI 2.0 (or ADSI 2.5 beta) on your web server. Obviously, the server of choice here is IIS4.0, but ADSI does run fine alongside Personal Web Server too. However, the lack of security on a Win9x platform suggests that this would be unwise. You can find all the necessary installation files on the download page of Microsoft's Backoffice site.

When set up, ADSI basically creates a super (directory) structure within which you access any directory service using the same universal commands. This structure contains two basic types of object:

❑ A container object, which holds a number of other objects as either children or 'members'

❑ A leaf object, which has neither children nor members

The keystone to the whole structure is the container named ADS://. Inside this container are stored a number of namespace containers. Each namespace represents a particular syntax with which you can access your target directory service. Unfortunately, your target service will not be found in a namespace unless it has an ADSI provider installed or you write one of your own and give it a namespace.

Currently, there are just six directory services that also run an ADSI provider, as shown below. However, ADSI is an open standard, and the incentive for other vendors to provide an ADSI implementation is very strong. At least one more – Windows 2000 Active Directory – is due in 1999. In the meantime, we have an abundance of things to do with the six providers that are currently available.

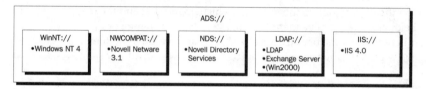

Beneath each namespace is a hierarchy of container objects and leaf objects. Each container and leaf has its own basic properties, which are dependent on the identity of the object. We can't go into them all here. However, as an example, you can begin to see the power and scale of ADSI by looking at the object hierarchy for the WinNT:// namespace:

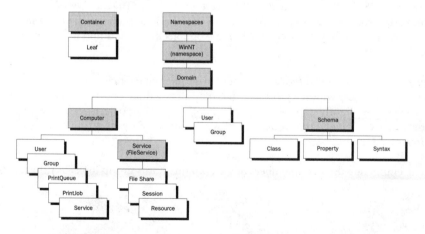

As you can see, Windows NT has a quite straightforward structure – you probably recognize most (or all) of the object names in the diagram above. Note that there is only one schema object for each namespace provider that ADSI recognizes – this is the object that stores the list of all the objects on the system, and their properties.

The real power in ADSI is via correct manipulation of the WinNT schema, a fact that will become abundantly clear when **Windows 2000** and its **Active Directory** are released. You can create new objects (with their own properties) for ADSI to recognize, or alter the property set of existing objects. For example, you could remove the need for a user to have a password by deleting a property.

We can go a step further. The schema also defines which of an object's properties are **mandatory** and which are **optional**. (If he'd known at the time that we'd have the potential to force information out of clients, by denying access to a terminal until each mandatory property had a value, then George Orwell might have called his book 1999...) ADSI has some security issues – for example, if you've created a completely functional remote administration site for your network the risks attached to unauthorized access are high. However – those concerns aside – the site itself is incredibly easy to implement, once a few basics are understood.

The Basic Concepts

Every ADSI object has six core properties: the `Parent` object, `ADsPath`, `Name`, `Guid` (a unique identification number), the `schema` (which governs it) and the object `class` (to which it belongs). Once you've identified that you want to change or monitor a particular item in the directory structure, you bind an object to that item. For example, suppose we want to change a user account:

```
Set objUser = GetObject("WinNT://DOMAIN/UserName")
```

Here, `DOMAIN` is the name of our local domain and `UserName` is the name of the account.

We can now access those six core properties with the simple *object.method* syntax, and print them on the screen. Since we've bound to a `User` object, we also have access to the properties and methods defined by the ADSI `User` object. The number of properties varies from one namespace provider to another; in `WinNT://`, there are 48 properties and three methods – more configurable options than you'd find in the User Manager.

The other key thing that's useful to know is how to enumerate the objects within a container – e.g. the users within a group, or the computers within a domain. In this case, the code varies slightly depending on whether the container objects are members or children of the container. For example, users are members of a group, while groups are children of a domain.

The code to enumerate the User members of the Administrators group looks like this:

```
<HTML>
<BODY>
<%
   Dim oGroup
   Dim oMember

   Set oGroup = GetObject("WinNT://DOMAIN/Administrators")
   For Each oMember in oGroup.Members
      Response.Write oMember.Name & "<BR>"
   Next
%>
</BODY>
</HTML>
```

If we want to list the children of an object, it's a simple case of altering the `For Each...Next` loop to read as follows:

```
Set oContainer = GetObject("WinNT://DOMAIN")
For Each oChild in oContainer
  Response.Write oChild.Name & "<BR>"
Next
```

These really are the two key coding methods to appreciate in an ADSI page. With these techniques safely under your belt, it's a matter of finding out what properties and methods each object class supports. To do that, you can either consult the ADSI help files or write a quick ASP page to enumerate the members of the `MandatoryProperties` and `OptionalProperties` properties of the schema for that object's class.

Suggested Applications

It may seem as though ADSI is oriented towards system administration – indeed, the obvious application for ADSI may well be creating a remote administration kit. However, by adding ADSI and ADO to ASP (and we could throw a few other things into the pot too) we can use any of the resources that are accessible via ADSI, in any namespace, for many practical applications. For example:

❑ **Personalized Intranet:** Instead of creating a user database with ADO, you could extend the user schema with personalization properties using ADSI, and then refer to this information to personalize your intranet to the user's taste.

❑ **Automated website providers:** With its access to the `IIS://` namespace, you could create a request page for users who wish to create their own homepages. You can then use ADSI or the `FileSystemObject` object to create a new virtual or physical directory respectively on which to locate the home page, and pass details back to the requester explaining how to access that page.

❑ **Project management:** A system could be set up such that each project in your company is represented by an 'ADSI Project Object' defined by the schema, with project-related status reports and facts defined as properties of the project object. Another property could perhaps point to a small database governed by ADO, which contains all communication about the project in a searchable format for reference purposes. This communication might take the form of many emails copied and put into the database using ADO and CDO.

ADSI is much more applicable than you might think. Moreover, with the approach of Web Based Enterprise Management (WBEM) (the ADSI counterpart for Enterprise management, finally heralded in with the release of Service Pack 4 for NT), we can expect ADSI's profile to keep on rising.

I Need to Know More

ADSI 2.0 is available as a download from Microsoft's Backoffice download page at `http://backoffice.microsoft.com`. In fact, ADSI comes in two different forms - the set of runtime libraries, and the SDK for writing your own namespace provider. To use ADSI with ASP, you need only the runtime libraries and the accompanying help files. However, it should be noted that the help files are intended to assist developers writing ADSI client applications in Visual Basic or C++.

There is only one book on ADSI website programming at the moment – it's *ADSI ASP Programmer's Reference* by Steven Hahn (Wrox Press, 1998, ISBN 1-861001-69-X). However, there are a few sites on the web which provide ADSI references and help pages. Once again, `www.15seconds.com` comes up trumps, hosting an ADSI listserv for those with problems on which you'd like to canvas others' opinions. There is also one ADSI newsgroup – `microsoft.public.active.directory.interfaces` – which has an active stream of Q&A threads on it (though it's not as busy as one might expect). Microsoft hasn't exactly pushed ADSI as yet – instead, it has been allowed simply to exist in the background until now. However, once Windows 2000 appears, we can expect that to change.

Collaborative Data Objects

Computers talk to themselves all the time, with conversations between components saying what to do and when to do it, and messages being sent to the applications that they're hosting. These inter-process calls do the nasty job of keeping track of which task is being done on what thread and keeping one component in contact with another.

At another level, computers are forever sending us messages that either we've sent ourselves, or others have sent to us; emails, reminders to attend meetings, calendar displays and PIMs. We have already seen how we can get to the data and directory service of a computer, using ADO and ADSI respectively. Not surprisingly, we can also tap into the flows of both kinds of messages, allowing us to send some of our own, and to manipulate those messages already received and create some output for the web as a result. Later (when we cover the rest of the NT Option Pack) we'll look at MSMQ, which deals with inter-process, inter-system and inter-applcation calls. But for now, we'll deal with mail messages – and that means using **Collaborative Data Objects (CDO)** in our ASP pages.

In the late 1980s, Microsoft saw the potential in mail systems and created the **Mail Application Programming Interfaces (MAPI)**. MAPI soon became the acknowledged standard around which to build any PC-based client/server mail program and create or make use of an already established MAPI-compliant mail transport layer. CDO is actually the fourth generation of the MAPI platform and was designed with access and utility for web programmers in mind. With it, ASP coders have the facility to extract and render any piece of information from any messaging system – including scheduling, calendaring and all other MAPI-based applications.

How Does it Work?

Previous incarnations of the MAPI standard have been almost all client-based, but of course, web technology tries to keep any client-side technology as thin as possible – so that the browser has less to do and performs at a faster rate. Therefore, CDO is based on the server-side, but as a consequence it's still faced with two problems:

❑ To get access to message stores, CDO needs client-side information like userid, password and location to be accessible on the server.

❑ The MAPI object model is pretty cumbersome and not suited to fast responses needed for the web of today.

Both of these issues are addressed by CDO, although the solutions bring their own stumbling blocks.

Dynamic Profiles

When you log in to your mailbox, the mail server needs to know where your mailbox is and how you want it presented. This configuration information is stored in a 'profile', on the client-side. Now, suppose we created a set of ASP/CDO pages on our web server, to access mailboxes and display their contents on the web. In order to access the *correct* mail folders, we would also need to find out the mail folder information from the profile – and as we know, the profile is on the client-side. Therefore, CDO generates user profiles dynamically on the web server, and stores them as .mmp files in the Exchsrv\webtemp directory.

Currently, this dynamic ability is limited only to generating profiles for use with Exchange Server; this means that any web-based mail activity is limited solely to interacting with this product.

> *There are still a few bugs in CDO, with respect to it working in a multi-Exchange Server environment – if you attempt to access the public folders of more than one server, they will find that only those of the Exchange Server bound to the web server are actually available for use. However, the same is not true of Private folders – which can be accessed from any server in the environment. For now, the solution is to replicate the remote folder's contents over to the local Exchange Server and set the local Exchange Server as the Home Server.*

The CDO Object Model

The previous versions of MAPI had quite a bulky object model that wasn't well-suited to working for the web. However, CDO's object model is lighter (though to be fair, it's still pretty heavy) and contains two object classes, MAPI and CDOHTML. Let's look at the MAPI object class first:

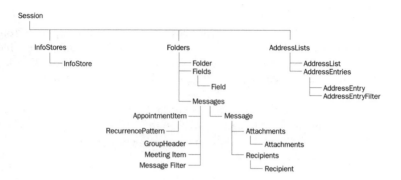

The MAPI class defines a set of 23 objects, which represent a fair collection of viewpoints within the mail application – from the InfoStore in which the message is contained, to the Message itself. These objects form a logical hierarchy, making it a lot easier to navigate your way to any item that you want.

Every CDO-based website begins with the creation of a MAPI.Session object, and with it a profile (either dynamically generated, or local). The profile presents us with the information that gives us access to one or more InfoStores and AddressLists.

Though they are likely to contain e-mail folders, Infostores may also hold calendars, schedules and tasks. If you're familiar with Exchange Server, you can think of an Infostore as being equivalent to the **Mailbox - Username** or **Public Folders** folders that you use every day. Within an Infostore is a set of Folders; each of these folders may contain other Folders or Messages. Each message may be an AppointmentItem, a MeetingItem or an email Message and can be sorted through with a MessageFilter. Meanwhile, AddressLists may hold a number of AddressEntries which may also be sorted through with an AddressEntryFilter.

While MAPI is the legacy, general object class, CDOHTML is the new addition to the object model in this incarnation of Mail API. Here's the CDOHTML class diagram:

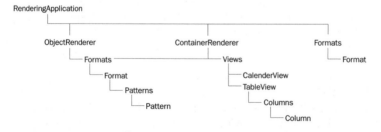

As far as web developers are concerned, it's from the CDOHTML class that the power of CDO stems. Once we've targeted what part of a user's messages we wish to access – whether it's a portion of one, some or all – the class's methods can render them dynamically into a customizable HTML table on a web page. Moreover, if those messages were previously stored in the Rich Text File format, their layout and formatting will be preserved.

*In the early releases of CDO (until version 1.1), this whole technology was known as **Active Messaging** and this object class was referred to as AMHTML. Since the release of Exchange 5.5, the current name for MAPI4 has been CDO and the object class known as CDOHTML.*

Going Through The Motions

Let's see how we use CDO to access Exchange and send a message. The first thing we need to do is log on to Windows NT.

Ideally, any CDO site should be in its own virtual directory with IIS Anonymous Access turned off, forcing users to log on. However, if IIS Anonymous Access is turned on then it's a simple matter to query AUTH_TYPE from the Request.ServerVariables collection, and force a log on box to appear if necessary. It is possible to log on as the anonymous guest user, IUSR_MachineName, but if we try to access any of the objects in the Session object, we'll get an error in return.

Assuming that we have logged on satisfactorily, the next task is to create the objects that will encompass the profile we want to use. A CDO session should last no longer than an ASP session, so it makes sense to instantiate MAPI (and CDOHTML if wanted) from global.asa. However, we still have a choice to make: Do we dynamically create a user profile on the client or on the server?

In the case of some distributed applications, it might be beneficial to create a specific profile under the browser, but it would be a little difficult to set up every browser that needed one correctly. Still, if we chose to create a client side profile, we would call

```
Set objClientsideSession = CreateObject("MAPI.Session") _
```

Else we declare

```
Set objServersideSession = Server.CreateObject("MAPI.Session")
```

to create a user profile on the server instead. Now we must see about logging onto a profile. This takes one call to the Logon method of MAPI.Session. This has seven parameters:

```
objServerSideSession.Logon ProfileName, Password, DialogBox, _
                   NewSession, PassDialog, NoMail, ProfileInfo
```

Here,

- ❑   ProfileName is the Profile name
- ❑   Password is the Profile's password
- ❑   DialogBox. If set to true, a Choose Profile dialog box will appear prompting for a profile and password – in a web application, this must be false

- ❏ NewSession is a Boolean variable that determines whether or not the new session should be part of the current shared MAPI session or a new session. This should be true to reduce the overhead on IIS.

- ❏ PassDialog refers to an option to pass the login dialog to a new or the parent window. Default is 0 or false

- ❏ NoMail is a Boolean variable, that determines whether or not the client will have permission to send or receive mail

- ❏ ProfileInfo is for use with dynamically created server-side profiles. This is a string that contains the Exchange Server computer's name and the Mailbox Recipients Alias name. It replaces the need to fill in the first two parameters.

Assuming we've chosen to create a profile dynamically, we query the client for the machine and mailbox that they want to log in to. With the information that they provide, we make the following call:

```
strProfileInfo = strServer + vbLF + strMailbox
objServerSideSession.Logon "", "", False, True, 0, True, bstrProfileInfo
```

If we don't get an error back from Exchange, we should look for something to latch onto. Every mail account in Exchange has an Inbox, so we'll try for that and see what its current name is:

```
Set objFolder = objSession.Inbox
Response.Write objFolder.Name
```

From here on, it's up to you what you do with CDO. Let's send a quick message to my brother at university for example.

```
Set objNewMail = objServerSideSession.Outbox.Messages.Add
objNewMail.Subject = "Hey Luke"
objNewMail.Text = "Good luck in your exams"

Set objAddressee = objNewMail.Recipients.Add
ObjAddressee.Name = "Luke Maharry"
ObjAddressee.Type = mapiTo
ObjAddressee.Resolve
ObjMessage.Send
```

The process of sending mail with CDO is not that intuitive to newcomers but is fairly straightforward otherwise. First we create a new mail item, place it in our outbox and give it a subject and message body. Next we add someone to the message's Recipients list. We give the addressee a name and identify that the message is being sent To him (as opposed to cc or bcc). Finally, we ask the mail client to resolve the name we've given the addressee. If it can't find an entry for the name in an address book somewhere, it will pop up a dialog box for us to select a name it does recognize. Finally we send the message.

Don't forget to log off the mailbox when you've finished. The call is simple:

```
ObjServerSideSession.Logoff
```

For the sake of completeness, don't neglect your obligation to free your server's resources – when you've finished using an object, set it to Nothing.

If you don't use Exchange Server, but you do have a copy of the NT Option Pack, then you might like to try and expand on this example using the simple SMTP Relay Server and the cut down version of CDO, CDO for NTS, that are available on it. CDONTS, as it is known, is designed purely for those who wish to manipulate mail messages, and supports none of the other features in CDO like calendaring, schedules or workflow. Such is its streamlined nature, that by using its additional object, NewMail, you can send an email message in three lines with the following code

```
Set objNewMail = CreateObject("CDONTS.NewMail")
ObjNewMail.Send ("FromAddress", "ToAddress", "MessageSubject", "MessageText")
Set objNewMail = Nothing
```

Quite an improvement over the eight lines it takes to do that using the full blown version of CDO.

Suggested Applications

It goes without saying that there's a lot you can do with CDO; in particular, if you combine it with ADSI it gives you access to any directory service or messaging application that supports the standard ADSI or Mail APIs. Rather than telling you what's possible, we suggest you take a look at Outlook Web Access (OWA).

OWA is a completely web-based version of Microsoft's Outlook that securely and reliably provides you with the basic mail and scheduling facilities of the standard version with little in the way of a drawback. You can find out more about it by having a look at http://www.microsoft.com/office/98/outlook/documents/WebAccessExchange.htm.

Where to Find More Information

At the time of writing, the current release of CDO is version 1.21. As this suggests, CDO is still pretty new; consequently, there's not much information available on CDO at the moment. There are currently no books that cover CDO to any great depth, but Wrox Press is in the process of developing a book – by Todd Mondor and Mikael Freidlitz – on the subject of ADSI and CDO web applications. Watch this space…

Out on the web, there are a few sites with information on CDO. The best place to look is the MSDN Online Library site, at http://premium.microsoft.com/msdn/library. Overviews and object model specifics on CDO can be found there, under Platform SDK\Database and Messaging Services\Collaboration Data Objects. There are also a few articles on CDO to be had at www.15seconds.com and www.activeserverpages.com.

Also in the NT Option Pack

The *Windows NT 4.0 Option Pack* is a veritable treasure trove of extensions and improvements. You already know that we can install ASP 2.0 from the Option Pack (as part of along PWS or IIS); and that ADO/RDS 1.5 are both available in the Option Pack (under the moniker of MDAC). If you chose the Custom installation option when you put these on your hard drive, you will have seen three more servers available for installation. These new servers don't offer us much in the way of new language – rather they offer new ways to manage our code:

- ❑ **MTS** offers us a greater degree of automation for our ASP components, along with support for transactions. It's actually installed automatically with ASP, but it's an option to install the documentation and samples.
- ❑ **MSMQ** offers messaging capabilities to our website
- ❑ **Certificate Server** adds extra security features

There are two other products — Index Server and Site Server Express — that also come in the Option Pack but they are not covered in this book.

Microsoft Transaction Server

The greater the complexity of your site, the more you need to fine-tune the site so that it's capable of looking after itself once it goes live. There are two parts to this: thorough testing and good coding. Let's focus for a moment on the second of these points. The importance of good coding comes from our need to make efficient use of our resources: instantiating objects only when we need them and releasing them when we're done. However, coding all this ourselves is a hassle, and it's not always clean. It's much easier, and tidier, to allow Microsoft Transaction Server (MTS) to take care of it automatically.

We can also ask MTS to make the actions of a component behave like **transactions**. When developing a stand-alone web application (be it for e-commerce, data referrals or whatever), you'll end up using at least a few Active Server components to encapsulate some of the lower level coding that runs the site. When a component performs an action, the complete action is usually made up of a number of tasks. Using MTS, we can check that all the tasks are performed correctly – in which case the transaction is **committed**. On the other hand, if any task is incorrectly performed, or fails, the whole transaction is **aborted** – in this case, we undo (or 'rollback') all of the other tasks in the action and return to the previous consistent state.

The classic illustration of this is to consider an e-bank situation. Suppose an employee is transferring $100 from account A to account B, *just* as the e-bank crashed. If this was not a transactional routine, there would be no way of knowing whether the complete transfer has taken place – if the crash occurs *after* the debit of A but *before* the credit of B, then $100 has disappeared! By implementing the transfer as a transaction, the system would realize that the 'credit' task had failed, and would therefore roll back the 'debit' task – thus maintaining consistency.

The Component Manager

If you decide to take advantage of MTS, then the components that you've designed must make use of the Application Programming Interfaces (APIs) that are installed with MTS. These new interfaces allow the component to inform MTS that its work has been completed successfully (with a call to `SetComplete`), to abort the work if an error occurred (with a call to `SetAbort`), and to create other objects that work within the MTS environment.

When you've completed writing the components for your application, you need to register their common usage and their presence with MTS. This is done by creating a 'package' for your application within MTS and installing the components in the package. Once in, they should look like this from MTS Explorer:

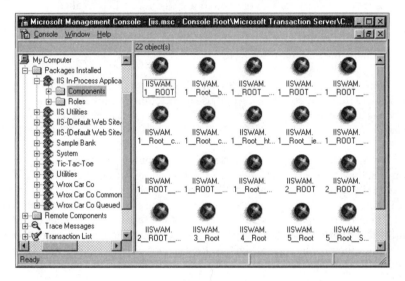

You can also use this screen to select the level of transactional support required by each of your components – this is done by right-clicking on the component's icon and choosing Properties. If you click on the Transaction tab, you'll see four choices for the component:

❑ Requires a transaction – the component must run within a transaction. If a component is called during a transaction, it can 'be active' within that transaction. If a component is called from outside of a transaction, then a transaction must be initiated in which to execute the component.

❑ Requires a new transaction – the component has to run within its own transaction, even if it is called in the middle of another transaction; MTS will create the new transaction.

❑ Supports transactions – the component can participate in a transaction if called from within one; but it's not necessary to create a new transaction if it's the component that is called initially.

❑ Does not support transactions – if called from within a transaction, the component will still be executed outside of that transaction. If the component is called before a transaction has been created, no new transaction will be created. This is the default setting for all newly-installed components in MTS.

Once installed in a package, a component's lifetime within the component manager has four simple stages:

❑ It is created within MTS, but is not activated yet, leaving resources free for other uses
❑ When a method of the object is called, MTS 'just-in-time' activates the component to execute it until the method is either completed (when SetComplete is called) or aborted (by SetAbort being called)
❑ When this happens, the component is 'deactivated', not destroyed, freeing up resources again
❑ Finally, the object is destroyed

Aside from a few extra lines of code (to tell MTS to commit or abort), MTS components are just standard COM components that use up machine resources until the point at which they are destroyed. However, they are also designed to either **have state** or be **stateless**.

Components with state are designed to retain their 'context'. In plain language, this means that they are designed to keep their settings from the last time they were used. However, if a component is deactivated as described above, the resources used to hold those settings are returned to the resource pool and used elsewhere, and their context is lost. Thus components with state cannot alert MTS that their action has either been committed or aborted with SetComplete or SetAbort and must lock down some resources for their continued survival. So they cannot be installed into an MTS package alongside the stateless components.

Unsurprisingly, applications that mostly use components with state do not scale very well in terms of frequency of hits on the server (compared with an application that mostly uses stateless components, which have no need to retain the resources they used when running a method). One solution to this problem however is to co-opt in the facilities that ASP itself has to retain state - i.e. the Session object and variables stored within it. If a component is designed to have some sort of state but will lose it if managed by MTS, the designer should store the information that defines the state of the component within one or more session variables. The component then has a quasi-state and the server will benefit from its management by MTS. Of course, the best solution and the one recommended for all MTS components is for a stateless design.

Transactional Active Server Pages

For ASP, a significant advantage of MTS is the ability to declare an ASP script as a transaction. Exactly the same transactional principles that are used by components are then applied to a script: either everything in the script completes and SetComplete is called, or something untoward happens and we call SetAbort. These scripts may also activate and use components in their execution, tying them all into a single transaction; and the script will always fire off an event when the transaction has ended, which you may or may not choose to make use of in your code.

There is one problem that comes with using transactional scripts. If a transaction aborts, any changes made using the script (such as changes to session or application variables) will *not* automatically be rolled back. We'll see a little further on look at how transactional events notify us whenever a transaction has aborted. When you handle this event, you can manually rollback any changes that MTS can't perform automatically.

None of this will happen unless we declare the level of transaction support that a script requires of MTS at the very top of the page (it must be the very first item in the ASP script):

```
<%@ TRANSACTION = TransSuppLevel %>
```

Here, TransSuppLevel can be one of four settings – Required, Requires_New, Supported or Not_Supported. These are equivalent to the options for a component's support level that we saw earlier. For ASP Required is really the only one that needs to be used. Since the largest granularity of transactions in ASP is the page itself, setting Requires_New is the same as setting Required, since no transaction can ever be active. Supported will not cause anything to happen, since no other entity can include an ASP page within a transaction. Not_Supported is the default.

Of course, if you are keeping to the 'good ASP' style guide that we included in Chapter 1, this line should actually read something like:

```
<%@ LANGUAGE = "VBScript" TRANSACTION = "Not_Supported" %>
```

This is because you should also declare the script's language, but ASP only allows one line beginning with <%@. Once you've done that, it's up to you to decide how to approach the script as a transaction. You can either allow MTS to automatically declare it complete or aborted (sloppy coding – avoid this if possible), or you can take some direct hand in it and make use of the ObjectContext object.

The ObjectContext Object

The ObjectContext object is installed with IIS, but doesn't become available until MTS is also installed on your server. It has two methods and two events that allow our ASP script logic to co-operate with the MTS environment that is hosting our components.

❑ The SetAbort method declares that the transaction initiated by the script has not completed successfully, which causes MTS to abort the current transaction. Any component that is participating in the transaction will be informed that the transaction was aborted and will roll back any changes it has made.

❑ The SetComplete method declares that the script is not aware of any reason for the transaction not to complete. If there are a number of components participating in the transaction, and they *all* call SetComplete, the transaction will complete.

One of two events will fire when the entire page has been processed. If no calls to SetAbort have been made, the OnTransactionCommit event will occur; otherwise the OnTransactionAbort event will fire.

The following script shows a possible transactional ASP page.

```
<%@ TRANSACTION = Required %>
<%
  Set objOnHand = Server.CreateObject("BookComp.OnHand")
  Set objSales = Server.CreateObject("BookComp.Sales")
  iQuantity = Request("Quantity")
  ProductID = Request("ProductID")
  strStatus = objOnHand.CheckOnHand(iQuantity, ProductID)

  If strStatus = "INS"
      ObjectContext.SetAbort
  Else
      ObjectContext.SetComplete
      acctInfo = Request("AcctInfo")
      Update = objSales.ProcessSale(acctInfo)
  End If
%>
```

If we take a look at this code in detail, you can see how the MTS code integrates very easily with the ASP code. As we have seen, the line

```
<%@ TRANSACTION = Required %>
```

indicates that this script must be within the bounds of a transaction. Since a transaction cannot span multiple ASP scripts, there will be no active transaction when this page starts. This will force MTS to create a new transaction, that will encompass this page and the two components referenced from within it. We create references to two components, the OnHand and Sales components, with a method which should be familiar from Chapter 7. Since MTS is providing the environment for this page, they will be created within the current object context of the transaction for this page. We then collect our quantity and product information, and call the CheckOnHand method to verify that we have enough of the item in stock.

A Failed Transaction

Let's assume that the method indicated that there was insufficient inventory to process the request, returning a value of INS. We need to check the return value of a method in order to know whether we need to abort the transaction. The SetAbort method is explicitly called by the script to indicate that this transaction should not be completed. If the CheckOnHand method performed any database modifications, such as requesting that items be removed from inventory, then the act of aborting the transaction will cause any changes to the database to be rolled back.

A Successful Transaction

If the inventory check was successful, then the sale transaction may continue. Since all of the processing that needs to be done by the script has completed successfully, the SetComplete method is called. It is not necessary to call this method explicitly, since it will be called once the script reaches the end. The final part of the script invokes the ProcessSale method to complete the sale.

We can also write an OnTransactionCommit or an OnTransactionAbort subroutine that will process when the event of that name fires. For example, you might want to execute the following code when a transaction is committed:

```
Sub OnTransactionCommit()
    Response.Write("<P>Thank you for placing your order.</P>")
    Response.Write("<P>Your order number is "& CStr(iOrderNum) & ".</P>")
    Response.Write("</BODY></HTML>")
End sub
```

We can display a message to the client indicating a successful order, using an order number that we have returned from a server component. Note that since this is called at the end of the page, we need to formally close the HTML stream by adding a </BODY></HTML> to the end of the page.

If the OnTransactionAbort event had fired however, we might want to execute some code like this:

```
Sub OnTransactionAbort()
    Response.Write("<P>An error has occurred in processing your order</P>")
    Response.Write("<P>We are unable to complete it at this time.</P>")
    Response.Write("</BODY></HTML>")
End sub
```

This message displays an indication on the client that the transaction was unsuccessful. Any changes to durable data that were made in the server component will be automatically rolled back. If there was any ASP session or application data that was changed in the transaction, those changes can be rolled back at this point. Since ASP does not provide for automatic rollback of changes made via ASP script, the code to support the rollback will need to be explicitly written. The OnTransactionAbort method is the ideal place to reference that code from.

Microsoft Message Queues

While the 'all-or-nothing' nature of a transaction is very useful, it can also create problems – you can't commit any of the component parts of a transaction until *all* have them been completed successfully. For example, suppose your transaction contains a component part that is to be performed over a distributed system, which depends on something as inherently unreliable as the Internet for communications. If the router is down, or the target machine is unavailable, or the target machine's operating system can't natively speak with your own server, then the whole transaction rolls back – not because it can't perform the action, but because of a 'hardware problem'.

Combining Microsoft Message Queues (MSMQ) with MTS provides a remedy for the temporary nature of the network across which a distributed application runs by offering:

❑   A means of communication between different systems and components
❑   Guaranteed message delivery over slow and unreliable connections through the use of asynchronous message queues
❑   Support for transactional messaging, allowing a rollback if the message is not received.

With these three facilities at our disposal, our applications are more robust, more 'patient' and more 'talkative'. The messages handled by MSMQ are not email messages (that's the realm of CDO); instead, they are a replacement for inter-process calls between machines for the continued execution of an application. They can also replace inter-application and inter-system calls as well.

Talking to Alien Systems

Microsoft's message queuing system is not the only one in existence, but it is the only one made for the COM/DCOM architecture upon which everything Windows DNA-based (including ASP) is run. Other messaging platforms include MD and IBM MQ, which exist for other computer architectures like OS/2, Sun, Solaris, HP-UNIX and AIX-UNIX.

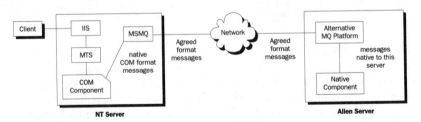

The key elements in enabling each messaging platform to talk to all the others are the components written for each platform – these control the messaging system. In the diagram above, the COM component and the Native component need to agree on a common format before they can begin to send and retrieve messages. They can then use this message format to translate to and from the native style for their operating system.

Connectionless Communication

We can use MSMQ to get around the 'no response' quandary mentioned earlier, because it supports the asynchronous queuing of messages. First the foundation must be laid – the calling computer and recipient computer decide together where (on the calling computer) the queue lives. When a message is to be sent, MSMQ wraps it up in a special COM package and appends it to the queue. While the recipient server is 'online', it picks up messages addressed to it by searching for this queue on the calling computer. If the recipient is 'offline' , the message remains in the queue until it is picked up (or until the 'dead letter' timeout is reached, in which case the message is transferred to the dead letter queue).

If you're using Windows NT 4.0, the message queues themselves are stored in a SQL Server database that is set up during the installation of MSMQ. If you haven't got a full copy of SQL Server then there's usually a scaled-down version of that product included with MSMQ, to get you around that sticking point.

Working with MSMQ

Like MTS, MSMQ comes with a set of APIs and a set of ActiveX objects that wrap up the API functions and make them available to ASP. There are ten such objects for working with MSMQ. Five of them allow us to interact with the queues and messages themselves, and exist in a nice logical hierarchy:

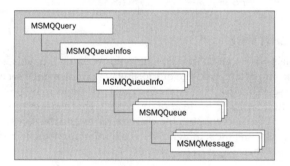

MSMQQuery is the parent container for the entire MSMQ environment. It holds MSMQQueueInfos, which maintains a list of all the queues that have been created. When you've found the queue you're looking for, you can create an MSMQQueueInfo object and alter some of that queue's basic properties and methods, if you wish. MSMQQueue represents unique, *open* instances of a queue, some of which may exist side-by-side if the queue is used by more than one application at the same time. Finally, MSMQMessage is the message object that allows us to create, send and refer to received messages.

With just these five objects, we can perform the basic tasks of creating, updating and deleting queues, locating and opening an existing queue and sending and receiving messages. In fact, to send a message we need only one object – MSMQMessage – and a reference to the destination queue. Rather than using the properties and methods of a queue to send a message, by using the MSMQMessage object we have the option to send the message to any queue, provided it is of the right type – it might be transactional or even encrypted.

For example, let's say that we want to send the latest score at a football game to CNN's vidiprinter for the Active Desktop. The code would look something like this:

```
...
If VidiprinterQueue.IsOpen Then
   Set LatestScores = Server.CreateObject("MSMQ.MSMQMessage")
   LatestScores.Priority = 2
   LatestScores.Label = "Latest Scores at " & FormatDateTime(Now, vTime)
   LatestScores.Body = "Patriots 45, Packers 0"
   LatestScores.Send VidiPrinterQueue
   Response.Write "Latest scores sent"
Else
   Response.Write "Vidiprinter offline"
End If
...
```

The MSMQMessage object has over 30 properties whose values you can set before the send method is called; but this short example should give you an idea of the kind of code you can use to interact with MSMQ. Like MTS, there's not much new code to learn but there are plenty of possibilities you can make real by using it.

Certificate Server

Perhaps the one subject we haven't covered at all in this book until now is how to secure our web site from prying eyes. The quickest way to implement a security measure is simply to send our pages over the Secure HTTP protocol by prefixing the links in our pages with https:// (instead of http://). This requires the use of the secure sockets layer (SSL) to encrypt both the client requests and the server responses going over the web, protecting their content. Many sites that implement credit card ordering facilities secure their pages in this way.

For the more paranoid clients and servers, Certificate Server allows you to create, issue, renew and revoke digital certificates of identity for a bit of extra security. Once a (client or server) machine has been issued with a digital certificate, it can present the certificate when it interacts with other machines, as proof that they are who they say they are. Servers can read and react to the certificate using the Request.ClientCertificate collection.

Certificates can also eradicate the hassle of multiple logons for clients as they navigate through the different security levels of a site. To do this, the certificate can contain an Access Control List (ACL) that states what the owner of the certificate can and cannot do on a system. A web site can access this ACL using the Response.ClientCertificate collection, and allow or deny access as appropriate.

If you are worried that certificates work only over one platform, there's no need. Certificate Server can produce and receive digital certificates that conform to any of three standard public key encryption techniques – PKCS #10, x509.3 and PKCS #7. Any platform that makes use of encryption for security purposes should be able to decrypt the information stored there without too much trouble. It can also produce certificates that conform to the Secure Sockets Layer (SSL), Secure MIME (S/MIME) and Secure Electronic Extensions (SET) protocols to make other applications secure as well.

For More Information

If you're looking for more information on how to incorporate MTS and MSMQ into your web applications, try *Professional MTS MSMQ Programming with VB and ASP* by Alex Homer and David Sussman (Wrox, 1998, ISBN 1-861001-46-0). In addition, there are a number of books coming out in early 1999 that focus more on the design of components to work with MTS. There's also *Designing Applications with MSMQ* by Alan Dickman (Addison-Wesley, 1998, ISBN 0-201325-81-0) – this looks at using MSMQ in your applications, but again, doesn't focus so much on using it within a web application. Again, Professional ASP 2.0 by Brian Francis et al, covers both of these technologies quite thoroughly.

Out on the web, there are now more than a few sites out there that deal with MTS and MSMQ. Try out Microsoft's NT Server pages to begin with at `http://www.microsoft.com/ntserver/appservice/default.asp` and then go from there.

Certificate Server, meanwhile, draws a big blank in terms of books covering it specifically, but any good ASP security book should contain a small section on its abilities and how to use it. See Appendix H for those available. Likewise, the web contains less material about it than you would guess. However, Microsoft's site does have a small amount of information within their security pages, that you can begin with, at http://www.microsoft.com/security/products/certserver.asp.

Summary

In this chapter, we have had a brief look at six technologies that extend and enhance ASP. Whether we are looking to access databases, directory services or MAPI-based systems or add transactional capability, asynchronous, multi-platform messaging, higher levels of security to our web site, we have seen the technologies that can provide the functionality to do so.

Of course, there are many other web technologies that aren't strictly within bounds of 'extending-ASP'. If you're looking for still more in your website, then don't forget that you have three very functional scripting languages at your disposal – VBScript, JScrit and JavaScript – and that new incarnations of all three are soon to be released. In addition, why not add to your static HTML pages using Dynamic HTML to animate a few things; or go one step further and investigate eXtensible Mark-up Language (XML) as a completely new base for your pages? You could make use of Index Server to make your site searchable, or add a few scriptlets and some ActiveX controls for nostalgia's sake.

As part of the Windows DNA plan, don't forget either that ASP has its roots in Microsoft's Component Object Model (COM) application architecture. With a low-level language like C++ we can access the ASP intrinsic objects as well as every other object mentioned in this chapter through their COM interface and build up applications and components completely from scratch. You'll see the various object models in a completely new light.

Of course, ASP itself is appearing in new colors within the release of Windows 2000, and it is to ASP 3.0 that we turn our attention in the next chapter.

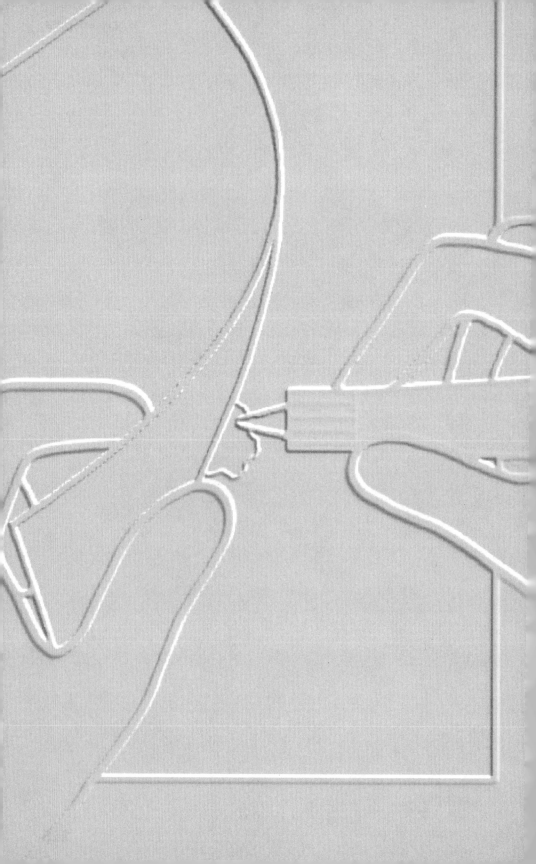

10

The Future: ASP 3.0

The Internet and its associated technologies are constantly and consistently evolving. New ideas and products continue to spring up – by the time we have learnt how to use them, they're being replaced by a newer, faster and flashier thing. All things considered, ASP has stood the test of time very well. It's been around for eighteen months, with only one slight change in that time. The differences between ASP 1.0 and ASP 2.0 were all for the better, and we can look out for similar improvements in the next version, which will arrive in the first half of next year as part of Internet Information Server 5.0, which is to be shipped with Windows 2000.

The second beta release of Windows 2000 (or NT5, as it was previously called) was actually feature-complete – this means that we've got a first look at ASP 3.0, albeit in a less-than-optimized state. The emphasis in this new release is on two things

❑   Improved performance from the parser and basic ASP components
❑   The scalability and robustness of web applications that build on the ASP 3.0 framework

It's not so much a complete overhaul (as with Windows 3.1 to Windows 95), but more of an enhancement (like Windows 95 to Windows 98). In this chapter, we'll have a look at what's new and what's improved in the forthcoming version of ASP.

Improvements Over ASP 2.0

ASP 3.0 includes some changes to the ASP object model. The Server object has gained the most, with three new methods added to its utility. There have also been two alterations to the object model itself. The first is a brand new object – the ASP Error object. The second is the inclusion of the existing ObjectContext object (which supports transactions) in the basic ASP object model. This means that in ASP 3.0 the methods and properties of the intrinsic ASP objects will be accessed through methods of the ObjectContext object, and not the ScriptingContext object.

A Changed Default

Putting those new features aside for a minute, ASP 3.0 also makes a change to one of its default operation settings, `Response.Buffer`. Response buffering is switched on by default. This means that (unless someone specifically calls `Response.Buffer = False`) none of the content will be sent to a client browser until the page has either been completely processed on the server, or `Response.Flush` is called. As we mentioned in Chapter 1, if buffering is on, the performance of ASP is enhanced – it doesn't have to worry about sending fragments of HTML and extra HTTP Headers back to the client in the middle of work. We will now have to remember to turn buffering off for debugging purposes and also, should the need arise, to send XML data. We'll look at the new XML support later on.

New Redirection Methods

If you're a regular visitor to the Microsoft website, you may well have noticed that the site has a facelift every 12 months or so. As a consequence, all the pages get reorganized and put into new areas. The end result is a new look to the site and a lot of ghost pages that still exist but simply say that the page has moved to a new location. Microsoft does at least explain this politely; but there are many sites which, when reorganized, merely display the standard '302 : Object Moved' page as a result of a `Response.Redirect` statement at the old address.

This client-side redirect method has now been joined by two server-side relocation methods attached to the server object – `Transfer` and `Execute`.

As you'll recall, `Redirect` works by sending '302 : Object Moved' back to the client in an HTTP Header, along with the new address of the page. If buffering is on, then the client invisibly requests the new page. If not, you get the Object Moved page:

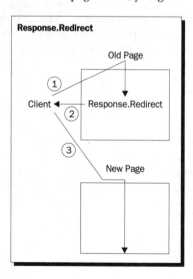

In contrast, the two new methods *don't* announce to the client that the page has moved. Instead, Server.Transfer simply asks the server to go to the new location and display it, with no questions asked. Server.Execute displays the target page within the page with the execute statement, effectively sandwiching one page into another.

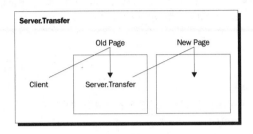

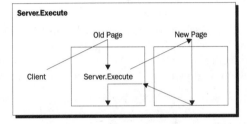

The variables created within the calling page are lost when you redirect to the new page, but the state of the intrinsic objects (their collections and the variables stored within them for Session) is retained from the calling page for use in the new one.

Moving to a Transactional Page

One more point to note with respect to these new flow controls is the transactional support for the page that's called. As we saw in Chapter 9, once MTS is installed alongside IIS and ASP, every ASP page may use the flags Required, Requires_new, Supported and Not_Supported to indicate the required level of transactional support. If Server.Transfer or Server.Execute points to a page that uses these flags, then the page's flag state will be upheld.

Furthermore, if the original page begins a transaction, and then the server's attention is transferred, if the new page either requires or supports transactions, then the transaction begun by the original page will be used (no new transaction will be started).

What role these methods leave for Response.Redirect, – apart from supporting legacy pages – is not immediately clear. With response buffering turned on, Response.Redirect's effect is the same as that of Server.Transfer but with a costly round trip to the client thrown in. Most likely, it will serve as a debugging check against the two new methods. The browser has no way of knowing if the new methods are being called, so Response.Redirect will change the URL shown in the address bar on the browser while Server.Transfer and Server.Execute will not. So it's a useful double-check to make sure those two methods are working correctly.

More Error Handling Capabilities

While we're on the subject of errors and debugging, a useful addition to the ASP object model here is the new ASPError object, which you can use to query information about an error that has occurred. The ASPError object is returned by another new method, Server.GetLastError, and exposes seven read-only properties, each containing a specific piece of information about the most recent error:

❑ The ASP error code

❑ The COM error code

❑ The source of the error

❑ The name of the file being processed when the error occurred

❑ The line number of the error

❑ Short and detailed descriptions of the error

The custom error pages in IIS 5.0, which currently cover all 4xx and 5xx HTTP 1.1 error codes, now also suggest corrective courses of action. In addition, they take advantage of the new server redirection methods in ASP 3.0. They can of course be replaced by your own error pages, which would do well to make use of the ASPError object and its facilities.

Enhanced Features In ASP 3.0

The majority of the improvements in ASP 3.0 are under the hood – we'll look at those in a minute. There are also a few things that we can 'see'. For example, the methodology of the Response.IsClientConnected method, has altered slightly to provide its answer to the server more quickly. In ASP 2.0, IsClientConnected could only detect that the client had disconnected *after* the server had attempted to send some content to the client (typically using Response.Write). In ASP 3.0, IsClientConnected can be queried *before* any content is sent to the client; moreover, IsClientConnected is called automatically if a response to the client has been queued for 3 seconds or more. In this case, if the client is no longer connected, the request will be disregarded.

The Active Server Components that come with ASP 2.0 have been rewritten to scale better for all sizes of application. The **Browser Capabilities** component in particular can now also read a client browser's capabilities, and update its record for that client, by reading name/value pairs from a cookie generated on the client. For example, if the client sends a cookie that contains a name/value pair userLanguage=Spanish, the Browser Capabilities component will add a userLanguage property and set the value for this property to Spanish.

A Souped-Up Engine

Behind the scenes of ASP, the parser has been improved both in speed and adaptability. Previously, a page of static content (i.e. only containing HTML and script) with a `.htm` or `.html` file extension would process slower if it were given an `.asp` extension instead. This is because the ASP 2.0 compiler scans through the `.asp` file for server-side code. In the new release, the compiler still scans any file with an `.asp` extension, but the processing of a static-content-only page with this extension is much faster than before. Processing is still slightly slower than for a `.htm` file, but the difference is now negligible. Thus, the cost of giving your static pages an `.asp` extension (perhaps with a view to adding ASP code later) is almost nil.

The compiler and runtime of the ASP Scripting Host will also have the ability to call upon more processing power from their host machine, if they find that the current resources are being blocked by external resources and other applications around their memory space. In this situation, both compiler and runtime will be able to generate new threads to execute extra requests simultaneously as required. Conversely, if compiler or runtime detect that the processor is starting to overload, then they can cut some of those threads and thus reduce the constant switching that results from too many simultaneously-executing non-blocking threads.

Removing the Waste

The ASP runtime has also improved its component-handling capabilities with the ability to release component instances automatically. This means that, when a component is instantiated by IIS4.0, the instance is only destroyed once the ASP page has finished. For example, in ASP 2.0, if you only use a component in the first five lines of a 1000-line page, it sits around and does nothing for the rest of the page's execution (bar taking up resources). In ASP 3.0, the instance will be destroyed prior to the end of the page if it is not being used. This will be true for all components that do not have the new OnEndPage flag set.

Script Encoding

One last addition to the ASP black box in time for version 3.0 is support for the encoding of client-side script generated from ASP scripts. This comes in response to developers who bemoan the fact that their client-side code is transmitted openly and unprotected from prying eyes over the web.

The actual BASE64 encoding algorithm is a feature of the new VBScript 5.0 and JScript 5.0 engines, both of which will have shipped with Internet Explorer 5.0 before Windows 2000 hits the shelves. Encoding is perhaps a strong word for the scrambling algorithm that the engines use – it will not stop any concerted effort to view your code, but it will prevent the general populace from copying the code and re-using it. The encoded scripts will be decoded at runtime so there will be no need to install a separate utility. Apparently, a function that will truly encrypt scripts will appear at a later date.

ASP 3.0 is Part of Windows 2000

Let's take a quick breather at this point. Within itself, ASP 3.0 is going to offer us a more mature product intent on getting the best performance out of what already exists. But let's not forget that ASP 3.0 will, for the time being, be available only as part of Windows 2000. Why? Simply because this new breed of our favorite web platform is inherently tied into its hosting operating system and it *won't* work without it – there are several changes under the hood of Windows 2000 which have affected ASP as well.

Introduction of COM+

One of the 'big' things touted about Windows 2000 is that it will be based upon the new version of Microsoft's Component Object Model, COM+. For casual ASP users, this means very little and has few consequences. Web application developers, on the other hand, might well notice a couple of changes in the way their components behave and take advantage of the new web-friendly features.

The first thing to notice is that Microsoft Transaction Server has been subsumed into COM+ itself. The same functionality of MTS remains as part of the operating system but the level of transaction and component management that we will get from Windows 2000 can't really be measured in comparison to MTS until we start developing with it.

The second is that COM+ also updates the security features for components. Using a new system known as 'cloaking', a component called from within an ASP page will have the security context of the web server instead of the security context of the client who owns the session. However, if the component needs to have access to the security context of the session's owner then it will do so – so that it can be recalled again later for use.

Changes in the Metabase

There have also been a few changes with regard to the ASP settings in the IIS metabase (IIS's very own registry). The most significant change is that all the ASP settings are in the metabase – and the Windows registry is now ASP free. In fact, two of the IIS registry settings have been moved to the metabase because they correspond to changes mentioned earlier. So now `ProcessorThreadMax` and `ErrorsToNTLog`, previously in `HKEY_LOCAL_MACHINE\SYSTEM\CurrentControlSet\Services\W3SVC\ASP\Parameters`, are both in the metabase.

Meanwhile, within the metabase the `AllowASPOutOfProcComponents` has been set to 1 by default, which means that ASP files can now instantiate components which run in their own process (i.e. `.exe` files) on the IIS machine by default. Previously, this default was switched off, because out-of-process components were always run in the security context of the first caller. They do not scale well, can't be run by MTS and simply slow down the server they're running on. In ASP 3.0, the option to use them is now yours.

New Technologies

Finally in this chapter, let's not forget the two 'new' technologies with which ASP will interact. Extensible Markup Language (XML) and Server Scriptlets have both been around in some form or another since the Spring of 1998, but it's only with ASP 3.0 and IIS 5.0 that both the XML parser and Server Scriptlets technology will have come out of beta.

XML

While Extensible Markup Language was initially billed as a web technology, it is rapidly attracting interest from many other areas. Originally created for document mark-up, it is receiving acceptance as a way of marking up all sorts of data. It enables people to use, re-use and transfer data marked up in XML across different platforms. This freedom arises because XML allows you to create your own tags for marking up data. Unlike HTML (which has a fixed set of tags, such as `<P>`, `<BR>`, `<H1>`) you can create tags that describe the data they are being used to mark up. So, if you were to mark up a library of books you could use tags such as this:

```
<book>
<title>Professional ASP Techniques for Webmasters</title>
<author>Alex Homer</author>
<ISBN>1-861001-79-7</ISBN>
</book>
```

As you can see, the tags actually describe their contents, meaning that it is far easier to perform general processing and retrieval on data marked up in XML. This allows you to represent complicated data structures with relative ease.

The simple example above does not show you how this data would be displayed, and that is because styling rules are kept separate from the data. The style rules are kept in a separate file called a stylesheet, which may be written in a language such as XSL (Extensible Stylesheet Language) or CSS. As you create your own tags, you will often need to define them in a schema so that applications using the XML know what the tags mean (the XML 1.0 specification uses Document Type Definitions, or DTDs). This may all seem like extra work; but once you've marked up your data in XML tags, it can be used and re-used in any application that can read XML. So our book list example could be used for a web site, a corporate intranet, a printed sales catalog, and so on. For ASP, the XML parser will produce HTML to be displayed. IE 5.0 will be the first Microsoft browser with an XML parser to let you view such files and IIS 5.0 will also support XML through ASP 3.0 and ADO 2.1.

Server Scriptlets

Reuse is the name of the game with scriptlets, a technology that's been around for quite a while now but with little or no subscription to it from the masses. As their name would suggest, Scriptlets are reusable fragments of code that can be plugged into a web page, and then executed as and when needed. Scriptlets, like include files, offer the developer another way to recycle code and save on the connection between client and server.

Server scriptlets take the reuse one level higher – we can write scriptlets that contain the information that allows it to function as a fully operational COM object. Thus, you can reuse it in web pages and also in other COM-compliant programs.

Microsoft already have areas of their website devoted to both these new technologies. You can find them at `http://www.microsoft.com/xml/` and `http://msdn.microsoft.com/scripting/`.

Summary

In this final chapter of *ASP 2.0 Programmer's Reference*, we have looked at the improved and the new features that the next version of ASP will bring with it. They fall into four basic categories:

❑ Changes to the ASP Object Model itself

❑ An enhanced ASP parser more suited to operate as the core of any site, large or small

❑ Improvements to ASP as a result of Windows 2000 integration

❑ New technologies with which you can enhance your ASP code

In these chapters, we have tried to provide a useful reference to the essential components of ASP and its extensions, what you can do with them at the moment, and where ASP is heading in the future.

The following appendices are intended to provide quick-check information for use as you code, and to complete the book as a foundation for your ASP development.

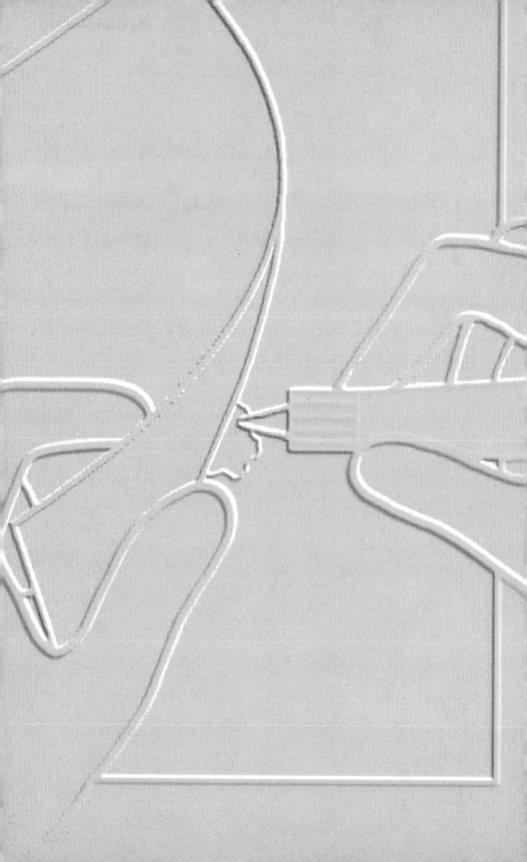

ASP 2.0 Object Model

Microsoft Active Server Pages Object Library Reference

Objects

Name	Description
Application	The main ASP application – defined as 'all the .asp files in a virtual directory and its sub-directories'.
Request	Retrieves the values passed from the client browser to the server during an HTTP request.
Response	Used for sending output to the client.
ScriptingContext	The Active Server Pages scripting context.
Server	Provides access to methods and properties on the server.
Session	Allows storage of information needed for an individual user session.

The Application Object

Methods

Name	Returns	Description
Lock		Prevents other Active Server Pages from modifying the Application
UnLock		Enables other Active Server Pages to modify the Application object

Properties

Name	Returns	Description
Contents	Dictionary	Collection of contents associated with application. Read only
StaticObjects	Dictionary	Collection of static objects associated with application. Read only

Events

Name	Returns	Description
OnStart		Occurs when a page in the application is first referenced
OnEnd		Occurs when the application ends

The Request Object

Methods

Name	Returns	Description
BinaryRead	Variant	Reads data returned by the client in a POST request

Properties

Name	Returns	Description
ClientCertificate	Dictionary	Collection of client certificate fields (specified in the X.509 standard). Read only
Cookies	Dictionary	Collection of cookies sent as part of the Request. Read only
Form	Dictionary	Collection of form elements. Read only
QueryString	Dictionary	Collection of query string values. Read only
ServerVariables	Dictionary	Collection of predetermined environment variables. Read only
TotalBytes	Integer	Total number of bytes that the client will return in the request body. Read only

The Response Object

Methods

Name	Returns	Description
AddHeader		Adds an HTTP header
AppendToLog		Adds a string to the end of the Web server log entry for this Request
BinaryWrite		Writes content without any character (Unicode to ANSI) conversion
Clear		Erases any buffered content
End		Causes Active Server Pages to stop processing and return any buffered output
Flush		Sends buffered output immediately
PICS		Adds an HTTP pics header. Read/Write
Redirect		Sends a '302 Redirect' status line
Write		Writes content with character (Unicode to ANSI) conversion

Properties

Name	Returns	Description
Buffer	Boolean	Indicates whether page output is buffered. Read/Write
CacheControl	String	The HTTP Cache-control header. Read/Write
CharSet	String	The HTTP Character set header. Read/Write
ContentType	String	The HTTP content type. Read/Write
Cookies	Dictionary	Collection of cookies sent as part of the Response. Write only
Expires	Integer	The length of time in minutes until the Response expires. Read/Write
ExpiresAbsolute	Date	The absolute date and time that the Response expires. Read/Write

Name	Returns	Description
IsClientConnected	Boolean	Indicates whether the client connection is still valid. Read only
Status	String	Value of the HTTP status line. Read only

The Server Object

Methods

Name	Returns	Description
CreateObject	Object	Creates an instance of a server component
HTMLEncode	String	Applies HTML encoding to a specified string
MapPath	String	Maps the specified relative or virtual path to the corresponding physical directory on the server
URLEncode	String	Applies URL query string encoding rules, including escape characters, to a specified string
URLPathEncode	String	Applies URL path encoding rules, including escape characters, to a specified string

Properties

Name	Returns	Description
ScriptTimeout	Integer	The maximum length of time in seconds before a script is terminated. Read/Write

The Session Object

Methods

Name	Returns	Description
Abandon		Destroys a Session object and releases its resources

Properties

Name	Returns	Description
Contents	Dictionary	Collection of all the items added to the Session through script commands. Read only
CodePage	Integer	The code page used when writing text to, or reading text from, the browser. Read/Write
LCID	Integer	The LCID used when writing text to, or reading text from, the browser. Read/Write
SessionID	String	Returns a Session ID for this user. Read only
StaticObjects	Dictionary	Collection of static objects associated with session. Read only
Timeout	Integer	The length of time in minutes before session state is destroyed after non-use by an individual user. Read/Write

Events

Name	Returns	Description
OnStart		Occurs when a page in the session is first referenced
OnEnd		Occurs when the session ends, is abandoned, or times out

The ObjectContext Object

Methods

Name	Returns	Description
SetAbort		Indicates that as far as the ASP page is concerned the transaction should not be completed
SetComplete		Indicates that as far as the ASP page is concerned the transaction can be completed

Events

Name	Returns	Description
onTransactionAbort		Raised when a transaction has been aborted
onTransactionComplete		Raised when a transaction has been completed

Method Calls Quick Reference

Application

Application.Lock
Application.UnLock

Request

Variant = Request.BinaryRead(*pvarCountToRead As Variant*)

Response

Response.AddHeader(*bstrHeaderName As String, bstrHeaderValue As String*)
Response.AppendToLog(*bstrLogEntry As String*)
Response.BinaryWrite(*varInput As Variant*)
Response.Clear
Response.End
Response.Flush
Response.Pics(*bstrHeaderValue As String*)
Response.Redirect(*bstrURL As String*)
Response.Write(*varText As Variant*)

Server

Set *Object = Server*.CreateObject(*bstrProgID As String*)
String = Server.HTMLEncode(*bstrIn As String*)
String = Server.MapPath(*bstrLogicalPath As String*)
String = Server.URLEncode(*bstrIn As String*)
String = Server.URLPathEncode(*bstrIn As String*)

Session

Session.Abandon

Microsoft Scripting Runtime Reference

Objects

Name	Description
Dictionary	The Dictionary object allows key-based storage of general items.
Drive	The Drive object allows you to gather information about drives attached to the system.
Drives	The Drives object contains a collection of Drive objects.
File	The File object allows you to create, delete and move files, and to query the system as to their names, paths, etc.
Files	The Files object contains a collection of File objects.
FileSystemObject	The FileSystemObject object is the main object of the Scripting group. It allows you to create, delete and gain information about (and generally manipulate) drives, folders, and files.
Folder	The Folder object allows you to create, delete and move folders, and to query the system as to their names, paths, etc.
Folders	The Folders object contains a collection of Folder objects.
TextStream	The TextStream object enables you to read and write text files.

The Dictionary Object

Methods

Name	Returns	Description
Add		Add a new key and item to the dictionary.
Exists	Boolean	Determine if a given key is in the dictionary.
Items	Variant	Get an array containing all items in the dictionary.
Keys	Variant	Get an array containing all keys in the dictionary.
Remove		Remove a given key from the dictionary.
RemoveAll		Remove all information from the dictionary.

Properties

Name	Returns	Description
CompareMode	CompareMethod	Set or get the string comparison method. Read/Write
Count	Integer	Get the number of key/item pairs in the dictionary. Read only
Item	Variant	Set or get the item for a given key. Read/Write
Key	Variant	Change a key to a different key. Write only

The Drive Object

Properties

Name	Returns	Description
AvailableSpace	Variant	Get available space. Read only
DriveLetter	String	Drive letter. Read only
DriveType	DriveTypeConst	Drive type. Read only
FileSystem	String	Filesystem type. Read only
FreeSpace	Variant	Get drive free space. Read only

Name	Returns	Description
IsReady	Boolean	Check if disk is available. Read only
Path	String	Path. Read only
RootFolder	IFolder	Root folder. Read only
SerialNumber	Integer	Serial number. Read only
ShareName	String	Share name. Read only
TotalSize	Variant	Get total drive size. Read only
VolumeName	String	Name of volume. Read/write

The Drives Collection

Properties

Name	Returns	Description
Count	Integer	Number of drives. Read only
Item	Drive	Get drive. Read only

The File Object

Methods

Name	Returns	Description
Copy		Copy this file
Delete		Delete this file
Move		Move this file
OpenAsTextStream	TextStream	Open a file as a TextStream

Properties

Name	Returns	Description
Attributes	FileAttribute	File attributes. Read/Write
DateCreated	Date	Date file was created. Read only

Table Continued on Following Page

Name	Returns	Description
DateLastAccessed	Date	Date file was last accessed. Read only
DateLastModified	Date	Date file was last modified. Read only
Drive	Drive	Get drive that contains file. Read only
Name	String	Get name of file. Read/Write
ParentFolder	Folder	Get folder that contains file. Read only
Path	String	Path to the file. Read only
ShortName	String	Short name. Read only
ShortPath	String	Short path. Read only
Size	Variant	File size. Read only
Type	String	Type description. Read only

The Files Collection

Properties

Name	Returns	Description
Count	Integer	Number of files. Read only
Item	File	Get file. Read only

The FileSystemObject Object

Methods

Name	Returns	Description
BuildPath	String	Generate a path from an existing path and a name
CopyFile		Copy a file
CopyFolder		Copy a folder
CreateFolder	Folder	Create a folder

Name	Returns	Description
CreateTextFile	TextStream	Create a file as a TextStream
DeleteFile		Delete a file
DeleteFolder		Delete a folder
DriveExists	Boolean	Check if a drive or a share exists
FileExists	Boolean	Check if a file exists
FolderExists	Boolean	Check if a path exists
GetAbsolutePathName	String	Return the canonical representation of the path
GetBaseName	String	Return base name from a path
GetDrive	Drive	Get drive or UNC share
GetDriveName	String	Return drive from a path
GetExtensionName	String	Return extension from path
GetFile	File	Get file
GetFileName	String	Return the file name from a path
GetFolder	Folder	Get folder
GetParentFolderName	String	Return path to the parent folder
GetSpecialFolder	Folder	Get location of various system folders
GetTempName	String	Generate name that can be used to name a temporary file
MoveFile		Move a file
MoveFolder		Move a folder
OpenTextFile	TextStream	Open a file as a TextStream

Properties

Name	Returns	Description
Drives	Drives	Get drives collection. Read only

The Folder Object

Methods

Name	Returns	Description
Copy		Copy this folder
CreateTextFile	TextStream	Create a file as a TextStream
Delete		Delete this folder
Move		Move this folder

Properties

Name	Returns	Description
Attributes	FileAttribute	Folder attributes. Read/write
DateCreated	Date	Date folder was created. Read only
DateLastAccessed	Date	Date folder was last accessed. Read only
DateLastModified	Date	Date folder was last modified. Read only
Drive	Drive	Get drive that contains folder. Read only
Files	Files	Get files collection. Read only
IsRootFolder	Boolean	True if folder is root. Read only
Name	String	Get name of folder. Read/write
ParentFolder	Folder	Get parent folder. Read only
Path	String	Path to folder. Read only
ShortName	String	Short name. Read only
ShortPath	String	Short path. Read only
Size	Variant	Sum of files and subfolders. Read only
SubFolders	Folders	Get folders collection. Read only

The Folders Collection

Methods

Name	Returns	Description
Add	Folder	Create a new folder

Properties

Name	Returns	Description
Count	Integer	Number of folders. Read only
Item	Folder	Get folder. Read only

The TextStream Object

Methods

Name	Returns	Description
Close		Close a text stream
Read	String	Read a specific number of characters into a string
ReadAll	String	Read the entire stream into a string
ReadLine	String	Read an entire line into a string
Skip		Skip a specific number of characters
SkipLine		Skip a line
Write		Write a string to the stream
WriteBlankLines		Write a number of blank lines to the stream
WriteLine		Write a string and an end of line to the stream

Properties

Name	Returns	Description
AtEndOfLine	Boolean	Is the current position at the end of a line? Read only
AtEndOfStream	Boolean	Is the current position at the end of the stream? Read only
Column	Integer	Current column number. Read only
Line	Integer	Current line number. Read only

Constants

CompareMethod

Name	Value	Description
BinaryCompare	0	Binary order comparison
DatabaseCompare	2	Database order comparison
TextCompare	1	Text order comparison

DriveTypeConst

Name	Value	Description
CDRom	4	Drive is a CD-ROM. No distinction is made between read only and read/write CD-ROM drives
Fixed	2	Drive has fixed (non-removable) media
RamDisk	5	Drive is a block of RAM on the local computer that behaves like a disk
Remote	3	Network drives
Removable	1	Drive has removable media
Unknown	0	Drive type can't be determined

FileAttribute

Name	Value	Description
Alias	64	File is an alias
Archive	32	File has been updated since last backup

Name	Value	Description
Compressed	2048	File is compressed
Directory	16	File is a directory
Hidden	2	File is a hidden file
Normal	0	File is a normal file
ReadOnly	1	File is read only
System	4	File is a system file
Volume	8	File is a network volume

IOMode

Name	Value	Description
ForAppending	8	Open a file and write to the end of the file.
ForReading	1	Open a file for reading only. You can't write to this file.
ForWriting	2	Open a file for writing. If a file with the same name exists, its previous contents are overwritten.

SpecialFolderConst

Name	Value	Description
SystemFolder	1	The System folder contains libraries, fonts and device drivers.
TemporaryFolder	2	The Temp folder is used to store temporary files.
WindowsFolder	0	The Windows folder contains files installed by the Windows operating system.

Tristate

Name	Value	Description
TristateFalse	0	Opens the file as ASCII
TristateTrue	-1	Opens the file as Unicode
TristateUseDefault	-2	Opens the file using the system default

Method Calls Quick Reference

Dictionary

Dictionary.Add(*Key As Variant, Item As Variant*)
Boolean = Dictionary.Exists(*Key As Variant*)
Variant = Dictionary.Items
Variant = Dictionary.Keys
Dictionary.Remove(*Key As Variant*)
Dictionary.RemoveAll

File

File.Copy(*Destination As String, OverWriteFiles As Boolean*)
File.Delete(*Force As Boolean*)
File.Move(*Destination As String*)
ITextStream = File.OpenAsTextStream(*IOMode As IOMode, Format As Tristate*)

FileSystemObject

String = FileSystemObject.BuildPath(*Path As String, Name As String*)
FileSystemObject.CopyFile(*Source As String, Destination As String, OverWriteFiles As Boolean*)
FileSystemObject.CopyFolder(*Source As String, Destination As String, OverWriteFiles As Boolean*)
IFolder = FileSystemObject.CreateFolder(*Path As String*)
ITextStream = FileSystemObject.CreateTextFile(*FileName As String, Overwrite As Boolean, Unicode As Boolean*)
FileSystemObject.DeleteFile(*FileSpec As String, Force As Boolean*)
FileSystemObject.DeleteFolder(*FolderSpec As String, Force As Boolean*)
Boolean = FileSystemObject.DriveExists(*DriveSpec As String*)
Boolean = FileSystemObject.FileExists(*FileSpec As String*)
Boolean = FileSystemObject.FolderExists(*FolderSpec As String*)
String = FileSystemObject.GetAbsolutePathName(*Path As String*)
String = FileSystemObject.GetBaseName(*Path As String*)
IDrive = FileSystemObject.GetDrive(*DriveSpec As String*)
String = FileSystemObject.GetDriveName(*Path As String*)
String = FileSystemObject.GetExtensionName(*Path As String*)
IFile = FileSystemObject.GetFile(*FilePath As String*)
String = FileSystemObject.GetFileName(*Path As String*)
IFolder = FileSystemObject.GetFolder(*FolderPath As String*)
String = FileSystemObject.GetParentFolderName(*Path As String*)
IFolder = FileSystemObject.GetSpecialFolder(*SpecialFolder As SpecialFolderConst*)
String = FileSystemObject.GetTempName
FileSystemObject.MoveFile(*Source As String, Destination As String*)
FileSystemObject.MoveFolder(*Source As String, Destination As String*)
ITextStream = FileSystemObject.OpenTextFile(*FileName As String, IOMode As IOMode, Create As Boolean, Format As Tristate*)

Folder

Folder.Copy(*Destination As String, OverWriteFiles As Boolean*)
ITextStream = Folder.CreateTextFile(*FileName As String, Overwrite As Boolean, Unicode As Boolean*)
Folder.Delete(*Force As Boolean*)
Folder.Move(*Destination As String*)

Folders

IFolder = Folders.Add(*Name As String*)

TextStream

TextStream.Close
String = TextStream.Read(*Characters As Integer*)
String = TextStream.ReadAll
String = TextStream.ReadLine
TextStream.Skip(*Characters As Integer*)
TextStream.SkipLine
TextStream.Write(*Text As String*)
TextStream.WriteBlankLines(*Lines As Integer*)
TextStream.WriteLine(*Text As String*)

C

ADO Object Model

Microsoft ActiveX Data Objects 2.0 Library Reference

All properties are read/write unless otherwise stated.

Objects

Name	Description
Command	A Command object is a definition of a specific command that you intend to execute against a data source.
Connection	A Connection object represents an open connection to a data store.
Error	An Error object contains the details about data access errors pertaining to a single operation involving the provider.
Errors	The Errors collection contains all of the Error objects created in response to a single failure involving the provider.
Field	A Field object represents a column of data within a common data type.
Fields	A Fields collection contains all of the Field objects of a Recordset object.
Parameter	A Parameter object represents a parameter or argument associated with a Command object based on a parameterized query or stored procedure.
Parameters	A Parameters collection contains all the Parameter objects of a Command object.

Table Continued on Following Page

Name	Description
Properties	A Properties collection contains all the Property objects for a specific instance of an object.
Property	A Property object represents a dynamic characteristic of an ADO object that is defined by the provider.
Recordset	A Recordset object represents the entire set of records from a base table or the results of an executed command. At any time, the Recordset object only refers to a single record within the set as the current record.

The Command Object

Methods

Name	Returns	Description
Cancel		Cancels execution of a pending Execute or Open call.
CreateParameter	Parameter	Creates a new Parameter object.
Execute	Recordset	Executes the query, SQL statement, or stored procedure specified in the CommandText property.

Properties

Name	Returns	Description
ActiveConnection	Variant	Indicates to which Connection object the command currently belongs.
CommandText	String	Contains the text of a command to be issued against a data provider.
CommandTimeout	Long	Indicates how long to wait, in seconds, while executing a command before terminating the command and generating an error. Default is 30.
CommandType	Command TypeEnum	Indicates the type of Command object.

Name	Returns	Description
Name	String	Indicates the name of the Command object.
Parameters	Parameters	Contains all of the Parameter objects for a Command object.
Prepared	Boolean	Indicates whether or not to save a compiled version of a command before execution.
Properties	Properties	Contains all of the Property objects for a Command object.
State	Long	Describes whether the Command object is open or closed. Read only.

The Connection Object

Methods

Name	Returns	Description
BeginTrans	Integer	Begins a new transaction.
Cancel		Cancels the execution of a pending, asynchronous Execute or Open operation.
Close		Closes an open connection and any dependent objects.
CommitTrans		Saves any changes and ends the current transaction.
Execute	Recordset	Executes the query, SQL statement, stored procedure, or provider specific text.
Open		Opens a connection to a data source, so that commands can be executed against it.
OpenSchema	Recordset	Obtains database schema information from the provider.
RollbackTrans		Cancels any changes made during the current transaction and ends the transaction.

Table Continued on Following Page

Properties

Name	Returns	Description
Attributes	Long	Indicates one or more characteristics of a `Connection` object. Default is 0.
CommandTimeout	Long	Indicates how long, in seconds, to wait while executing a command before terminating the command and generating an error. Default is 30.
ConnectionString	String	Contains the information used to establish a connection to a data source.
ConnectionTimeout	Long	Indicates how long, in seconds, to wait while establishing a connection before terminating the attempt and generating an error. Default is 15.
CursorLocation	CursorLocationEnum	Sets or returns the location of the cursor engine.
DefaultDatabase	String	Indicates the default database for a `Connection` object.
Errors	Errors	Contains all of the `Error` objects created in response to a single failure involving the provider.
IsolationLevel	IsolationLevelEnum	Indicates the level of transaction isolation for a `Connection` object. Write only.
Mode	ConnectModeEnum	Indicates the available permissions for modifying data in a `Connection`.

Name	Returns	Description
Properties	Properties	Contains all of the Property objects for a Connection object.
Provider	String	Indicates the name of the provider for a Connection object.
State	Long	Describes whether the Connection object is open or closed. Read only.
Version	String	Indicates the ADO version number. Read only.

Events

Name	Description
BeginTransComplete	Fired after a BeginTrans operation finishes executing.
CommitTransComplete	Fired after a CommitTrans operation finishes executing.
ConnectComplete	Fired after a connection starts.
Disconnect	Fired after a connection ends.
ExecuteComplete	Fired after a command has finished executing.
InfoMessage	Fired whenever a ConnectionEvent operation completes successfully and additional information is returned by the provider.
RollbackTransComplete	Fired after a RollbackTrans operation has finished executing.
WillConnect	Fired before a connection starts.
WillExecute	Fired before a pending command executes on the connection.

The Error Object

Properties

Name	Returns	Description
Description	String	A description string associated with the error. Read only.
HelpContext	Integer	Indicates the ContextID in the help file for the associated error. Read only.
HelpFile	String	Indicates the name of the help file. Read only.
NativeError	Long	Indicates the provider-specific error code for the associated error. Read only.
Number	Long	Indicates the number that uniquely identifies an Error object. Read only.
Source	String	Indicates the name of the object or application that originally generated the error. Read only.
SQLState	String	Indicates the SQL state for a given Error object. It is a five-character string that follows the ANSI SQL standard. Read only.

The Errors Collection

Methods

Name	Returns	Description
Clear		Removes all of the Error objects from the Errors collection.
Refresh		Updates the Error objects with information from the provider.

Properties

Name	Returns	Description
Count	Long	Indicates the number of Error objects in the Errors collection. Read only.
Item	Error	Allows indexing into the Errors collection to reference a specific Error object. Read only.

The Field Object

Methods

Name	Returns	Description
AppendChunk		Appends data to a large or binary Field object.
GetChunk	Variant	Returns all or a portion of the contents of a large or binary Field object.

Properties

Name	Returns	Description
ActualSize	Long	Indicates the actual length of a field's value. Read only.
Attributes	Long	Indicates one or more characteristics of a Field object.
DataFormat	Variant	Write only.
DefinedSize	Long	Indicates the defined size of the Field object. Write only.
Name	String	Indicates the name of the Field object.
NumericScale	Byte	Indicates the scale of numeric values for the Field object. Write only.
OriginalValue	Variant	Indicates the value of a Field object that existed in the record before any changes were made. Read only.
Precision	Byte	Indicates the degree of precision for numeric values in the Field object. Read only.
Properties	Properties	Contains all of the Property objects for a Field object.
Type	DataTypeEnum	Indicates the data type of the Field object.

Table Continued on Following Page

Name	Returns	Description
UnderlyingValue	Variant	Indicates a Field object's current value in the database. Read only.
Value	Variant	Indicates the value assigned to the Field object.

The Fields Collection

Methods

Name	Returns	Description
Append		Appends a Field object to the Fields collection.
Delete		Deletes a Field object from the Fields collection.
Refresh		Updates the Field objects in the Fields collection.

Properties

Name	Returns	Description
Count	Long	Indicates the number of Field objects in the Fields collection. Read only.
Item	Field	Allows indexing into the Fields collection to reference a specific Field object. Read only.

The Parameter Object

Methods

Name	Returns	Description
AppendChunk		Appends data to a large or binary Parameter object.

Properties

Name	Returns	Description
Attributes	Long	Indicates one or more characteristics of a Parameter object.
Direction	ParameterDirectionEnum	Indicates whether the Parameter object represents an input parameter, an output parameter, or both, or if the parameter is a return value from a stored procedure.
Name	String	Indicates the name of the Parameter object.
NumericScale	Byte	Indicates the scale of numeric values for the Parameter object.
Precision	Byte	Indicates the degree of precision for numeric values in the Parameter object.
Properties	Properties	Contains all of the Property objects for a Parameter object.
Size	Long	Indicates the maximum size, in bytes or characters, of a Parameter object.
Type	DataTypeEnum	Indicates the data type of the Parameter object.
Value	Variant	Indicates the value assigned to the Parameter object.

The Parameters Collection

Methods

Name	Returns	Description
Append		Appends a Parameter object to the Parameters collection.
Delete		Deletes a Parameter object from the Parameters collection.
Refresh		Updates the Parameter objects in the Parameters collection.

Properties

Name	Returns	Description
Count	Long	Indicates the number of Parameter objects in the Parameters collection. Read only.
Item	Parameter	Allows indexing into the Parameters collection to reference a specific Parameter object. Read only.

The Properties Collection

Methods

Name	Returns	Description
Refresh		Updates the Property objects in the Properties collection with the details from the provider.

Properties

Name	Returns	Description
Count	Long	Indicates the number of Property objects in the Properties collection. Read only.
Item	Property	Allows indexing into the Properties collection to reference a specific Property object. Read only.

The Property Object

Properties

Name	Returns	Description
Attributes	Long	Indicates one or more characteristics of a Property object.
Name	String	Indicates the name of the Property object. Read only.
Type	DataTypeEnum	Indicates the data type of the Property object.
Value	Variant	Indicates the value assigned to the Property object.

The Recordset Object

Methods

Name	Returns	Description
AddNew		Creates a new record for an updateable Recordset object.
Cancel		Cancels execution of a pending asynchronous Open operation.
CancelBatch		Cancels a pending batch update.
CancelUpdate		Cancels any changes made to the current record, or to a new record prior to calling the Update method.
Clone	Recordset	Creates a duplicate Recordset object from an existing Recordset object.
Close		Closes the Recordset object and any dependent objects.
CompareBookmarks	CompareEnum	Compares two bookmarks and returns an indication of the relative values.

Table Continued on Following Page

Name	Returns	Description
Delete		Deletes the current record or group of records.
Find		Searches the Recordset for a record that matches the specified criteria.
GetRows	Variant	Retrieves multiple records of a Recordset object into an array.
GetString	String	Returns a Recordset as a string.
Move		Moves the position of the current record in a Recordset.
MoveFirst		Moves the position of the current record to the first record in the Recordset.
MoveLast		Moves the position of the current record to the last record in the Recordset.
MoveNext		Moves the position of the current record to the next record in the Recordset.
MovePrevious		Moves the position of the current record to the previous record in the Recordset.
NextRecordset	Recordset	Clears the current Recordset object and returns the next Recordset by advancing through a series of commands.
Open		Opens a Recordset.
Requery		Updates the data in a Recordset object by re-executing the query on which the object is based.
Resync		Refreshes the data in the current Recordset object from the underlying database.
Save		Saves the Recordset to a file.
Supports	Boolean	Determines whether a specified Recordset object supports particular functionality.

Name	Returns	Description
Update		Saves any changes made to the current `Recordset` object.
UpdateBatch		Writes all pending batch updates to disk.

Properties

Name	Returns	Description
AbsolutePage	PositionEnum	Specifies in which page the current record resides.
AbsolutePosition	PositionEnum	Specifies the ordinal position of a `Recordset` object's current record.
ActiveCommand	Object	Indicates the `Command` object that created the associated `Recordset` object. Read only.
ActiveConnection	Variant	Indicates to which `Connection` object the specified `Recordset` object currently belongs.
BOF	Boolean	Indicates whether the current record is before the first record in a `Recordset` object. Read only.
Bookmark	Variant	Returns a bookmark that uniquely identifies the current record in a `Recordset` object, or sets the current record to the record identified by a valid bookmark.
CacheSize	Long	Indicates the number of records from a `Recordset` object that are cached locally in memory.
CursorLocation	CursorLocationEnum	Sets or returns the location of the cursor engine.

Table Continued on Following Page

Name	Returns	Description
CursorType	CursorTypeEnum	Indicates the type of cursor used in a Recordset object.
DataMember	String	Specifies the name of the data member to retrieve from the object referenced by the DataSource property. Write only.
DataSource	Object	Specifies an object containing data to be represented as a Recordset object. Write only.
EditMode	EditModeEnum	Indicates the editing status of the current record. Read only.
EOF	Boolean	Indicates whether the current record is after the last record in a Recordset object. Read only.
Fields	Fields	Contains all of the Field objects for the current Recordset object.
Filter	Variant	Indicates a filter for data in the Recordset.
LockType	LockTypeEnum	Indicates the type of locks placed on records during editing.
MarshalOptions	MarshalOptionsEnum	Indicates which records are to be marshaled back to the server.
MaxRecords	Long	Indicates the maximum number of records to return to a Recordset object from a query. Default is zero (no limit).
PageCount	Long	Indicates how many pages of data the Recordset object contains. Read only.

Name	Returns	Description
PageSize	Long	Indicates how many records constitute one page in the Recordset.
Properties	Properties	Contains all of the Property objects for the current Recordset object.
RecordCount	Long	Indicates the current number of records in the Recordset object. Read only.
Sort	String	Specifies one or more field names the Recordset is sorted on, and the direction of the sort.
Source	String	Indicates the source for the data in a Recordset object.
State	Long	Indicates whether the recordset is open, closed, or whether it is executing an asynchronous operation. Read only.
Status	Integer	Indicates the status of the current record with respect to match updates or other bulk operations. Read only.
StayInSync	Boolean	Indicates, in a hierarchical Recordset object, whether the parent row should change when the set of underlying child records changes. Read only.

Events

Name	Description
EndOfRecordset	Fired when there is an attempt to move to a row past the end of the Recordset.
FetchComplete	Fired after all the records in an asynchronous operation have been retrieved into the Recordset.
FetchProgress	Fired periodically during a lengthy asynchronous operation, to report how many rows have currently been retrieved.
FieldChangeComplete	Fired after the value of one or more Field objects have been changed.
MoveComplete	Fired after the current position in the Recordset changes.
RecordChangeComplete	Fired after one or more records change.
RecordsetChangeComplete	Fired after the Recordset has changed.
WillChangeField	Fired before a pending operation changes the value of one or more Field objects.
WillChangeRecord	Fired before one or more rows in the Recordset change.
WillChangeRecordset	Fired before a pending operation changes the Recordset.
WillMove	Fired before a pending operation changes the current position in the Recordset.

Method Calls Quick Reference

Command

Command.Cancel
Parameter = Command.CreateParameter(*Name As String, Type As DataTypeEnum, Direction As ParameterDirectionEnum, Size As Integer, [Value As Variant]*)
Recordset = Command.Execute(*RecordsAffected As Variant, Parameters As Variant, Options As Integer*)

Connection

Integer = Connection.BeginTrans
Connection.Cancel
Connection.Close
Connection.CommitTrans
Recordset = Connection.Execute(*CommandText As String, RecordsAffected As Variant, Options As Integer*)
Connection.Open(*ConnectionString As String, UserID As String, Password As String, Options As Integer*)
Recordset = Connection.OpenSchema(*Schema As SchemaEnum, [Restrictions As Variant], [SchemaID As Variant]*)
Connection.RollbackTrans

Errors

Errors.Clear
Errors.Refresh

Field

Field.AppendChunk(*Data As Variant*)
Variant = Field.GetChunk(*Length As Integer*)

Fields

Fields.Append(*Name As String, Type As DataTypeEnum, DefinedSize As Integer, Attrib As FieldAttributeEnum*)
Fields.Delete(*Index As Variant*)
Fields.Refresh

Parameter

Parameter.AppendChunk(*Val As Variant*)

Parameters

Parameters.Append(*Object As Object*)
Parameters.Delete(*Index As Variant*)
Parameters.Refresh

Properties

Properties.Refresh

Recordset

Recordset.AddNew(*[FieldList As Variant], [Values As Variant]*)

Recordset.Cancel

Recordset.CancelBatch(*AffectRecords As AffectEnum*)

Recordset.CancelUpdate

Recordset = Recordset.Clone(*LockType As LockTypeEnum*)

Recordset.Close

CompareEnum = Recordset.CompareBookmarks(*Bookmark1 As Variant, Bookmark2 As Variant*)

Recordset.Delete(*AffectRecords As AffectEnum*)

Recordset.Find(*Criteria As String, SkipRecords As Integer, SearchDirection As SearchDirectionEnum, [Start As Variant]*)

Variant = Recordset.GetRows(*Rows As Integer, [Start As Variant], [Fields As Variant]*)

String = Recordset.GetString(*StringFormat As StringFormatEnum, NumRows As Integer, ColumnDelimeter As String, RowDelimeter As String, NullExpr As String*)

Recordset.Move(*NumRecords As Integer, [Start As Variant]*)

Recordset.MoveFirst

Recordset.MoveLast

Recordset.MoveNext

Recordset.MovePrevious

Recordset = Recordset.NextRecordset(*[RecordsAffected As Variant]*)

Recordset.Open(*Source As Variant, ActiveConnection As Variant, CursorType As CursorTypeEnum, LockType As LockTypeEnum, Options As Integer*)

Recordset.Requery(*Options As Integer*)

Recordset.Resync(*AffectRecords As AffectEnum, ResyncValues As ResyncEnum*)

Recordset.Save(*FileName As String, PersistFormat As PersistFormatEnum*)

Boolean = Recordset.Supports(*CursorOptions As CursorOptionEnum*)

Recordset.Update(*[Fields As Variant], [Values As Variant]*)

Recordset.UpdateBatch(*AffectRecords As AffectEnum*)

HTTP 1.1 Header Codes

Code	Reason Phrase
Group 1: Information	
100	Continue
101	Switching Protocols
Group 2: Success	
200	OK
201	Created
202	Accepted
203	Non-Authoritative Information
204	No Content
205	Reset Content
206	Partial Content
Group 3: Redirection	
300	Multiple Choices
301	Moved Permanently
302	Moved Temporarily
303	See Other
304	Not Modified
305	Use Proxy

Code	Reason Phrase
Group 4: Client Error	
400	Bad Request
401	Unauthorized
402	Payment Required
403	Forbidden
404	Not Found
405	Method Not Allowed
406	Not Acceptable
407	Proxy Authentication Required
408	Request Time-out
409	Conflict
410	Gone
411	Length Required
412	Precondition Failed
413	Request Entity Too Large
414	Request-URI Too Large
415	Unsupported Media Type

Table Continued on Following Page

Code	Reason Phrase
Group 5: Server Error	
500	Internal Server Error
501	Not Implemented
502	Bad Gateway
503	Service Unavailable
504	Gateway Time-out
505	HTTP Version not supported

Client error and server error codes – with default explanations as provided by Microsoft Internet Information Server – are listed below.

Error Code	Short Text	Explanation
400	Bad Request	Due to malformed syntax, the request could not be understood by the server. The client should not repeat the request without modifications.
401.1	Unauthorized. Logon Failed	This error indicates that the credentials passed to the server do not match the credentials required to log on to the server. Please contact the Web server's administrator to verify that you have permission to access the requested resource.
401.2	Unauthorized: Logon Failed due to server configuration	This error indicates that the credentials passed to the server do not match the credentials required to log on to the server. This is usually caused by not sending the proper WWW-Authenticate header field. Please contact the Web server's administrator to verify that you have permission to access to requested resource.
401.3	Unauthorized: Unauthorized due to ACL on resource	This error indicates that the credentials passed by the client do not have access to the particular resource on the server. This resource could be either the page or file listed in the address line of the client, or it could be another file on the server that is needed to process the file listed on the address line of the client. Please make a note of the entire address you were trying to access and then contact the Web server's administrator to verify that you have permission to access the requested resource.

Error Code	Short Text	Explanation
401.4	Unauthorized: Authorization failed by filter	This error indicates that the Web server has a filter program installed to verify users connecting to the server. The authentication used to connect to the server was denied access by this filter program. Please make a note of the entire address you were trying to access and then contact the Web server's administrator to verify that you have permission to access the requested resource.
401.5	Unauthorized: Authorization failed by ISAPI/CGI app	This error indicates that the address on the Web server you attempted to use has an ISAPI or CGI program installed that verifies user credentials before proceeding. The authentication used to connect to the server was denied access by this program. Please make a note of the entire address you were trying to access and then contact the Web server's administrator to verify that you have permission to access the requested resource.
403.1	Forbidden: Execute Access Forbidden	This error can be caused if you try to execute a CGI, ISAPI, or other executable program from a directory that does not allow programs to be executed. Please contact the Web server's administrator if the problem persists.
403.2	Forbidden: Read Access Forbidden	This error can be caused if there is no default page available and directory browsing has not been enabled for the directory, or if you are trying to display an HTML page that resides in a directory marked for Execute or Script permissions only. Please contact the Web server's administrator if the problem persists.
403.3	Forbidden: Write Access Forbidden	This error can be caused if you attempt to upload to, or modify a file in, a directory that does not allow Write access. Please contact the Web server's administrator if the problem persists.
403.4	Forbidden: SSL required	This error indicates that the page you are trying to access is secured with Secure Sockets Layer (SSL). In order to view it, you need to enable SSL by typing "https://" at the beginning of the address you are attempting to reach. Please contact the Web server's administrator if the problem persists.

Error Code	Short Text	Explanation
403.5	Forbidden: SSL 128 required	This error message indicates that the resource you are trying to access is secured with a 128-bit version of Secure Sockets Layer (SSL). In order to view this resource, you need a browser that supports this level of SSL. Please confirm that your browser supports 128-bit SSL security. If it does, contact the Web server's administrator and report the problem.
403.6	Forbidden: IP address rejected	This error is caused when the server has a list of IP addresses that are not allowed to access the site and the IP address you are using is in this list. Please contact the Web server's administrator if the problem persists.
403.7	Forbidden: Client certificate required	This error occurs when the resource you are attempting to access requires your browser to have a client Secure Sockets Layer (SSL) certificate that the server recognizes. This is used for authenticating you as a valid user of the resource. Please contact the Web server's administrator to obtain a valid client certificate.
403.8	Forbidden: Site access denied	This error can be caused if the Web server is not servicing requests, or if you do not have permission to connect to the site. Please contact the Web server's administrator.
403.9	Access Forbidden: Too many users are connected	This error can be caused if the Web server is busy and cannot process your request due to heavy traffic. Please try to connect again later. Please contact the Web server's administrator if the problem persists.
403.10	Access Forbidden: Invalid Configuration	There is a configuration problem on the Web server at this time. Please contact the Web server's administrator if the problem persists.
403.11	Access Forbidden: Password Change	This error can be caused if the user has entered the wrong password during authentication. Please refresh the page and try again. Please contact the Web server's administrator if the problem persists.
403.12	Access Forbidden: Mapper Denied Access	Your client certificate map has been denied access to this Web site. Please contact the site administrator to establish client certificate permissions. You can also change your client certificate and retry, if appropriate.

Error Code	Short Text	Explanation
404	Not Found	The Web server cannot find the file or script you asked for. Please check the URL to ensure that the path is correct. Please contact the server's administrator if this problem persists.
405	Method Not Allowed	The method specified in the Request Line is not allowed for the resource identified by the request. Please ensure that you have the proper MIME type set up for the resource you are requesting. Please contact the server's administrator if this problem persists.
406	Not Acceptable	The resource identified by the request can only generate response entities that have content characteristics that are "not acceptable" according to the Accept headers sent in the request. Please contact the server's administrator if this problem persists.
407	Proxy Authentica-tion Required	You must authenticate with a proxy server before this request can be serviced. Please log on to your proxy server, and then try again. Please contact the Web server's administrator if this problem persists.
412	Precondition Failed	The precondition given in one or more of the Request-header fields evaluated to FALSE when it was tested on the server. The client placed preconditions on the current resource meta-information (header field data) to prevent the requested method from being applied to a resource other than the one intended. Please contact the Web server's administrator if the problem persists.

Table continued on Following Page

Error Code	Short Text	Explanation
414	Request-URI Too Long	The server is refusing to service the request because the Request-URI is too long. This rare condition is likely to occur only in the following situations: A client has improperly converted a POST request to a GET request with long query information. A client has encountered a redirection problem (for example, a redirected URL prefix that points to a suffix of itself). The server is under attack by a client attempting to exploit security holes present in some servers using fixed-length buffers for reading or manipulating the Request-URI. Please contact the Web server's administrator if this problem persists.
500	Internal Server Error	The Web server is incapable of performing the request. Please try your request again later. Please contact the Web server's administrator if this problem persists.
501	Not Implemented	The Web server does not support the functionality required to fulfill the request. Please check your URL for errors, and contact the Web server's administrator if the problem persists.
502	Bad Gateway	The server, while acting as a gateway or proxy, received an invalid response from the upstream server it accessed in attempting to fulfill the request. Please contact the Web server's administrator if the problem persists.

Note that Server error message files are placed in HELP\COMMON folder of Windows or Windows NT.

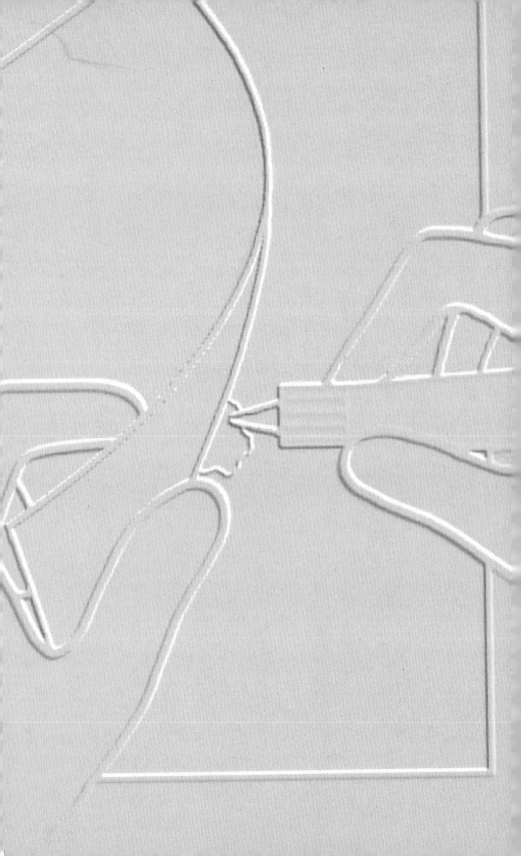

E

HTTP Server Variables

In Chapter 2, we saw how the ASP Scripting Host identifies various items about an HTTP request and stores the information in individual variables. These items can then be retrieved from the ASP script logic using the `ServerVariables` collection that is exposed by the `Request` object.

The complete set of server variables is listed in the table below:

Variable	Meaning
ALL_HTTP	Complete set of HTTP Headers. In this variable, the headers have been capitalized and prefixed with HTTP_.
ALL_RAW	Complete set of HTTP Headers. Similar to ALL_HTTP, but the header names are left unchanged.
APPL_MD_PATH	Path in the Metabase for the web application (the Metabase contains the IIS4 configuration).
APPL_PHYSICAL_PATH	Physical path of the web application, i.e. the location on disk.
AUTH_PASSWORD	User's password, if the user has been authenticated using Basic Authentication.
AUTH_TYPE	Authentication type, if the user has been authenticated. Set to Basic for Basic Authentication or NTLM for Windows NT Challenge/Response Authentication.
AUTH_USER	User's name, if the user has been authenticated.
CERT_COOKIE	Unique identifier for client certificate.
CERT_FLAGS	Flags: bit 0 is set if client certificate is present; bit 1 is set if the certificate authority that issued the certificate is not recognized.

Table Continued on Following Page

Variable	Meaning
CERT_ISSUER	Certificate issuer, from the Issuer field in the client certificate.
CERT_KEYSIZE	Number of bits used to encrypt the secure channel session.
CERT_SECRETKEYSIZE	Number of bits in the server certificate's private key.
CERT_SERIALNUMBER	Serial number of certificate allocated by issuer.
CERT_SERVER_ISSUER	Certificate issuer, from the Issuer field in the server certificate.
CERT_SERVER_SUBJECT	Certificate owner, from the Subject field in the server certificate.
CERT_SUBJECT	Certificate owner, from the Subject field in the client certificate.
CONTENT_LENGTH	Number of bytes sent by the client.
CONTENT_TYPE	Type of data in HTTP Request.
GATEWAY_INTERFACE	Version of the CGI gateway specification implemented.
HTTP_headername	See "HTTP Headers" section later
HTTPS	ON if a secure channel is used; OFF otherwise
HTTPS_KEYSIZE	Number of bits used to encrypt the secure channel session.
HTTPS_SECRETKEYSIZE	Number of bits in the server certificate's private key.
HTTPS_SERVER_ISSUER	Certificate issuer, from the Issuer field in the server certificate.
HTTPS_SERVER_SUBJECT	Certificate owner, from the Subject field in the server certificate.
INSTANCE_ID	Identifies the instance of the web server in the Metabase.
INSTANCE_META_PATH	Path in the Metabase for the IIS instance.
LOCAL_ADDR	IP address on the server that received the HTTP request.
LOGON_USER	User's Windows NT account name, if the user has been authenticated.

Variable	Meaning
PATH_INFO	The part of the URL after the server name but before any query string.
PATH_TRANSLATED	Value of PATH_INFO with any virtual path converted to a physical directory name.
QUERY_STRING	Information following the question mark (?) in the URL string.
REMOTE_ADDR	IP address of the client that issued the HTTP request.
REMOTE_HOST	Hostname (if known) of the client that issued the HTTP request.
REMOTE_USER	User's name, if the user has been authenticated. This will be the name released from the client and will not be affected by any ISAPI authentication filters.
REQUEST_METHOD	Type of HTTP Request, defines how the payload is carried, i.e. GET, POST or PUT
SCRIPT_NAME	Virtual pathname to the script or application being executed.
SERVER_NAME	Hostname or IP address of server.
SERVER_PORT	TCP/IP port number on the server that received the HTTP request.
SERVER_PORT_SECURE	Set to 1 if the HTTP Request is on an encrypted port; otherwise set to 0.
SERVER_PROTOCOL	Protocol name and version (usually HTTP/1.1) that the software on the server and the client are using to satisfy the information request.
SERVER_SOFTWARE	Name and version of the server software that is handling the information request.
URL	The part of the URL after the server name but before any query string.

HTTP Headers

The HTTP Request includes a number of items on information about the request and the capabilities of the client; these items are name / value pairs and are known as HTTP Headers. Any of the HTTP Headers that are not parsed into one of the variables listed above can be obtained using the server variable name HTTP_headername, where headername is the name of the header item. Commonly used examples are:

Variable	Meaning
HTTP_ACCEPT	List of the MIME data types that the client can accept.
HTTP_ACCEPT_ENCODING	List of encoding types that the client can accept.
HTTP_ACCEPT_LANGUAGE	List of the human languages that the client prefers
HTTP_CONNECTION	Type of connection
HTTP_USER_AGENT	Client software information, usually consisting of the browser version, plus the operating system, plus the browser type
HTTP_REFERER	URL of the page containing the link used to get to this page
HTTP_COOKIE	Cookies sent from the client's browser

Displaying the HTTP Server Variables

We can display the values of all HTTP Server Variables by invoking the following ASP script that enumerates through the Request.ServerVariables collection:

```
<!------------------------------------------------------------------
              HTTPLIST.ASP - Shows how to iterate through
                   Request.ServerVariables collection
----------------------------------------------------------------->
<% @language = VBScript %>
<HTML>
<HEAD>
<TITLE>HTTP Server Variables</TITLE>
</HEAD>
<BODY>
<H2>HTTP Server Variables</H2>
<TABLE>
  <% for each item in Request.ServerVariables %>
<TR>
<TD>
<FONT face="Verdana" SIZE=1>
  <% Response.Write item %>
</FONT>
</TD>
<TD>
```

```
<FONT face="Verdana" SIZE=1>
    <% Response.Write Request.ServerVariables(item) %>
</FONT>
</TD>
</TR>
    <% next %>
</TABLE>
</BODY>
```

It generates the following page:

Microsoft Server Components

This appendix is designed to be a quick reference for the Microsoft Active Server Components that are supplied as part of IIS, PWS or the IIS Resource Kit. For each component there's a full list of objects, methods and properties, in as much detail as we've been able to find. Where the return column is left empty for a particular method, this indicates that the method does not have a return value (although of course it will still return a value for success (0) or failure). In addition to methods and properties we've named the DLL for the component where appropriate, and the PROGID you can use to create an instance of that component. At the end of this appendix you can find a separate quick reference for all the method calls, including any parameters and parameter types.

The AdRotator Component

This component can be found in ADROT.DLL. To create an instance of this component use a PROGID of MSWC.AdRotator.

Properties

Name	Returns	Description
Border	SmallInt	Specifies the size of the advertisement border. Read/Write.
Clickable	Integer	Specifies whether the advertisement is a link. Read/Write
GetAdvertisement	String	Returns the next advertisement. Read-only.
TargetFrame	String	The frame where the advertisement will be displayed. Read/Write

The ASP2HTML Component

This is a Java component. To create an instance of it use a `PROGID` of
`IISSample.Asp2Htm`.

Methods

Name	Description
Body	Retrieves the body of the HTML document
ContentEncoding	Retrieves the content-encoding header field of the document
ContentLength	Gets the length of the content in the document
ContentType	Gets the type of the content in the document
Date	Gets the sending date of the URL
Expiration	Gets the expiration date of the URL
File	Retrieves the name of the file at the given URL
GetData	Retrieves the necessary data about the URL
Host	Retrieves the host of the URL
LastModified	Gets the last date of modification for the document
Port	Retrieves the port number of the URL
Protocol	Retrieves the protocol of the given URL
Ref	Retrieves the anchor of the given URL
Server	Gets the server name from the document
Title	Retrieves the title of the HTML document
URL	Sets the URL to connect to
WriteToFile	Writes the retrieved document to the given file

The Browser Capabilities Component

An instance of the Browser Capabilities component takes its properties from the client
browser type that it is representing, so there are no properties to list here – we looked
at some of the commonest browser properties in chapter 7. The `PROGID` for this
component is `MSWC.BrowserType`, and you can find it in `BROWSCAP.DLL`.

The Collaborative Data Objects Component

The full Object Library Reference for both CDO and CDONTS is available for
download from `http://webdev.wrox.co.uk/books/2459`. At over a hundred
pages it was not feasible to include it here!

The Content Linking Component

The Content Linker can be found in NEXTLINK.DLL. To create an instance of it use a PROGID of MSWC.NextLink.

Methods

Name	Returns	Description
About	String	No description of this method is available. Read only
GetListCount	Integer	The number of links in the listfile. Read only
GetListIndex	Integer	The position in the listfile of the current page. Read only
GetNextDescription	String	The description of the next link in the listfile. Read only
GetNextURL	String	The URL of the next link in the listfile. Read only
GetNthDescription	String	The description of the link at position n in the listfile. Read only
GetNthURL	String	The URL of the link at position n in the listfile. Read only
GetPreviousDescription	String	The description of the previous link in the listfile. Read only
GetPreviousURL	String	The URL of the previous link in the listfile. Read only

The Content Rotator Component

The Content Rotator can be found in CONTROT.DLL. To create an instance of it use a PROGID of IISSample.ContentRotator

Objects

Name
ContentRotator

283

Methods

Name	Returns	Description
ChooseContent	String	Gets one random entry from the content schedule file
GetAllContent		Gets all entries from the content schedule file

The Counters Component

The PROGID to create an instance of this component is MSWC.Counters, and it is found in COUNTERS.DLL.

Objects

Name
CounterCtl

Methods

Name	Returns	Description
Get	Integer	Returns the value of a counter
Increment	Integer	Increments the value of a counter by 1
OnEndPage		Object destruction
OnStartPage		Object initialization
Remove		Removes a counter
Set	Integer	Sets the value of a counter

The HTML Table Formatter Component

This is a Java component. The PROGID to create an instance of this component is .IISSample.HTMLTable.

Methods

Name	Returns	Description
AutoFormat		Converts data into an HTML-formatted table

Properties

Name	Description
Borders	Indicates whether there is a border around the table cells
Caption	Sets the caption for the table
CaptionStyle	Sets a style of the table's caption
HeadingRow	Indicates whether the first row of the table contains column headers

The Load Balancer Component

The Load Balancer component has a PROGID of mcs.loadbalancer and is found in LOADBAL.DLL.

Objects

Name
RateLoad

Methods

Name	Returns	Description
AddServer		Adds a new server to the list of servers for which the instance gathers PerfMon statistics
DeInit		Clear all current server rankings
GetPreferredServer	String	Returns the name of the server currently ranked highest in the server ranking table
Init		Initialize the Load Balancer instance ready to read Perfmon statistics from servers
OnEndPage		Object destruction
OnStartPage		Object initialization
ReadCounter	Integer	Reads one Perfmon statistic from one specific server
Start		Starts a thread to sort the server ranking table based on Perfmon statistics
Stop		Stops the thread started with the Start method

Properties

Name	Returns	Description
Sort Ascending	Boolean	Whether servers in the server ranking table should be sorted in ascending order, according to Perfmon statistics (default is true). Read/Write
Sound	Boolean	Whether the instance will produce a tone at different stages of its operation (default is false). Read/Write

The MyInfo Component

The PROGID for this component is MSWC.MyInfo. Remember that you won't have to create an instance of it under PWS. The MyInfo component is found in MYINFO.DLL.

Methods

Name	Description
PageType	Returns a number corresponding to the value in the "This site is..." pop-up menu in the Personal Web Server control panel.
PersonalName	Returns the owner's name
PersonalAddress	Returns the owner's address
PersonalPhone	Returns the owner's phone number
PersonalMail	Returns the owner's e-mail address
PersonalWords	Returns additional text associated with the owner
CompanyName	Returns the name of the owner's company
CompanyAddress	Returns the address of the owner's company
CompanyPhone	Returns the phone number of the owner's company
CompanyDepartment	Returns the owner's department name
CompanyWords	Returns additional text associated with the owner's company
HomeOccupation	Returns the owner's occupation
HomePeople	Returns text listing the people the owner lives with
HomeWords	Returns additional text associated with the owner
SchoolName	Returns the name of the owner's school
SchoolAddress	Returns the address of the owner's school

Name	Description
SchoolPhone	Returns the phone number of the owner's school
SchoolDepartment	Returns the owner's department or class
SchoolWords	Returns text associated with the owner's school
OrganizationName	Returns the name of the organization featured on the site
OrganizationAddress	Returns the address of the organization
OrganizationPhone	Returns the phone number of the organization
OrganizationWords	Returns text describing the organization
CommunityName	Returns the name of the community featured on the site
CommunityLocation	Returns the location of the community
CommunityPopulation	Returns the population of the community
CommunityWords	Returns text describing the community
URL	Returns the Nth user-defined URL. Corresponds to the Nth link description in URLWords
URLWords	Returns string containing the Nth user-defined description of a link. Corresponds to the Nth URL in URL
Style	Returns the relative URL of a style sheet
Background	Returns the background for the site
Title	Returns the user-defined title for the home page
Guestbook	Returns −1 if the guest book should be available on the site. Otherwise returns 0
Messages	Returns −1 if the private message form should be available on the site. Otherwise returns 0

The Page Counter Component

The **PROGID** for this component is **IISSample.PageCounter**, and it is found in PAGECNT.DLL.

Methods

Name	Returns	Description
Hits	Integer	Returns the number of hits on a URL
PageHit	Integer	Increments the counter for a page by one
Reset		Resets the number of hits on a URL to 0

The Permission Checker Component

The PROGID for this component is IISSample.PermissionChecker, and it is found in PERMCHK.DLL.

Methods

Name	Returns	Description
HasAccess	Boolean	check file access permission
OnEndPage		object destruction
OnStartPage		object initialization

The Registry Access Component

The PROGID to create an instance of this component is IISSample.Registry. The Registry Access component can be found in REG.DLL.

Methods

Name	Returns	Description
CopyKey		Copies a registry key and all subkeys and values
DeleteKey		Deletes a registry key and all of its subkeys
DeleteValue		Removes a named value from a registry key
ExpandString	String	Expands a string containing environment variables
Get	Variant	Gets a registry key's value
GetExpand	Variant	Gets a value from registry key, expanding any embedded environment variables

Name	Returns	Description
KeyExists	Boolean	Is the key already present in the registry?
Set		Sets a registry key's value
SetExpand		Sets a registry key's value as data type REG_EXPAND_SZ
SubKeys	Variant	Returns a collection of a key's subkeys
Values	Variant	Returns a collection of a key's values
ValueType	String	Returns the data type of a registry value

RegSubKeysCollection

Properties

Name	Returns	Description
Count	Integer	Returns number of items in collection. Read-only
Item	Variant	Given an index, returns an item in the collection. Read-only

RegValue

Properties

Name	Returns	Description
Name	String	Returns the name of a collection element. Read only.
Value	Variant	Returns the value of a collection element. Read-only

RegValuesCollection

Properties

Name	Returns	Description
Count	Integer	Returns number of items in collection. Read-only.
Item	Variant	Given an index, returns an item in the collection. Read-only.

The Status Component

The Status component is only available on PWS for Macintosh. The PROGID for this component is MSWC.Status, and it can be found in STATUS.DLL.

Properties

Name	Description
VisitorsSinceStart	The number of unique visitors (IP addresses or domain names) since the server started up
RequestsSinceStart	The number of requests since the server started up
ActiveHTTPSessions	The current number of http connections
HighHTTPSessions	The highest number of concurrent http connections since the server started up
ServerVersion	The Personal Web Server version string
StartTime	The time the server started up
StartDate	The date the server started up
FreeMem	The amount of unused memory available to the server
FreeLowMem	The lowest value for the amount of unused memory available to the server since it started up
VisitorsToday	Number of unique visitors (IP addresses or domain names) since midnight
RequestsToday	The number of requests received since midnight
BusyConnections	The total number of requests that were rejected because the server was already handling the maximum number of connections it can handle
RefusedConnections	The total number of requests that were refused because authentication was invalid
TimedoutConnections	The total number of connections that were closed without request having been received
Ktransferred	The total number of kilobytes sent by the server since the server started up
TotalRequests	The total number of requests received since the status counters were reset using the admin tool
CurrentThreads	The sum of the number active http connections and the number of threads in the connection thread pool that are not currently handling connections

Name	Description
AvailableThreads	The number of threads in the connection thread pool that are not currently handling connections
RecentVisitors	An HTML table listing the 32 most recent unique visitors. This table includes each visitor's domain name (or IP address) and the number of requests generated by each visitor
PopularPages	An HTML table listing the 32 most recently visited pages. This table includes each page's URL and the number of requests for each page

The Document Summary Information Component

The PROGID for this component is IISSample.SummaryInfos, and it is found in SUMINFO.DLL. Before accessing properties of the document, such as Author, Title, Date Created or Subject, check what kind of properties are available for this document or document type. To do this you can right-click on the required file in Windows Explorer, select Properties and click on the Summary tab.

Objects

Name
SumInfo
SumInfos

The SumInfo Object

Methods

Name	Returns	Description
SetFile		Attaches the object to a structured storage file.
Write		Writes the summary information to the Response object in HTML.

Properties

Name	Returns	Description
Application	Variant	The application which created the document. Read only
Author	Variant	The author of the document. Read only
Bytes	Variant	The size of the document in bytes. Read only
Category	Variant	The document category. Read only
CharCount	Variant	The number of characters in the document. Read only
Comments	Variant	Document comments. Read only
Company	Variant	Company name. Read only
CreateTime	Variant	When the document was created. Read only
EditTime	Variant	When the document was last edited. Read only
HeadingPairs	Variant	No extra description available. Read only
HiddenSlides	Variant	No extra description available. Read only
Keywords	Variant	Document keywords. Read only
LastPrinted	Variant	When the document was last printed. Read only
LastSavedBy	Variant	Who last saved the document. Read only
LastSaveTime	Variant	When the document was last saved. Read only
Lines	Variant	The number of lines in the document. Read only
LinksUpToDate	Variant	No extra description available. Read only
Manager	Variant	No extra description available. Read only
MMClips	Variant	No extra description available. Read only

Name	Returns	Description
Notes	Variant	No extra description available. Read only
PageCount	Variant	The number of pages in the document. Read only
Paragraphs	Variant	No extra description available. Read only
PresentationTarget	Variant	No extra description available. Read only
RevNumber	Variant	Number of revisions to the document. Read only
ScaleCrop	Variant	No extra description available. Read only
Slides	Variant	No extra description available. Read only
Style	Integer	Output style (0 = paragraph format [the default]; 1=full listing, HTML table format). Read/Write
Subject	Variant	The subject of the document. Read only
Template	Variant	The template used by the document. Read only
ThumbNail	Variant	Thumbnail graphics. Read only
Title	Variant	The title of the document. Read only
TitlesOfParts	Variant	No extra description available. Read only
URL	Variant	No extra description available. Read only
WordCount	Variant	The number of words in the document. Read only

The SumInfos Object

Methods

Name	Returns	Description
SetFileSpec		Sets the list of files from which properties are extracted
Write		Outputs properties according to the style property listed in the table above

Properties

Name	Returns	Description
Count	Integer	Indicates the number of items in the enumeration. Read-only
Item	SumInfo	Returns a specific member of the enumeration. Read-only
Style	Integer	Sets the style of property listing – plain text or table format. Read/Write

The Tools Component

The PROGID for this component is MSWC.Tool, and you can find it in TOOLS.DLL.

Objects

Name
ToolsCtl
ToolsResponse

The ToolsCtl Object

Methods

Name	Returns	Description
FileExists	Boolean	Checks if file exists or not
Owner	Boolean	Checks if the current user is the owner of the site (*Macintosh only*)
PluginExists	Boolean	Checks the existence of a server plug-in (*Macintosh only*)
ProcessForm		Processes an HTML form

Name	Returns	Description
Random	Integer	Generates a random integer
Test	String	No extra description is available.

The ToolsResponse Object

Methods

Name	Returns	Description
Write		No extra description is available.
WriteSafe		No extra description is available.

The Tracer Component

To create an instance of the Tracer component use a PROGID of IISSample.Tracer. This component is found in TRACER.DLL.

Objects

Name
Tracer

Methods

Name	Returns	Description
TimerSplit		No extra description is available
TimerStart		No extra description is available
TimerStop		No extra description is available
TimerTotal		No extra description is available
Trace		No extra description is available

Properties

Name	Returns	Description
Name	String	No extra description is available. Read/Write

Method Calls Quick Reference

The ContentRotator object of the ContentRotator component

String = ContentRotator.ChooseContent(bstrDataFile As String)
ContentRotator.GetAllContent(bstrDataFile As String)

The CounterCtl object of the Counters component

Integer = CounterCtl.Get(counterName As String)
Integer = CounterCtl.Increment(counterName As String)
CounterCtl.OnEndPage
CounterCtl.OnStartPage(piUnk As VT_UNKNOWN)
CounterCtl.Remove(counterName As String)
Integer = CounterCtl.Set(counterName As String, newValue As Integer)

The RateLoad object of the LoadBalancer component

RateLoad.AddServer(szServerName As String)
RateLoad.DeInit
String = RateLoad.GetPreferredServer
RateLoad.Init(szObjectName As String, szCounterName As String)
RateLoad.OnEndPage
RateLoad.OnStartPage(piUnk As VT_UNKNOWN)
Integer = RateLoad.ReadCounter(szServerName As String, szObjectName As String, szCounterName As String)
RateLoad.Start
RateLoad.Stop

The PgCntObj object of the PageCounter component

Integer = PgCntObj.Hits(bstrURL As String)
Integer = PgCntObj.PageHit
PgCntObj.Reset(bstrURL As String)

The PermissionChecker component

Boolean = PermissionChecker.HasAccess(bstrLocalUrl As String)
PermissionChecker.OnEndPage
PermissionChecker.OnStartPage(pUnk As VT_UNKNOWN)

The RegObj object of the RegistryAccess component

RegObj.CopyKey(bstrRegFullKeynameSource As String, bstrRegFullKeynameDest As String, fFlush As Boolean)
RegObj.DeleteKey(bstrRegFullKeyname As String, fFlush As Boolean)
RegObj.DeleteValue(bstrRegFullKeyValuename As String, fFlush As Boolean)
String = RegObj.ExpandString(bstr As String)
Variant = RegObj.Get(bstrRegFullKeyValuename As String)

Variant = RegObj.GetExpand(*bstrRegFullKeyValuename As String*)
Boolean = RegObj.KeyExists(*bstrRegFullKeyname As String*)
RegObj.Set(*bstrRegFullKeyValuename As String, vtValue As Variant, fFlush As Boolean*)
RegObj.SetExpand(*bstrRegFullKeyValuename As String, bstrValue As String, fFlush As Boolean*)
Variant = RegObj.SubKeys(*bstrRegFullKeyname As String*)
Variant = RegObj.Values(*bstrRegFullKeyname As String*)
String = RegObj.ValueType(*bstrRegFullKeyValuename As String*)

The SumInfo object of the Summary Information component

SumInfo.SetFile(*FileName As String*)
SumInfo.Write

The SumInfos object of the Summary Information component

SumInfos.SetFileSpec(*Path As String, FileSpec As String*)
SumInfos.Write

The ToolsCtl object of the Tools component

Boolean = ToolsCtl.FileExists(*fileURL As String*)
Boolean = ToolsCtl.Owner
Boolean = ToolsCtl.PluginExists(*pluginName As String*)
ToolsCtl.ProcessForm(*outputFile As String, templateFile As String, insertionPoint As String*)
Integer = ToolsCtl.Random
String = ToolsCtl.Test

The ToolsResponse object of the Tools component

ToolsResponse.Write(*bstrData As String*)
ToolsResponse.WriteSafe(*bstrData As String*)

The Tracer object of the Tracer component

Tracer.TimerSplit(*bstrLabel As String*)
Tracer.TimerStart
Tracer.TimerStop
Tracer.TimerTotal(*bstrLabel As String*)
Tracer.Trace(*bstrTrace As String*)

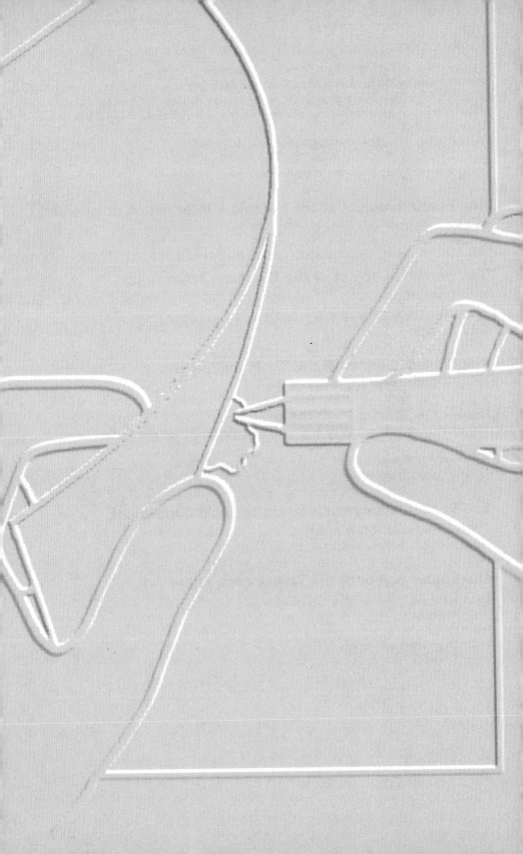

G

Useful Information

Language Codes Supported by Microsoft Internet Explorer 4/5

ASP script logic can determine the user's language(s) by inspecting the HTTP_ACCEPT_LANGUAGE server variable (via the Request.ServerVariables collection). This can be used to provide multi-language support, and to return web content that is automatically in the language that is suitable for the user. Such automatic detection is much smarter than asking the user to click on a hyperlink (perhaps a flag) to select their choice of language.

A user can select their spoken languages and their order of preference by means of the Languages... button on the General property sheet – accessed via the View | Internet Options menu option.

The national languages (and their associated mnemonic abbreviations) that are supported by Internet Explorer are listed in the table below:

Language	Abbreviation
Afrikaans	af
Albanian	sq
Arabic	ar
Arabic (Algeria)	ar-dz
Arabic (Bahrain)	ar-bh
Arabic (Egypt)	ar-eg

Language	Abbreviation
Arabic (Iraq)	ar-iq
Arabic (Jordan)	ar-jo
Arabic (Kuwait)	ar-kw
Arabic (Lebanon)	ar-lb
Arabic (Libya)	ar-ly
Arabic (Morocco)	ar-ma

Table Continued on Following Page

Language	Abbreviation	Language	Abbreviation
Arabic (Oman)	ar-om	Danish	da
Arabic (Qatar)	ar-qa	Dutch (Belgian)	nl-be
Arabic (Saudi Arabia)	ar-sa	Dutch (Standard)	nl
Arabic (Syria)	ar-sy	English	en
Arabic (Tunisia)	ar-tn	English (Australian)	en-au
Arabic (U.A.E.)	ar-ae	English (Belize)	en-bz
Arabic (Yemen)	ar-ye	English (British)	en-gb
Basque	eu	English (Canadian)	en-ca
Belarusian	be	English (Ireland)	en-ie
Bulgarian	bg	English (Jamaica)	en-jm
Catalan	ca	English (New Zealand)	en-nz
Chinese	zh	English (South Africa)	en-za
Chinese (Hong Kong)	zh-hk	English (Trinidad)	en-tt
Chinese (PRC)	zh-cn	English (United States)	en-us
Chinese (Singapore)	zh-sg	Estonian	et
Chinese (Taiwan)	zh-tw	Faeroese	fo
Croatian	hr	Farsi	fa
Czech	cs	Finnish	fi

Language	Abbreviation	Language	Abbreviation
French (Belgian)	fr-be	Latvian	lv
French (Canadian)	fr-ca	Lithuanian	lt
French (Luxembourg)	fr-lu	Macedonian	mk
French (Standard)	fr	Malaysian	ms
French (Swiss)	fr-ch	Maltese	mt
Gaelic	gd	Norwegian (Bokmal)	no
German (Austrian)	de-at	Norwegian (Nynorsk)	no
German (Liechtenstein)	de-li	Polish	pl
German (Luxembourg)	de-lu	Portuguese (Brazilian)	pt-br
German (Standard)	de	Portuguese (Standard)	pt
German (Swiss)	de-ch	Rhaeto-Romanic	rm
Greek	el	Romanian	ro
Hebrew	he	Romanian (Moldavia)	ro-mo
Hindi	hi	Russian	ru
Hungarian	hu	Russian (Moldavia)	ru-mo
Icelandic	is	Serbian (Cyrillic)	sr
Indonesian	in	Serbian (Latin)	sr
Italian (Standard)	it	Slovak	sk
Italian (Swiss)	it-ch	Slovenian	sl
Japanese	ja	Sorbian	sb
Korean	ko		

Table Continued on Following Page

Language	Abbreviation	Language	Abbreviation
Spanish	es	Spanish (Puerto Rico)	es-pr
Spanish (Argentina)	es-ar	Spanish (Uruguay)	es-uy
Spanish (Bolivia)	es-bo	Spanish (Venezuela)	es-ve
Spanish (Chile)	es-cl	Sutu	sx
Spanish (Colombia)	es-co	Swedish	sv
Spanish (Costa Rica)	es-cr	Swedish (Finland)	sv-fi
Spanish (Dominican Republic)	es-do	Thai	th
Spanish (Ecuador)	es-ec	Tsonga	ts
Spanish (El Salvador)	es-sv	Tswana	tn
Spanish (Guatemala)	es-gt	Turkish	tr
Spanish (Honduras)	es-hn	Ukrainian	uk
Spanish (Mexican)	es-mx	Urdu	ur
Spanish (Nicaragua)	es-ni	Vietnamese	vi
Spanish (Panama)	es-pa	Xhosa	xh
Spanish (Paraguay)	es-py	Yiddish	ji
Spanish (Peru)	es-pe	Zulu	zu

Some Common MIME Types and File Extensions

ASP script logic can generate and return web content *other* than the normal HTML documents, by setting the `Response` object's `ContentType` property to a string that identifies the type of information. This string is known as the **Multipurpose Internet Mail Extensions type** (or **MIME type**) and is sent in the HTTP Response Headers along with the web content.

Alternatively, if the web user navigates directly to a web resource (not via ASP), the web server will determine the MIME type to include in the HTTP response; this is achieved by using a table that maps file extensions to an associated MIME type.

The web browser uses this information to identify the type of web content and to determine how to process the information; this might involve handling it within the browser or invoking another helper application to handle the task. The web browser uses the MIME type/file extension mapping to determine the application that is associated with the web content.

The set of common MIME types and their associated file extensions are given in the table below:

MIME Type	Description	File Extension
application/acad	AutoCAD Drawing Files	.dwg
application/clariscad	ClarisCAD Files	.ccad
application/dxf	DXF (AutoCAD)	.dxf
application/msaccess	Microsoft Access File	.mdb
application/msword	Microsoft Word File	.doc
application/octet-stream	Uninterpreted Binary	.bin
application/pdf	PDF (Adobe Acrobat)	.pdf
application/postscript	PostScript, encapsulated PostScript, Adobe Illustrator	.ai, .ps, .eps
application/rtf	Rich Text Format	.rtf
application/vnd.ms-excel	Microsoft Excel File	.xls
application/vnd.ms-powerpoint	Microsoft Power Point File	.ppt
application/x-cdf	Channel Definition File	.cdf

Table Continued on Following Page

303

MIME Type	Description	File Extension
application/x-csh	C-shell script	.csh
application/x-dvi	TeX	.dvi
application/x-javascript	JavaScript Source File	.js
application/x-latex	LaTeX Source	.latex
application/x-mif	FrameMaker MIF format	.mif
application/x-msexcel	Microsoft Excel File	.xls
application/x-mspowerpoint	Microsoft Power Point File	.ppt
application/x-tcl	TCL Script	.tcl
application/x-tex	TeX Source	.tex
application/x-texinfo	Texinfo (emacs)	.texinfo, .texi
application/x-troff	troff	.t, .tr, .roff
application/x-troff-man	troff with MAN macros	.man
application/x-troff-me	troff with ME macros	.me
application/x-troff-ms	troff with MS macros	.ms
application/x-wais-source	WAIS Source	.src
application/zip	ZIP Archive	.zip
audio/basic	Basic Audio (usually m-law)	.au, .snd
audio/x-aiff	AIFF Audio	.aif, .aiff, .aifc
audio/x-wav	Windows WAVE Audio	.wav
image/gif	GIF Image	.gif
image/ief	Image Exchange Format	.ief
image/jpeg	JPEG Image	.jpeg, .jpg, .jpe
image/tiff	TIFF Image	.tiff, .tif

MIME Type	Description	File Extension
image/x-cmu-raster	CMU Raster	.ras
image/x-portable-anymap	PBM Anymap Format	.pnm
image/x-portable-bitmap	PBM Bitmap Format	.pbm
image/x-portable-graymap	PBM Graymap Format	.pgm
image/x-portable-pixmap	PBM Pixmap Format	.ppm
image/x-rgb	RGB Image	.rgb
image/x-xbitmap	X Bitmap	.xbm
image/x-xpixmap	X Pixmap	.xpm
image/x-xwindowdump	X Windows Dump (xwd) Format	.xwd
multipart/x-gzip	GNU zIP Archive	.gzip
multipart/x-zip	PKZIP Archive	.zip
text/css	Cascading Style Sheet Source	.css
text/html	HTML File	.html, .htm
text/plain	Plain Text	.txt
text/richtext	MIME Rich Text	.rtx
text/tab-separated-values	Text with Tab-Separated Values	.tsv
text/x-setext	Struct-Enhanced Text	.etx
video/mpeg	MPEG Video	.mpeg, .mpg, .mpe
video/quicktime	QuickTime Video	.qt, .mov
video/x-msvideo	Microsoft Windows Video	.avi
video/x-sgi-movie	SGI Movieplayer Format	.movie

For more information look at: ftp://ftp.isi.edu/in-notes/iana/assignments/media-types

Common Codepages

We can use the CodePage property of the Session object (or the @CODEPAGE directive) to support the various international character encoding schemes.

The ASP internals use the standard Unicode character set; however, web content and the information received from web browsers can frequently be written in alternative character encoding schemes, such as those to support non-English characters sets.

By specifying a codepage, the ASP will automatically convert all strings in the script logic between Unicode and the scheme specified by the codepage. Furthermore, by changing the Session.CodePage property before calling Response.Write (and then afterwards returning the codepage back to its original value) it is possible to send web content that is coded in a different scheme to the base scheme used by the web server. This approach could be used, for example, to send data in Arabic from an English web site.

A list of character encoding schemes, and the associated CodePage numbers, is given in the table below:

Codepage	Name	Alias
1200	Universal Alphabet	unicode
1201	Universal Alphabet (Big-Endian)	unicodeFEFF
1250	Central European Alphabet (Windows)	windows-1250
1251	Cyrillic Alphabet (Windows)	windows-1251
1252	Western Alphabet	iso-8859-1
1253	Greek Alphabet (Windows)	windows-1253
1254	Turkish Alphabet	iso-8859-9
1255	Hebrew Alphabet (Windows)	iso-8859-8
1256	Arabic Alphabet (Windows)	windows-1256
1257	Baltic Alphabet (Windows)	windows-1257
1258	Vietnamese Alphabet (Windows)	windows-1258
20866	Cyrillic Alphabet (KOI8-R)	koi8-r
21866	Ukrainian Alphabet (KOI8-RU)	koi8-ru

Codepage	Name	Alias
28592	Central European Alphabet (ISO)	iso-8859-2
28593	Latin 3 Alphabet (ISO)	iso-8859-3
28594	Baltic Alphabet (ISO)	iso-8859-4
28595	Cyrillic Alphabet (ISO)	iso-8859-5
28596	Arabic Alphabet (ISO)	iso-8859-6
28597	Greek Alphabet (ISO)	iso-8859-7
50220	Japanese (JIS)	iso-2022-jp
50221	Japanese (JIS-Allow 1 byte Kana)	csISO2022JP
50222	Japanese (JIS-Allow 1 byte Kana)	iso-2022-jp
50225	Korean (ISO)	iso-2022-kr
50932	Japanese (Auto Select)	none
50949	Korean (Auto Select)	none
51932	Japanese (EUC)	euc-jp
51949	Korean (EUC)	euc-kr
52936	Chinese Simplified (HZ)	hz-gb-2312
65000	Universal Alphabet (UTF-7)	utf-7
65001	Universal Alphabet (UTF-8)	utf-8
852	Central European (DOS)	ibm852
866	Cyrillic Alphabet (DOS)	cp866
874	Thai (Windows)	windows-874
932	Japanese (Shift-JIS)	shift_jis
936	Chinese Simplified (GB2312)	gb2312
949	Korean	ks_c_5601-1987
950	Chinese Traditional (Big5)	big5

Locale IDs (LCIDs)

We can use the `LCID` property of the `Session` object (or the `@LCID` directive) to override the default locale of the web server and specify the user's locale setting. This defines various items that correspond to the user's particular language and country, such as how numbers are displayed, how dates are formatted and how lists are sorted.

A list of locales (and their associated LCID numbers) is given in the table below:

Country/ Region	Language	LCID (Hex)
Albania	Albanian	041c
Algeria	Arabic	1401
Argentina	Spanish	2c0a
Australia	English	0c09
Austria	German	0c07
Bahrain	Arabic	3c01
Belarus	Belarusian	0423
Belgium	French	0813
Belize	English	2809
Bolivia	Spanish	400a
Brazil	Portuguese	0416
Brunei Darussalam	Malay	083e
Bulgaria	Bulgarian	0402
Canada	English	1009
Canada	French	0c0c
Caribbean	English	2409
Chile	Spanish	340a
Colombia	Spanish	240a
Costa Rica	Spanish	140a
Croatia	Croatian	041a

Country/ Region	Language	LCID (Hex)
Czech Republic	Czech	0405
Denmark	Danish	0406
Dominican Republic	Spanish	1c0a
Ecuador	Spanish	300a
Egypt	Arabic	0c01
El Salvador	Spanish	440a
Estonia	Estonian	0425
Faeroe Islands	Faeroese	0438
Finland	Finnish	040b
France	French	040c
Germany	German	0407
Greece	Greek	0408
Guatemala	Spanish	100a
Honduras	Spanish	480a
Hong Kong	Chinese	0c04
Hungary	Hungarian	040e
Iceland	Icelandic	040f
India	Hindi	0439
Indonesia	Indonesian	0421
Iran	Farsi	0429

Country/Region	Language	LCID (Hex)
Iraq	Arabic	0801
Ireland	English	1809
Israel	Hebrew	040d
Italy	Italian	0410
Jamaica	English	2009
Japan	Japanese	0411
Jordan	Arabic	2c01
Kenya	Swahili	0441
Korea	Korean (Ext. Wansung)	0412
Korea	Korean (Johab)	0812
Kuwait	Arabic	3401
Latvia	Latvian	0426
Lebanon	Arabic	3401
Libya	Arabic	3001
Liechtenstein	German	1407
Lithuania	Classic Lithuanian	0827
Lithuania	Lithuanian	0427
Luxembourg	French	140c
Luxembourg	German	1007
Macau	Chinese	1404
Macedonia	Macedonian	042f
Malaysia	Malay	043e

Country/Region	Language	LCID (Hex)
Mexico	Spanish	080a
Monaco	French	180c
Morocco	Arabic	1801
Netherlands	Dutch	0413
New Zealand	English	1409
Nicaragua	Spanish	4c0a
Norway (Bokmal)	Norwegian	0414
Norway (Nynorsk)	Norwegian	0814
Oman	Arabic	2001
Pakistan	Urdu	0420
Panama	Spanish	180a
Paraguay	Spanish	280a
Peru	Spanish	280a
Philippines	English	3409
Poland	Polish	0415
Portugal	Portuguese	0816
PRC	Chinese	0804
Puerto Rico	Spanish	500a
Qatar	Arabic	4001
Romania	Romanian	0418
Russia	Russian	0419
Saudi Arabia	Arabic	0401

Table Continued on Following Page

Country/Region	Language	LCID (Hex)
Serbia (Cyrillic)	Serbian	0c1a
Serbia (Latin)	Serbian	081a
Singapore	Chinese	1004
Slovakia	Slovak	041b
Slovenia	Slovene	0424
South Africa	English	1c09
South Africa	Afrikaans	0436
Spain	Basque	042d
Spain	Catalan	0403
Spain (Mod. Sort)	Spanish	0c0a
Spain (Trad. Sort)	Spanish	040a
Sweden	Swedish	041d
Switzerland	French	100c
Switzerland	German	0807
Switzerland	Italian	0810

Country/Region	Language	LCID (Hex)
Syria	Arabic	2801
Taiwan	Chinese	0404
Thailand	Thai	041e
Trinidad	English	2c09
Tunisia	Arabic	1c01
Turkey	Turkish	041f
U.A.E.	Arabic	3801
Ukraine	Ukrainian	0422
United Kingdom	English	0809
United States	English	0409
Uruguay	Spanish	380a
Venezuela	Spanish	200a
Vietnam	Vietnamese	042a
Yemen	Arabic	2401
Zimbabwe	English	3009

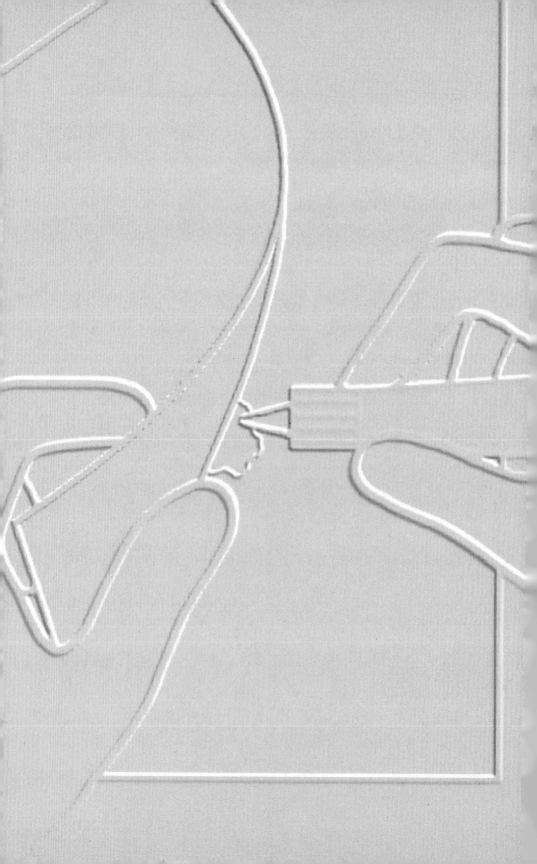

Further References and URLs

This appendix collects together the further reading and websites mentioned in this book, and adds some more suggestions. Of course, there are many places to turn to should you get stuck. This section will try and cut a good cross section of what's out there to be had.

Books

Beginning Active Server Pages 2.0 by Brian Francis *et al.*
(Wrox, ISBN 1-861001-34-7)
Professional Active Server Pages 2.0 by Brian Francis *et al.*
(Wrox, ISBN 1-861001-26-6)
Beginning... establishes the ASP foundations; then *Professional...* expands upon them, bringing in the associated web technologies like ADO, CDO and CDF and addressing the issues of E-Commerce and community websites.

ADO 2.0 Programmer's Reference by David Sussman & Alex Homer
(Wrox, ISBN 1-861001-83-5)
The most complete guide to using ADO that you can buy and the companion piece to this book.

ADSI ASP Programmer's Reference by Steven Hahn
(Wrox, ISBN 1-861001-69-X)

Professional MTS/MSMQ with VB and ASP by Alex Homer and David Sussman
(Wrox, ISBN 1-861001-46-0)

Professional ASP Techniques for Webmasters by Alex Homer
(Wrox, ISBN 1-861001-79-7)

ASP Troubleshooting by Juan T. Llibre
(Wrox, ISBN 1-861002-32-7) *to appear Feb 1999*

ADO RDS Programming with ASP by Johnny Papa *et al.*
(Wrox, ISBN 1-861001-64-9) *to appear Feb 1999*

Professional IE4 Programming by Mike Barta *et al.*
(Wrox, ISBN 1-861-000-70-7)

ASP, MTS, ADSI Web Security by Richard Harrison
(Prentice Hall, ISBN 0-13-084465-9)
Useful tome on how to implement a secure Web infrastructure using Microsoft
development tools and Internet-enabled products.

Designing Applications with MSMQ by Alan Dickman
(Addison-Wesley, ISBN 0-201325-81-0)

Journals

ASP Today is the new subscription journal about Active Server Pages from Wrox Press.
It covers the latest hardcore techniques and code for professionals, delivered in chunks
you can read easily and adapt for use in your continuing development of ASP-based
web applications. For more information and subscription details see
`http://www.wrox.com`.

Newsgroups

At the other end of the interaction scale, there are several Internet newsgroups on the
net that focus purely on ASP posers and queries. The official Microsoft ASP
newsgroups can be found at:

```
microsoft.public.inetserver.asp.general

microsoft.public.inetserver.asp.db

microsoft.public.inetserver.asp.components

microsoft.public.inetserver.iis
```

There are also several other groups that can be found to discuss and pose ASP
problems, as follows:

```
microsoft.public.vi.general

microsoft.public.vi.setup

microsoft.public.vi.dtc

microsoft.public.vi.debugging

microsoft.public.inetserver.misc

microsoft.public.frontpage.client

alt.destroy.microsoft (believe it or not!)
```

If you want a slightly different approach, *15Seconds.com* host the busiest ASP listserver
in the land. Details of how to subscribe can be found at
`http://www.15seconds.com/listserv.htm`

Websites

Of course the major resource for a web technology is the web itself and there are many sites which proffer their advice, time and solutions for your ASP problems.

Resources

15Seconds.com - www.15seconds.com
ActiveServerPages.com - www.activeserverpages.com
Active Server Pages Forum - www.zdjournals.com/m_sbn4/
ASP Developer network - www.aspdeveloper.net
ASP Forum - www.vallin.com/forum/
ASP Hole - www.asphole.com
ASP101 - www.asp101.com
ASPSite - www.aspsite.com
ASPToday - www.asptoday.com
ASP Toolbox - www.tcp-ip.com
ASP Xtras – www.aspxtras.com
ASPZone – www.aspzone.com
The ASP Alliance - www.aspalliance.com
The Active Corner - www.kamath.com
The ASP Developer's Site - www.genusa.com/asp/
Ultimate ASP – www.ultimateasp.com
FAQ for ASP - homepages.id.ibs.se/henrik/aspfaq/
Jazzbo's Tech Jam - www.fidalgo.net/~jazzbo/
Microsoft ASP Pages - www.microsoft.com/workshop/server
Server Objects Repository - www.serverobjects.com
Wrox Web Development Community Pages - webdev.wrox.co.uk

Downloads

Microsoft download site:
http://www.microsoft.com/windows/downloads
NT 4 Option Pack:
http://www.microsoft.com/windows/downloads/contents/Updates/NT40
ptPk/
Inet Monitor 3.0:
http://www.microsoft.com/msdownload/#itool
Cookie Munger
http://backoffice.microsoft.com/downtrial/moreinfo/iissamples/Ck
yMunge.asp
Browscap.ini file:
http://www.aspalliance.com/juan/browscap.zip

This isn't intended to be a complete list; if you can't find the information you're looking for here, these pages provide a plethora of links to other sites that should help you to find the answers.

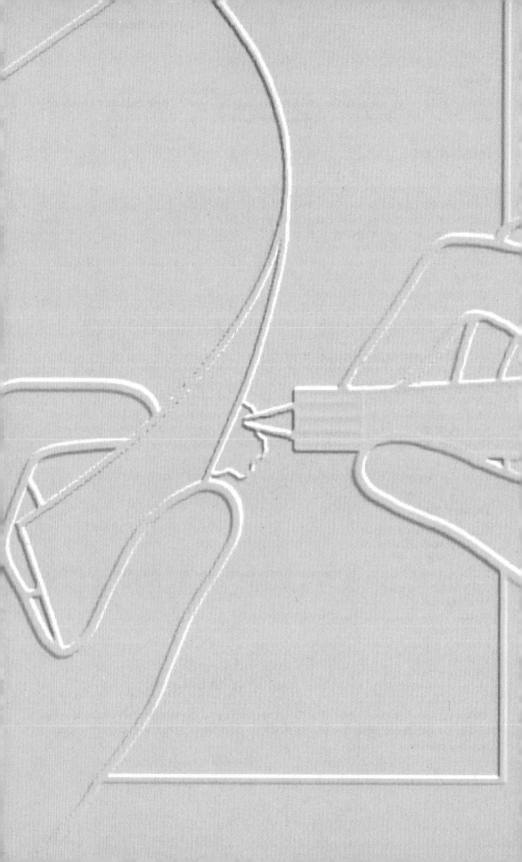

Support and Errata

One of the most irritating things about any programming book is when you find that bit of code you've just spent an hour typing simply doesn't work. You check it a hundred times to see if you've set it up correctly and then you notice the spelling mistake in the variable name on the book page. Of course, you can blame the authors for not taking enough care and testing the code, the editors for not doing their job properly, or the proofreaders for not being eagle-eyed enough, but this doesn't get around the fact that mistakes do happen.

We try hard to ensure no mistakes sneak out into the real world, but we can't promise that this book is 100% error free. What we can do is offer the next best thing by providing you with immediate support and feedback from experts who have worked on the book and try to ensure that future editions eliminate these gremlins. The following section will take you step by step through the process of posting errata to our web site to get that help. The sections that follow, therefore, are:

- ❑ Wrox Developers Membership
- ❑ Finding a list of existing errata on the web site
- ❑ Adding your own errata to the existing list
- ❑ What happens to your errata once you've posted it (why doesn't it appear immediately)?

There is also a section covering how to e-mail a question for technical support. This comprises:

- ❑ What your e-mail should include
- ❑ What happens to your e-mail once it has been received by us

So that you only need view information relevant to yourself, we ask that you register as a Wrox Developer Member. This is a quick and easy process, that will save you time in the long-run. If you are already a member, just update membership to include this book.

Wrox Developer's Membership

To get your FREE Wrox Developer's Membership click on Membership in the navigation bar of our home site:

www.wrox.com

This is shown in the following screenshot:

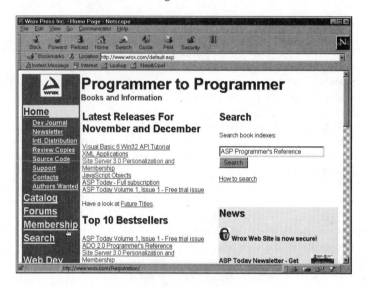

Then, on the next screen (not shown), click on **New User**. This will display a form. Fill in the details on the form and submit the details using the **Send Form** button at the bottom. Before you can say 'The best read books come in Wrox Red' you will get the following screen:

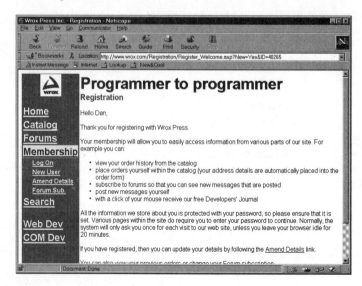

Finding an Errata on the Web Site

Before you send in a query, you might be able to save time by finding the answer to your problem on our web site: http:\\www.wrox.com.

Each book we publish has its own page and its own errata sheet. You can get to any book's page by clicking on Support from the left hand side navigation bar.

From this page you can locate any book's errata page on our site. Select your book from the pop-up menu and click on it.

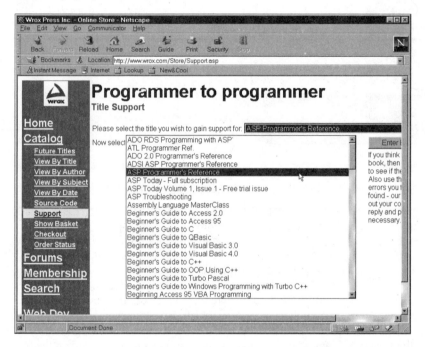

Then click on Enter Book Errata. This will take you to the errata page for the book. Select the criteria by which you want to view the errata, and click the Apply criteria... button. This will provide you with links to specific errata. For an initial search, you are advised to view the errata by page numbers. If you have looked for an error previously, then you may wish to limit your search using dates. We update these pages daily to ensure that you have the latest information on bugs and errors.

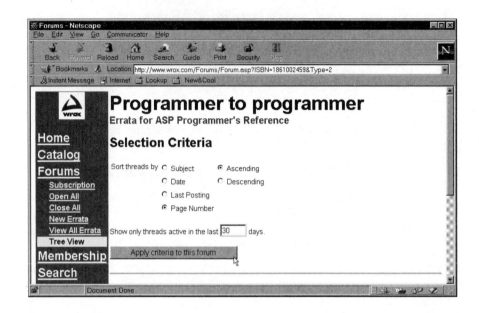

Adding an Errata to the Sheet Yourself

It's always possible that you may find your error is not listed, in which case you can enter details of the fault yourself. It might be anything from a spelling mistake to a faulty piece of code in the book. Sometimes you'll find useful hints that aren't really errors on the listing. By entering errata you may save another reader hours of frustration, and of course, you will be helping us provide even higher quality information. We're very grateful for this sort of advice and feedback. You can enter errata using the 'ask a question' of our editors link at the bottom of the errata page. Click on this link and you will get a form on which to post your message.

Fill in the subject box, and then type your message in the space provided on the form. Once you have done this, click on the Post Now button at the bottom of the page. The message will be forwarded to our editors. They'll then test your submission and check that the error exists, and that the suggestions you make are valid. Then your submission, together with a solution, is posted on the site for public consumption. Obviously this stage of the process can take a day or two, but we will endeavor to get a fix up sooner than that.

E-mail Support

If you wish to directly query a problem in the book with an expert who knows the book in detail then e-mail support@wrox.com, with the title of the book and the last four numbers of the ISBN in the subject field of the e-mail. A typical email should include the following things:

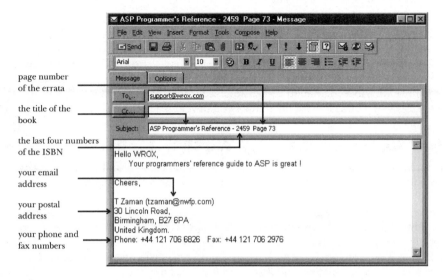

page number of the errata

the title of the book

the last four numbers of the ISBN

your email address

your postal address

your phone and fax numbers

We won't send you junk mail. We need the details to save your time and ours. If we need to replace a disk or CD we'll be able to get it to you straight away. When you send an e-mail it will go through the following chain of support:

Customer Support

Your message is delivered to one of our customer support staff who are the first people to read it. They have files on most frequently asked questions and will answer anything general immediately. They answer general questions about the book and the web site.

Editorial

Deeper queries are forwarded to the technical editor responsible for that book. They have experience with the programming language or particular product and are able to answer detailed technical questions on the subject. Once an issue has been resolved, the editor can post the errata to the web site.

The Authors

Finally, in the unlikely event that the editor can't answer your problem, s/he will forward the request to the author. We try to protect the author from any distractions from writing. However, we are quite happy to forward specific requests to them. All Wrox authors help with the support on their books. They'll mail the customer and the editor with their response, and again all readers should benefit.

What We Can't Answer

Obviously with an ever growing range of books and an ever-changing technology base, there is an increasing volume of data requiring support. While we endeavor to answer all questions about the book, we can't answer bugs in your own programs that you've adapted from our code. So, while you might have loved the help desk systems in our Active Server Pages book, don't expect too much sympathy if you cripple your company with a live adaptation you customized from Chapter 12. But do tell us if you're especially pleased with the routine you developed with our help.

How to Tell Us Exactly What You Think

We understand that errors can destroy the enjoyment of a book and can cause many wasted and frustrated hours, so we seek to minimize the distress that they can cause.

You might just wish to tell us how much you liked or loathed the book in question. Or you might have ideas about how this whole process could be improved. In which case you should e-mail `feedback@wrox.com`. You'll always find a sympathetic ear, no matter what the problem is. Above all you should remember that we do care about what you have to say and we will do our utmost to act upon it.

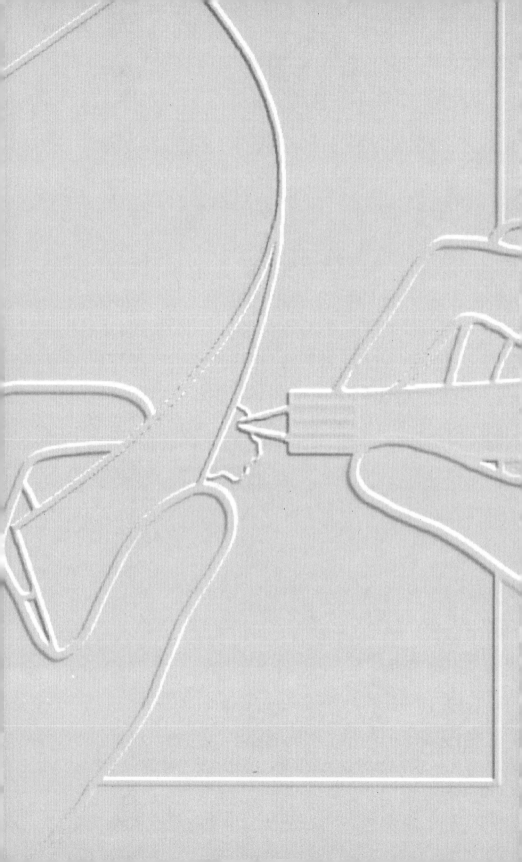

Index

F

global-scope objects. *see* application-scope objects
Go. *see* Lotus Go
graphics. *see* images
Guid property (ADSI), 196

H

HasAccess Method, 144
HasKeys Property (Request.Cookies Collection), 36, 55
HasKeys Property (Response.Cookies Collection), 55
<HEAD> section
  PICS labels in, 64
headers. *see* HTTP headers
HEIGHT attribute, 146
Hidden value (file attribute), 121
Hit Count Data file, 144
Hits method, 144
homepages
  automated creation of, 197
housekeeping
  event handler for, 88
HP-UNIX operating system, 210
.htm file extension, 221
.htm files
  accessing through TextStream Object, 17
  folder for, 23
HTML
  formatting advertisements as, 148
  static content created with, 10
  submitting forms in, 38
HTML checkboxes. *see* checkboxes
HTML combo boxes. *see* combo boxes
HTML controls
  naming, 41
  with multiple options, 41
HTML documents
  generating dynamically, 151
  retrieving contents of, 144
.html file extension, 221
HTML forms. *see* forms
HTML output stream
  character set, 60
  closing, 209
  creation of, 58
  erasing buffered, 68
  splitting with buffering, 59
HTML Table Formatter Component, 145
HTML tables
  checking browser support for, 150

converting data from ADO data source into, 145
creating from recordsets, 178
rendering messages into, 200
HTML tags
  adding to table, 178
  interpreting as characters, 97, 137
  sending within ASP script, 71
  vs. XML tags, 223
HTMLEncode method, 97, 137
HTTP 200 OK message, 65
HTTP 302 Object Moved message, 19, 65, 70, 218
HTTP 404 Not Found error message, 19, 65
HTTP content type
  default, 61
  description, 61
  for images, 61
  header for, 60
HTTP headers
  adding new, 66
  custom, 48
  function, 46
  minimizing number sent, 24
  retrieving value of, 48
  rewritten by Cookie Munger, 58
  sent to client during redirection, 70
  sent to client when cookies modified, 54
HTTP protocol
  ASP and, 30
  description, 29
  secure variant of. see HTTPS protocol
  stateless nature of, 16, 20, 165
HTTP Requests
  analysed by ASP Scripting Host, 30
  cookies appended to, 35
  definition, 29
  encrypting, 212
  extracting information from, 30
  form elements in, 38
  initiation of, 38
  number of bytes in, 50
HTTP Responses
  clearing, 68
  controlling content of, 53
  definition, 30
  encrypting, 212
HTTP Server Variables. *see* Server Variables
HTTP_ACCEPT_LANGUAGE variable, 48
HTTP_USER_AGENT variable, 47, 149

Q

query strings
definition, 39, 43
generating, 43
multiple-valued, 45
name value pairs in, 38, 39
retrieving unparsed version of, 45
QUERY_STRING variable, 43
QueryString Collection, 43–45
name/value pairs accessed by, 38, 39
question mark. *see* **? character**
queues. *see* **message queues**
quote marks
in PICS labels, 64

R

RDO. *see* **Remote Data Objects (RDO)**
RDS. *see* **Remote Data Services (RDS)**
Read Method, 132
Read Permission, 14
ReadAll Method, 133, 136
ReadLine Method, 133, 136
read-only files
checking for, 121
deleting, 112, 124
overwriting, 110
ReadOnly value (file attribute), 121
Recipients list, 202
record pointer
moving to new record, 180
records
adding to database, 180–81
deleting, 183
locking, 176
reading, 177
updating, 182
    with Oracle, 186
Recordset Object (ADO), 169
instantiating, 176, 177
Recordset.Charset property. *see* **Charset**
Property
recordsets
adding records to, 180
caching, 185
converting to a string, 178
creating HTML combo boxes from, 178
creating HTML tables from, 178
definition, 169
deleting records from, 183

hierarchical
    OLEDB provider for, 167
    represented by Field Object, 170
iterating through, 177
locally saved
    manipulating, 191
    OLEDB provider for, 167
lock type, 176
opening, 176, 183
updating, 182
REDIRECT attribute, 146, 147
Redirect method, 19, 65, 69–70, 218, 219
redirection. *see* **client: redirecting; server:**
    redirection methods on
redirection file, 145
Redirection File, 147
Refresh method (ADO Parameters
    Collection), 184
registry
accessing, 144
accessing during component
    creation/unloading, 159
Active Server Components have entries in,
    17
DSNs stored in, 173
entering Active Server Components into,
    163
no ASP 3.0 settings in, 222
Registry Access Component, 144
remote data access. *see* **data:remote**
    access of
Remote Data Objects (RDO), 166
Remote Data Services (RDS), 187, 191–93
availability, 192
further references for, 193
object model, 192
performance enhancements of, 193
remote disk drive
retrieving network name for, 119
Remove Method, 104
RemoveAll Method, 104
Request Object, 29–51
collections, 31–49
    listed, 31
    referring to, 49
definition, 30
function, 16, 30
information placed into, 30
interface, 31
method, 50
property, 50
sources of information for, 31

W

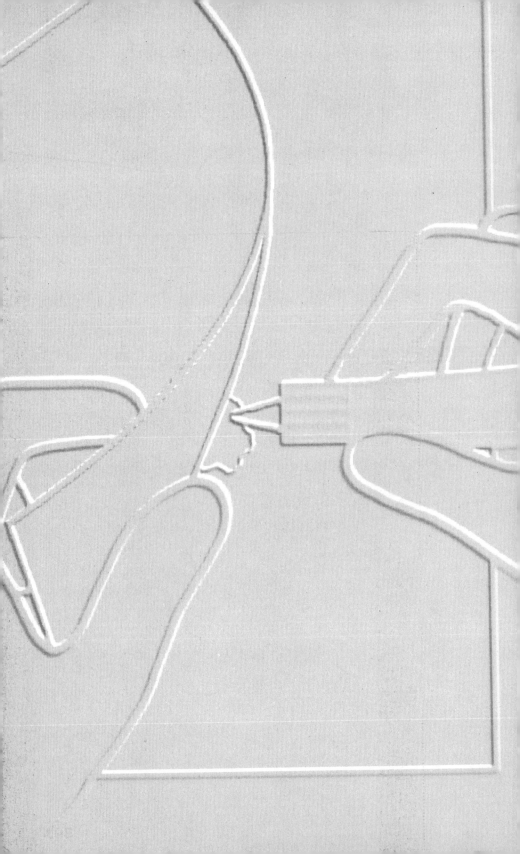